CLIMATE CHANGE, UNTOLD TRUTHS AND THE ULTIMATE SOLUTION

T0078360

CLIMATE CHANGE, UNTOLD TRUTHS AND THE ULTIMATE SOLUTION

Also guides to end Poverty, Unemployment, Corruption, Crime, Terrorism, Pollution, Environmental Degradation and other evils

DR. S. J. P. THOMPSON

PARTRIDGE
A Penguin Random House Company

ISBN: Softcover   978-1-4828-1379-1
            Ebook   978-1-4828-1378-4

The author loves every child and youth of every race, country, and religion, social and economic status as his own grandchild and wants the billions of them reach adulthood with dignity, freedom, peace, hope and happiness and without disparities, inequalities, hatred, poverty, exploitations or destitution. The ideas of this book alone can do that within a time frame of about twenty years in a predictable and measurable way. This book was written only with that desire and not for profit or fame. Hence he does not wish to slap any restrictions on use of his ideas and parts of or even the whole book. He also encourages translations and even economic publications in poor countries.

To order additional copies of this book, contact
Partridge India
000 800 10062 62
www.partridgepublishing.com/india
orders.india@partridgepublishing.com

Contents

Dedication vii

About the author ix

Preface xi

1   Understanding the Origin and
    Course of Global ills 1
2   From Private Affairs to Global Responsibility 9
3   A Simile that Connects the Unthinkable................................... 14
4   Family, the Ultimate Nation-Building Unit 20
5   Sustainability or Sustainable Living... 30
6   Status of Unsustainability 37
7   Arithmetic of Sustainability 42
8   Why We Failed to Recognize The End of Sustainability.............. 49
9   HIF—The Hellish Fountainhead of
    Unsustainability.. 54
10 The Long Trails of HIF.. 64
11 Highly Detrimental Population Density 69
12 Understanding the
    Warning-Signals of Deficits 81
13 The Sequential Evolution of Calamitous Curses........................ 85
14 Aspects of Poverty... 95
15 Unemployment and Unworthy Employment............................ 99
16 Unhealthy Competitions and Challenges................................. 105
17 Blood-Sucking Professions in HPD Regions 110
18 Urbanization.. 115
19 Violence, Terrorism, and Ungovernable Conditions.................. 123
20 Migrations—General Aspects 133

21   Migration and Mutual Emancipation 141
22   Sweet are the (Prudent) Uses of
     Adverse Migration 146
23   Don't Kill Peace-Making Through Migrations 158
24   Pollution.. 168
25   Reversing Pollution.. 177
26   Global Warming and Climate Change are Real Threats,
     Yet We Do More to Heighten Them 182
27   Ending GW and CC 189
28   Cancer of Planet Earth 195
29   The Panacea that Ends Man-Made Curses 198
30   Toward a Stable and Sustainable Economy 205
31   Timetable for a Great Green Living 217
32   Implementing PSCHHF 228
33   Crossing the Hurdles 239
34   The Cost of Imprudent Benevolence..................................... 248
35   The Precious By-Products of the PSCHHF Norm 253
36   Rational Action-Plans to Regain Sustainability 257

Dedication

I dedicate this book to the dear living and the departed souls who kept my spirits high and kept my life going with their affection, love, respect, concern and gratitude.

About the author

Author is a product of Madras Medical College. His professional and social life taught him the truths behind the good, bad and the ugly happenings.

Through the vast media he confirmed that the same truths, in magnified form, are behind the curses of modern humanity such as resisting poverty, unending crime, 9/11, terrorism, Arab uprising, unstoppable forest destruction, pollution and others and hence climate change.

In order to bring these to the notice of the world he voluntarily reduced his professional practice.

Preface

With anxiety I had been watching mankind's fight against evils, from poverty, crime, violence and terrorism to environmental degradation, forest destruction and pollution, for many decades and that against climate change for the last two decades. I was apprehensive because the truths I had learned by observing many families, societies and countries since my childhood days very clearly told that the above efforts cannot be successful, because they have never addressed the true causative factor behind those evils.

I was absolutely sure that the responsible leaders and common man will be able to explain the "biology" and "biography" of these evil when they understand those truths and will be able to create the right policies. So I published my first book *"Give Yourself a Sane Happy World"* in the year 2008 which turned out to be a huge one. (Available on amazon. com). I have liberally drawn points from that book, which is referred to in this book as *Book G*.

I took the pain to publish these books because I am sure that these truths alone can end those evils in the most natural way which further ensure a worthy life as global village.

The author can be contacted through e-mail at sanerworld@gmail. com or at the following postal address or telephones.

Dr. S. J. P. Thompson
Justin Hospital, Kulasekaram
Kanyakumari District, Tamil Nadu
India—629 161
Ph: +91 9443377309, 4651 277309, 4651 277608.

1

Understanding the Origin and Course of Global ills

Costly Wars and the Harsher New Enemies

It is a hard fact that despite astronomical developments, responsible democracies and the best plans and policies of experienced, well-read people, the intelligent species, *Homo sapiens*, are not able to enjoy a peaceful, happy, and hopeful life. While unimaginable newer developments have been happening in science, technologies, computers, atomic energy, space, medicine, agriculture, and other fields, humanity is forced to fight a wide-fronted, unending war against curses like poverty, crime, violence, and terrorism, using huge funds and significant manpower. Despite these protracted fights over decades, proud achievers could not claim any worthy victory, but have earned tougher "enemies" and catastrophes in the form of pollution, global warming (GW), and climate change (CC).

We have recognized the dangers caused by environmental degradation, pollution, GW, and CC, and so have come together and initiated efforts to alleviate the damage. The Rio Declaration on Environment and Development (1992) and the Kyoto Protocol (1997) are two major "united" efforts in that direction. Other than these, every worthy country has its own plans to protect the environment and to reduce pollution and other causative factors of GW. But we are forced to accept these efforts also as failures because we keep destroying more green cover and causing more pollution and, consequently, the impact of GW and CC on the world is harsher than what it was at the time the Kyoto Protocol was initiated. Our efforts for a definite accord at

Copenhagen and at the meetings that followed it did not yield any positive result.

Everybody's Worry

Every rational and worthy policy and plan must have a time-limit or time-scale. Such a well-conceived policy must bring the expected result at the expected time—at least to reasonable satisfaction. So our failures indicate that we were wrong somewhere or everywhere. Like every normal human, I also worried a lot because of the persistence of socio-economic, political, religion-based, environmental, and other ills, evils, and curses, and had been trying to understand why we failed and why new evils kept cropping up despite our costly fight against already existing evils.

Confident Diagnosis to Institute the Right Regimen for a Cure

Now, with my observations and studies over the last five decades, I can very confidently say that our policies and efforts have been highly imperfect because we never understood the true causative factor of the evils we have been fighting against and so have never addressed the real initiator. We cannot blame anyone for that mistake because, as we will see, everyone has been deceived by the manifestations of this causative factor, the real disease. The manifestations of the causative factor look like unrelated entities and often appear too terrible when compared with the real causative factor. Now I can say with confidence that the terrible ills and evils like poverty, crime, violence, terrorism, pollution, etc., against which we had been fighting are not real diseases but are signs and symptoms of a contrasting, "hidden," humble disease, and so this real disease escaped the attention it deserves.

When we closely observe evils like corruption, forest destruction, crime, terrorism, polluting activities, etc., we can see that the perpetrators are all desperately trying to gain something. If we go still deeper, we can always find them burdened with some kind of deficits or deficiencies which make their life unsustainable. We must understand that deficiencies are life-threatening, so basic survival instincts force them to do something—decently or indecently—to minimize or end those deficiencies. Some of them work hard for a longer time and others who don't have opportunities earn a livelihood by engaging in crime, forest destruction, terrorism, hate campaigns, and polluting activities. It is not at all an exaggeration, because if they stop those acts of ill-repute, most of them will have to starve.

Thus we failed because we just fought against their bizarre attempts (like crime and polluting activities) to end the deficits they have created; but never did any worthy attempt to understand how people created deficits and so never did anything to prevent the creation of deficits.

It can be understood soon that the real disease or originator of all those ills, evils, and curses is deficits of various necessities, ranging from basic natural resources to polluting energy. For all practical purposes, **deficits, deficiencies, insufficiencies, shortages, and unsustainable living conditions (ULC)** are synonymous.

Prevalence of the Disease

Today, a vast majority of human families suffer considerable deficits or unsustainable living conditions (the real disease), and the population of too many countries has crossed (outgrown) sustainable levels. The industrialized Western countries have inadvertently created a highly detrimental economic structure for them with its gluttonous appetite for energy which cannot presently be supplied by Nature. Thus all are destined to do some kind of desperate activities to minimize their deficits and in that process create those evils which directly or indirectly bring about GW and CC.

Happenings that Diverted Attention

Observations and studies very clearly indicate that the ignorant poor people at the lower strata of society are the topmost creators of deficiencies and their prominent sufferers; they indirectly aid too many factors at higher levels which favour pollution, GW, and CC. They obviously endure poverty and suffer starvation, malnutrition and related hardships. The first spontaneous reaction of every normal observer of such families is sympathy; and with that comes the willingness to help them with food or other materials. So no one cares about their multi-dimensional deficits or deficit-creating situation. Again, at this juncture, it may sound awkward and indecent to indict them for their lapses. In the same way people act fast to end crime, violence, etc. without understanding why they do so or what forces them to those situations.

The deficits of highly polluting industrialized countries are different. For too many reasons, they have developed their industries far more than what they can consume (and so are unsustainable) and allowed their urban centres to grow to unnatural levels (this, too, is unsustainable). To make good their unsustainable economy and living conditions, they require very high quantities of polluting energy, without which they cannot sustain. Thus they have lost the freedom to prevent/ stop polluting activities. Expecting them to oblige by accepting a pollution-reduction accord is impracticable. Yet the right time will come for them to reduce it—which we will see later.

Most Rational and Practical Act

The world knows that billions of people in poor and developing countries suffer pathetically because of deficits at their family levels. Studies show that their deficits also contribute in some indirect ways to the super pollution of developed countries, which we can call "proxy pollution" (this is further explained later). Studies also say that it is easier to uplift the poor toward sustainable living than to do the same with polluting economies. When the poor gain freedom from deficits, the factors which promote "proxy pollution" end and prompt the polluting countries to restructure their economic activities.

Course of Deficits

Since we failed to recognize and address the deficits of poor families in time, they have been growing in numbers and now verge on dangerous levels. The accumulated deficits have grown to such high levels in so many regions that they cannot be balanced or compensated for even with the total resources and opportunities available in those regions or countries. In other words, the people of that region have outgrown their resources.

When the deficits remain with some families, they alone suffered poverty; but when the total needs of the people of that region outgrow the total resources of the region, it becomes a kind of regional deficit/poverty, and its harsh manifestations affect almost every person in that region and augment all those existing curses. We will see that this is a highly consequential transformation and we can call this situation Generalized Unsustainable Living Conditions (**GULC**) or High Population Density (**HPD**), or Unsustainable Population Density (**UPD**).

Presently, regional deficits have grown to engulf most countries, and today, the total deficits created by humans have outgrown the total life-supportive resources of the world. Then how do we live? Understanding this gives the clue to the evolution of evils including pollution, GW, and CC.

Nutty Truths

As we saw, GULC augments and complicates all the evils we discussed and creates more. Yet, those are not too specific to affect any particular people in a particular pattern and so GULC, too, failed to attract the right attention to the huge deficits.

Today, considerable numbers of people of GULC countries, especially the enlightened, the influential, and the affluent, live a happy, "sustainable" life; but do so at the heavy cost of carbon emissions—by compensating for their deficits with dirty energy. The euphoria of such living makes them oblivious to the deficits they are burdened with and so the "disease" remains unsolved.

Understanding GULC gives the answers for many distressing questions. Why do people pollute? Why do the regions which have successfully stabilized their population still suffer from crime, violence, pollution, and other evils? Why are the rich, developed countries not able to stop pollution?

Well Adapted Deficient Life (WADL)

If we analyse our present-day life, we can certainly understand that we have deficiencies in almost every field of our life, such as family life, economy, society, politics, employment-related affairs, and religion-related life, and also have huge shortages in natural resources like water, fertile lands, living space, energy sources, and even clean air to breathe. To everybody's surprise, even basic virtues like love, honesty, integrity, gratitude, dignity, safety, hope, amity, etc., are deficient in many individuals, societies, and nations to a great extent. Yet we live "well" and do not even realize that we have these deficiencies because we have adapted ourselves smoothly to the transformations and to what we have around us.

We can call our life a "well adapted deficient life" (WADL). We can realize the degree and quantum of WADL if we list the deficiencies and quantify each one of them.

Adaptations Blunt Senses of Sufferers

Nobody's life is a wholesomely contented and sustainable one, despite adaptations. It is basic knowledge that deficiencies are threat to life and so, instead of "wasting" time to find the cause for their ills, people have used all their time and energy to adapt themselves to the threatening, deficient conditions. This early response or adaptation is "tightening the belt" where people learn to live with a lesser quantity of water, substandard food, "artificially boosted" farming techniques, compromised shelter and environment, riskier jobs, longer hours of work, and compromising on non-vital needs like education, and many more.

At the same time, people tried for a dignified adapted life; and in that process, there appeared new inventions, innovations, discoveries, better education and entertainments, which created newer jobs and enriched urban life. These eased their lives and even made life happy, joyous, and flourishing, which naturally blinded them further to understanding the harsh realities of unsustainable conditions. Today, people adapting these successfully do not know that they themselves live a highly unsustainable life. But they are the people who occupy the most powerful and vital positions in politics, bureaucracy, industry, and other deciding activities. Then how can we expect them to bother about unsustainable living conditions, the deep disease?

We must also understand that these newer inventions and the adapted lives do not promote any carbon-fixing activity like agriculture; but on the contrary, GW is favoured.

Comprehending the Enormity of Deficits

Today the quantities of various deficits/shortages that cause unsustainability at a global level are so high that if we add together the unfulfilled needs such as water, fertile land (for sustainable agriculture), living space, energy resources, education facilities, job opportunities, infrastructure, the facilities to neutralize day-to-day pollution and accumulated pollution, etc. of the billions of needy people around the world, it will come to such a huge sum that it cannot be compensated for, even by creating another planet Earth. Can you understand the enormity of the deficits and the severity of unsustainability?

End Human Miseries and Global Ills

The one and the only way to end all the human miseries and global ills is to prevent the factors which create deficiencies or unsustainability. When the world understands the systematically explained course in the following chapters and acts with determination, all those ills, evils, and curses will end in the most natural way.

Points to Remember

We have been making our life unsustainable by creating and accumulating huge deficits of all sorts. With time, these multiplied and morphed and now threaten us with GW and CC. We failed to recognize these deficits and their growth because:

When compared to the horrific consequences, the issues of deficits appear inconsequential and insignificant.

As and when deficiencies grew and their consequences troubled us, we started adapting to the changing realities and in that process forgot the progenitor.

Most often, the well-adapted life, like urban living with newer jobs, new energy sources, and facilities like entertainments took the responsible people far away from reality and so they failed to make relevant policies.

2

From Private Affairs to Global Responsibility

From Unpredictable Living Conditions to Stability

Until about seven decades ago, vast sections of people of poor and developing countries lived under highly unpredictable and dangerous conditions because of frequent wars, famines, and other natural calamities, and mass-killer diseases like small pox, cholera, and many other infectious diseases, exploitation, socio-religious superstitions, and many other such ills and evils. Life expectancy was short. These took away the much desired hope, peace, happiness, and security and affected their orderly, planned lives. Yet the simultaneous gradual global developments during the last few centuries and the favourable regional changes after the Second World War (World War II) have significantly helped those people to reverse those unfavourable situations. Humanity has found solutions to most of the above sorrows, and every corner of the world has enjoyed the developments in science, technology, medical research, energy sources, green revolution, splitting of atoms, deciphering genes, computers, instant communications, and many more.

European colorizations since the sixteenth century created a situation that we can call the first globalization. When they left their colonies around the middle of the twentieth century, they left behind many positive legacies. Along with the end of colonialism, the irresponsible and selfish monarchies and other irresponsible "governments" disappeared from most regions and gave way to responsible democratic governments and rule of law. As a synergy to these, the international understanding, world bodies like UNO, international trade, modern education, communication-media like European languages, and many more such developments brought people together and promoted unity, cooperation, and stability.

Shifting Responsibility

Until World War II, vast sections of people had reasons to blame colonial powers and other irresponsible governments for all their sufferings. But now, they themselves wield power and they have the duty, privilege, right, and responsibility to plan a life which must give them contentment and joy.

In fact, vast sections of people and leaders have been doing that. As a result, their life expectancy tripled or quadrupled. Longevity has given them more experiences, more realistic (practical) knowledge, and also more responsibilities. Yet too many families and leaders have failed to understand or foresee that longevity naturally increases their population, and so families and regions will need more resources and facilities.

Irresponsibility and Ignorance Ruined Precious Lives

Modern living insists that one must have many additional possessions which, in turn, increase the cost of living and so the burden of every breadwinner. As a result, they easily run into deficits and suffer. Again, the natural resources that support people of a region are static. Because of longevity, fast-growing populations have depleted the resources which had been supporting them for generations, causing shortages in all the poor and developing countries (GULC).

Unfortunately, vast sections of people have failed to take note of these and so have been creating deficiencies, to their eventual ruin. Ignorance and indifference are so stark that even after suffering an unworthy life, millions of families have repeated the same mistake and have multiplied deficiencies at family and regional levels. Their leaders, too, never warned them appropriately and so everybody suffers in many ways.

Finding a Scapegoat is the Most Stupid Act

Blaming the government, bureaucracy, or others for somebody's poverty and suffering is not at all a sensible act today. The duty of governments is to ensure social order, to prevent exploitation, to help people recover from calamities, to build infrastructures and other facilities, to defend their countries from all kinds of threats, and above all, to let their people understand the pleasant or unpleasant truths about their country—like water shortages, unemployment, predators of sorts, etc. All these must help even a very ordinary family to weigh the positive factors against the negative ones and plan a life which will be free from deficiencies and dependence.

It is a moral responsibility that able-bodied couples must plan their families in such a way as to live respectably and to save enough to support their country, too; but expecting (with healthy limbs) governments to feed them during normal times is a shameful and immoral act. There are uncommon situations which necessitate government freebies for a period, but continuing freebies for decades indicates that something is basically wrong with those recipients as well as the governments.

Unpleasant Truth

Contrary to rational expectations, modern humanity suffers more poverty (in absolute numbers), more varieties of crime, more violence and terrorism and more threats through pollution, global warming (GW), and climate change (CC). These catastrophes evolved because no one has properly linked the deficits or unsustainable living conditions to the evolving ills, evils, and curses. When I say that the deficit or the unsustainable living condition is the factor which generated, worsened, and complicated all those ills and evils, my assertions may sound strange. Happenings are so stark that deficits in families and generalized unsustainable (deficient) living conditions (GULC) can be compared with the innocuous gun powder, which can explode violently and blast even mighty mountains—as we witness in the form of explosive revolutions and other terrible acts of disgruntled people, and at last, the same through GW and CC. Despite these happenings, there are too many ignorant people to laugh at the fact that it is man-made deficiencies which initiate and propagate all those evils and curses, including pollution, GW, and CC. They will understand the reality when they read the coming chapters carefully.

Unpleasant Sight

It is rational planning and disciplined life that make man a species above other animals. But many do not mind even the most elementary aspects of sustainable family formation. Deficits are not natural curses of families or societies; but are man-made. Every family, including the very poor, starts as a happy sustainable one with a favourable equation of two supportive parents to one child. Yet despite modern facilities and widely available knowledge, millions of families earn for themselves a sorrowful life by disregarding the sustainable family equation (size) appropriate to them and are living an undignified life at the mercy of others; because they failed to mind that advantageous situation. It is a heart-rending sight to see the pathetic sufferings of the innocent children of those foolish parents. If those moronic parents had been a little more careful, their children would not have come to suffer inequalities, indignities, hunger, and a painful life and early death. It is not at all a trivial mistake but a heinous crime to deny their children their right to live in dignity. Deficits force those families to "beg, borrow, or steal" and even to "cheat, beat, and kill" others, and thus they degrade themselves economically and morally in society. After committing such horrible mistakes, they demand assistance from their governments and even from well-to-do people, and even claim that it is their right. It is not uncommon to see such people blaming others for their poverty and miseries. If such situations had arisen in the dark ages, they would have been pardonable. But if a family is bent upon, in these enlightened days, living in poverty and unsustainability, it becomes the duty of the government and every rational and right-thinking people to interfere and prevent those sorrows in the interest of its innocent children.

From Private to Public Affair

Family-level unsustainability and sufferings may be a private affair; but, as we will see, the deficits they have created have grown to engulf regions, countries, and now the whole planet. These overgrown deficits hurt and threaten every human with a variety of curses, like crime, violence, terrorism, green cover destruction, and other evils, and devitalize the whole planet with deadly pollution, GW, and CC. Further these evils hurt and demoralize even the most humble and patriotic families who wish to live a simple life and force them to shell out their hard-earned wealth and time in order to end/mitigate the deficits and curses created by others. So now family-level deficits have become a public and global issue. Expecting the millions of ignorant families to correct the deficits on their own is not at all going to bring any worthy result; but the delay of a day will take us nearer to a greater catastrophe and put the perpetrators, too, into greater danger. So it becomes the duty of every responsible human to understand the real deep ill or disease of deficit-creation at lower levels and help the innocent families to gain contentment through the formula we will construct rationally.

An Attempt to Make a Wholesome Understanding

We now know that the "signs and symptoms" (consequences like crime, terrorism, and pollution) of simple looking deficiencies (the real disease) are really too horrible, and so we deceptively divert our attention to make imperfect policies—just to deal with the consequences. Such deceptions are not isolated issues. When we go through the following simile in the next chapter, we will have a wholesome understanding of the "disease" and deception.

Life-threatening infectious diseases are cured by extracts of inconsequential fungi (like penicillin) and we solve many tough problems with simple formulae. Similarly, we have a very simple (probably the only) formula to end all those evils and to arrest the course of GW and CC.

3

A Simile that Connects the Unthinkable

Unthinkable Derivatives

Can anyone imagine a rat begetting an elephant or a frog giving birth to a whale? Generating such un-identical, unrelated, and monstrous creatures or bringing about unimaginable transformations (morphing) or expressions in day-to-day life may appear unthinkable. Yet they do happen everywhere. People everywhere suffer monster-attacks through starvation, crime, violence, pollution, GW, and CC. If we go behind these monsters, we can see that they are created by simple-looking, humble deficits or unsustainable living conditions (ULC). People may not believe such unpalatable realities, so, in order to make them realize a deceptive course of events, I would like to explain it with a simile.

This simile is about a person with a lung infection and its similarities with the above harsh course of families, societies, countries, and the world. Here, this deep-seated infection with silly-looking microbes creates signs and symptoms which appear harsh and unrelated to the primary cause. Such deceptive (strange and severe) signs and symptoms (expressions) invariably make ordinary people ignore the primary factor.

The Simile

We now have vast knowledge about infectious diseases like pneumonia. A lung infection like bronchitis or pneumonia is caused by pathogenic microbes. When such pathogens invade any part of a person, his defensive mechanisms are activated. The immunological mechanism tries to suppress the invaders. But, when the invading bacteria have the freedom to proliferate, the victim succumbs to the infectious disease. No one sees what is happening inside; but the victim suffers strange discomforts and pain that we call the signs and symptoms of disease.

A typical patient with such a lung infection develops fever, cough, general weakness, headache, chest pain, general aches, difficulty in breathing (dyspnoea), and if mismanaged or neglected, conditions worsen with very high fever, dehydration, severe difficulty in breathing, and even delirium. If mismanaged further, death is the certain outcome. Ordinary people never think of that deep-seated infection (the real disease), but worry about the threatening symptoms.

Well-learned physicians use the knowledge and wisdom of great souls like Edward Jenner, Louis Pasteur, Robert Koch, Alexander Fleming, Wilhelm Roentgen, and many others to examine, investigate, diagnose, and treat the disease. We can treat them empirically or even find out the exact causative bacteria and select the most suitable weapon (antibiotics) with which to exterminate the organisms. The more precise we are, the faster will be the recovery, the costs of treatment will be reduced, and the complications and suffering will be minimized.

Early Course of Infections

Like the virulent bacteria challenging the defensive immune mechanism of individuals, deficits of families challenge the abilities of the breadwinners' and family's resources and cause poverty and related indignities (symptoms). When the numbers of families with deficits multiply beyond the limits, their total needs exceed the resources of that region, and then the regional deficits challenge the whole community and the life-supportive resources of the whole region. Then that community suffers more poverty and unemployment (more signs and symptoms). In order to overcome these "challenges" (deficits), people may go for corrupt deeds, crime, forest destruction, and polluting industrial activities (further more signs and symptoms).

Overwhelming Infections

If the mild infection is left uncared for or is wrongly treated, it flares up to overcome immunological defence mechanisms and cause life-threatening pneumonia with the generalized suffering discussed above.

Similarly, when unsustainable families multiply unhindered, their total deficiencies (requirements) outgrow far beyond the region's supportive capacity and create more and more severe "symptoms" corresponding to the rising quantities of deficits—more of the above "symptoms" and more serious "symptoms and signs," like ruthless crime, violence, terrorism, highly polluting industrial activities, GW, and CC.

Rational Mode of Treatment

The usual plan for a cure consists of symptomatic, supportive, and curative treatment. Of these, curative treatment, with the aim of eliminating pathogens with the right antibiotics, is the most important step. The disease is cured only when the infecting bacteria are eliminated. When infecting microbes are eliminated, all those harsh symptoms and signs will vanish.

Yet during the course of eliminating the bacteria, the victims must be freed from the painful symptoms, like aches and fever. So, symptomatic treatment is a necessity. It consists of antipyretics (for fever), painkillers, and drugs to ease cough. Similarly, "symptoms and signs" like poverty, crime, terrorism, and pollution must be fought to prevent more complications while action is taken to prevent the generation of deficits in families.

Weak and dehydrated patients need supportive treatment with vitamins, easily digestible nutritious food, intravenous fluids, intravenous nutrients, etc. Similarly, the ignorant victims of ULC/deficits must be supported with necessary food, shelter, clothing, and education. At the same time, they must be enlightened on the evolution of their disease—creating deficits/ULC—so as to prevent the formation of unsustainable huge families with deficits, to ensure a permanent cure, wellbeing, and dignity.

The Prognosis with Different Modes of Treatment

Symptomatic and Supportive Treatment—
Alleviation Efforts or Euphoric Feel-Good Treatment?

A lay person or a quack may not take into account the role of bacteria and so may try to alleviate the harsh symptoms and signs like fever, headache, cough, etc., lessen the weakness with supportive care, and wait for results.

With these, the patient may feel comfortable to a considerable extent and feel hopeful; at the same time, the causative bacteria too celebrate these treatments because they are not at all disturbed, but given a long life. So they silently proliferate. When their growth crosses certain levels, the patient experiences very severe symptoms and a downward course that leads, eventually, to death.

Most policy makers, economists, and planners of most countries, including rich, developed countries and well-respected service organizations, have been doing what these quacks had been doing with their treatment approach, and continue to commit the same fooleries even today, despite the monumental failures of the past. Hence the initial symptoms, like poverty, crime, corruption, etc., have "advanced" to violence, terrorism, pollution, GW, and CC. Every person must understand that, today, the sufferers are not just the creators of deficits but the effects of those curses, from corruption to CC, have engulfed even honest patriots, hard-working humble poor and the tax payers who have a planned living and above all, the billions of absolutely innocent children of every stratum of society and of every country.

Exploitation and devitalisation of hard-working and tax-paying people ultimately debilitate them and their country. Today, the youth of such families are fed up with living in the motherlands and are queuing up to move to other countries which can assure them peace and a life without exploitation. These youths include descendants of freedom fighters, politicians, and "respectable" bureaucrats. Can anyone think of a worse symptom than this?

These horrible symptoms are the reflections of the incompetence of their own forefathers who, as responsible people, failed to understand the deficits in families and society and so failed to give their children a better tomorrow.

Wholesome Combined Treatment

No one disputes the necessity for the above mode of palliative and comforting treatment. But every person with common sense definitely disputes the negligence to add curative treatment, because in the absence of curative efforts, the mitigation-treatment would silently drive the patient to complications and death.

Similarly, alleviation measures to those in poverty and threats of crime, violence and terror-strikes, ungovernable conditions, and pollution are necessities to protect humanity from torturing life and premature death. But this symptomatic and supportive treatment will never end the real disease of deficit-generation in families, especially in poor and developing countries.

Today, billions of people around the world generate deficits through unsustainable huge families and the developed countries are mired in a highly unsustainable huge industrial economy. In order to narrow the deficits or shortages like fertile lands, water, living space, and money to meet the day-to-day expenditures including those for education and health care, people engage in many desperate acts like forest destruction, crime, and polluting industrial acts which at last lead to harsher symptoms, like GW and CC. So, for us, the curative treatment is preventing the formation of deficits in families; that means helping people to form sustainable contented families. When compared to the feel-good treatment, the financial and other necessities of curative treatment constitute just a fraction. Ending ULC in poor and developing countries will help the developed countries "cure" their deficit-causing economy.

We will discuss the practical way of doing it in later chapters.

Target of Treatment

Families are the ultimate building blocks of a nation and a global community. Today's families face far more challenges and liabilities than those of yesteryear. Understanding these is vital for a wholesome planning for deficit-free families, so that they will build a world free from deficiencies and all its associated evils and curses.

4

Family, the Ultimate Nation-Building Unit

(And the ultimate breeder of the good, the bad, and the ugly)

Family, a Responsible Mini-Nation

Families are the ultimate wholesome units of human society and the building-blocks of a nation. A family is a self-governed mini-nation in all respects. And so, parents as the heads of families have the rights, duties, and responsibilities to plan for their happy, sustainable life just as governments plan for their countries.

It is families (not the lonely individuals) which generate succeeding generations. A faulty or deficient family affects the whole nation and the whole world. Other than ensuring a sustainable life, the modern family has many functions and duties which affect the quality of its lives and the worth of the citizens it creates.

Importance of Making Families Healthy and Content

A nation built with contented, respectable and sustainable families can give everyone a great life with peace and happiness. But defective and deficient families are real torments that torture their own members and ruin the health of their nation, too. It is time for the world to understand that most of the socio-economic and other ills and evils, like forest destruction, environmental degradation, crime, violence, and unpatriotic acts, are done in the process of correcting or making good the deficiencies at the family level. The creation of more such deficient families worsens the above ills further and promotes GW and CC, directly or indirectly, as we will discuss.

VIPs

Children are the purpose of families and it is children who make families wholesome, and so they are the VIPs (Very Important Persons). Children carry forward the genome of the family and the legacies of the nation—its culture, individuality, natural gifts, and treasures—toward eternity. Yet too many VIPs in a family means an abundance of responsibilities and expenditures to the parents, which they cannot fulfil, and so creates deficiencies. Deficiencies reduce the efficiency and chances of their journey toward infinity. Yet instincts pressurize people to ensure that journey by forcing them to reduce or make good their deficits somehow, and in that process, the above-mentioned ills evolve. Thus, when a deficient family creates ills and evils, it hurts others and Nature and brings disrepute to them. Hence, modern parents must plan meticulously in accordance with the prevailing tough living conditions to avoid physical deficits and also to spare time in order to take care of the social, intellectual, and psychological needs of their children.

Child is Not a "Private/Family Property"

Even though children are the purpose of a family, children are not at all their "private properties." Infants depend entirely on their parents; but gradually become less dependent and, in due course, become distinct individuals or citizens. As citizens and members of the society, they have to interact with people from vastly different backgrounds. Together they must understand and face social, economic, national, and international problems, plan appropriately, and do things rationally to ensure amity and stability in society. They must also contribute to economic viability and do whatever is possible to make their nation sustainable, independent, and respectable.

Again, children, when they grow up, will spend a longer part of their lives with their spouses who come from an entirely different family with different experiences and ideas. Every parent must keep this in mind and train their children (as directed below) so that family life continues in harmony.

When children are brought up in well-planned, content families with the right care, relevant education, ample exposure to a wide range of real-life situations and diverse people, adequate knowledge about changing socio-economic course and their life-supportive resources, and are taught to use basic resources like fertile lands, they grow into future citizens with great confidence and care for their family and country.

Most crowded societies have varieties of evil predators to poach on and exploit innocent children and youths. So, parents have the duty to warn their children and even their children's friends of evils like drugs, gambling, sexual perversions, fanaticism, crime, and treacherous people in social, religious, and political circles with deceitful ideologies, and other such "traps" prevalent in their society and country.

Furthermore, children must be encouraged to explore everything that makes their life more meaningful and progressive and to do appreciable deeds. All these help those growing youth to plan with forethought and live as respectable, responsible, and self-sacrificing patriotic citizens who interact with others with dignity and protect every distinct feature of their nation.

These responsible acts of parents are almost continuous and life-long and take a lot of their time, energy, and wealth and so parents must take these into account while planning their families.

Visible and Invisible Factors That Make a Person

Human beings are not just visible physical entities with physical needs; they have individual minds and souls. Nourishing and developing the mind and soul are as important as feeding and caring for physical developments, because it is the mind and soul which act as software and control the person and decide their ambitions, endeavours, and other worthy or unworthy acts. When an individual's mind is conditioned with virtues and worthy ideologies, he lives a respectable life; wrong ideologies could convert him into a criminal, a terrorist, or into an unworthy, undesirable person such as a suicide-bomber. Such children, influenced by harmful "software," are a curse to their families and nation. They cause damage to humanity and retard the progress of their motherland.

Children start interacting with family members from infancy and gradually widen their area of interaction to the vast society. As they grow, children learn more and more from observations, experiences, trial and error, and from what people teach them. Parents are the first and the best teachers, and family alone tolerates the stupidities and absurd acts of children and corrects children without hurting them mentally.

Multiplying Duties of Modern Parents

Love and related virtues like tolerance, self-sacrifice, encouragement, mutual care, etc. are the most important factors that bond family members and make a home. A child or any other person who does not have trustworthy people to give and take love can never have a perfect life.

Basic manners and emotional reactions have a strong and direct bearing on the life of people in a great way. Such intricate matters are best taught and conditioned by senior family members. They clear the doubts of children and do all they can to make children feel safe and hopeful, by "loading" their empty minds with worthy "software" (ideologies), by timely corrections, and by teaching them to be empathetic and tolerant.

Today, the world is literally exploding with vast knowledge, which may be good, bad, or ugly, and reaches even illiterate people in remote regions through the different media. Perverted fanatics in various fields, with vested interests, spread damaging knowledge. Today's parents must be vigilant in providing for and protecting their children throughout their lives from those evil poachers.

These responsible acts cannot be done by any normal parents and so they must take their innocent children to the right schools and teachers, introduce them to worthy religious leaders, honest political circles, and respectable social circles and even must help them to find worthy friends.

Leisure may appear as innocuous and pleasant free time; but improper utilization of it pushes too many youths into irredeemable dangers. For some people, twenty-four hours a day may appear insufficient. Yet even for them there come times when they feel like doing nothing and are bored. There are youths with no proper employment, and they feel lonely with nothing to do.

Such idle minds can turn into a devil's workshop. This is not an exaggeration, so children must be guided, equipped, and trained to spend every bit of their leisure or even longer periods of their free time with interesting and worthy deeds so that their leisure ends as a happy and useful event. Encouraging children to play group games, to develop reading habits and good hobbies, helping them to enjoy good entertainments and undertake explorations and similar harmless and worthy activities will help them beat their loneliness and undesirable thoughts and acts. Such purposeful involvements even help them to overcome tension and mental disorders.

Every Child is a Future Home Builder

As mentioned, each child of every family will be a spouse of someone coming from another and sometimes even contrasting background and will spend a long part of life with him/her. Made-for-each-other couples are very rare, so the partners in each marriage must understand their life-partners, make compromises, adjustments, and even sacrifices in order to make family life worthy, sustainable, and harmonious. It is immaturity, selfishness, distrust, and suspicion which break most families. Everyone must understand that virtues such as empathy, tolerance, and forgiveness make one a civilized, respectable, and successful partner. Making children understand the role of love, sex (cf. chapters 16 and 17 of *Book G*), and forgiveness, and inculcating in them the sagacity to prevent circumstances which create suspicions, makes their family life wonderful.

Elders must be watchful and help new couples remove the commonly occurring misunderstandings during early married life. Further, guiding and helping them stand on their own legs with respect and dignity will go a long way in ensuring the creation of a new worthy family and a new generation to take the family and nation forward.

Ideal Home

When parents are wise enough to understand the above positive and negative factors and plan rationally to form a sustainable contented family, they are certain to build an ideal home. In such a home, everyone loves every other member and spontaneously cares about the other. For them, caring about others or making sacrifices for others is not a burden but a pleasure. As mentioned, the worst stupidities or tantrums of members, especially those of growing children, are never taken as offending, damaging, or something to be ridiculed; everyone tries to correct others' mistakes and fooleries in the most natural way, with no room for guilt, ill-feelings, blackmailing, or ridiculous nicknaming. Such harmony and cooperation always work toward contentment and sustainability.

A normal home is bound together by such abundantly flowing pure love from every member, the greatest tonic that nourishes life itself and makes people altruistic and self-sacrificial to the extent to sacrifice even life for those who are bound by love. In an ideal home, no one is left alone and the concern and care about others naturally saves everyone from the strain, tension, and anxieties of today's life. Even the physical feeling of tiredness and exhaustion from hard labour melt away when family members treat them with love and gratitude. In such families, mental illnesses, drug addictions, and suicidal tendencies are rare.

Home is the place where everyone can have the maximum freedom and can demand every right; every member has utmost responsibilities and duties toward it. When people have very high stakes in the form of loving families, which are more precious than the most precious material wealth, they spontaneously protect it with all their strength and wealth because without it they cannot think of a life. So, patriotism, altruism, courage, readiness for self-sacrifice, and such virtues come most naturally to them.

When parents form such ideal homes, many negatives like quarrels and litigations which drag their families toward unsustainable or deficient conditions do not arise. Such contented lives never allow them to voluntarily involve themselves in ugly acts which harm others and create situations which lead to GW and CC—like forest felling, environmental degradation, and polluting activities.

Harmony Favours Economy and Hope

Life in harmony as a family is the most advantageous, economical, pleasing, and desirable reality. A normal person's life revolves around it and home always attracts its members toward it like centripetal physical force. Normal persons can never think of a greater life than the one they normally enjoy in a normal home.

Usually, rural communes or villages are constituted by closely related and well known homes with many common attributes which, again, ensure a life in harmony; where one can think of the best possible life. Such harmony and uniformity get diluted with every outward move. A youth who enjoyed a worthy childhood would never like to settle permanently in unfamiliar, contrasting regions which would undo his and other people's socio-cultural assets and demographic equilibrium.

Unworthy Citizen

Children and youths, as dependants, are pure consumers and do almost nothing for carbon-fixing. By the time they reach adulthood, they have used a lot of natural resources, energy, and products of polluting industries. These make them indebted to Nature.

Adulthood is the time for people to repay their carbon-related debts to Nature. It depends to a large extent upon the way they form their own families as adults. If they plan a small sustainable family, they can spare natural resources, energy, and time to do carbon-friendly activities; but if they form unsustainable huge families, they naturally engage in activities which promote GW and CC and become a burden again to the world. It is more than a three-fold loss or harm to Mother Nature; he has consumed a lot to reach adulthood; he continues to consume a lot as an adult, and by creating an unsustainable family, he has created more consumers.

By such insane acts, these unworthy people lose the joy of living and also deny it to their dear children and to others and, above all, help the ruinous GW and CC.

Why People Fail to Form Worthy Families

Every responsible leader and planner must understand that most young couples who are going to build their families by having children are not at all mentally or intellectually mature persons. In almost all developing and poor countries, and among the poor communities or migrant populations of developed countries, these new couples are just grown-up children. For many reasons, it is foolish to expect such young couples to plan relevantly-formed, worthy families.

Since they had been dependent on their parents, they could not have had enough exposure to real life situations like strained resources, unemployment, crime, corruption, competition, etc. These young new couples normally enjoy the best health, youthful vigour, confidence (bliss of ignorance), and enthusiasm to do more work, but they may not realize that these will gradually decline while their responsibilities grow with their growing children. In most instances, these childish couples have the support of their parents. But the couples may not understand that their supportive parents will soon become dependent on them because of ageing. The cumulative effects of all these "mirages" easily deceive them to exceed their limits by having more children than their real attributes can support. This simple-looking mistake seals their fate and confirms their and their children's sufferings for a very long time.

Contribution of Worthless Governments

People-friendly democratic governments never bother to help the "immature" young couples to form sustainable small families because they are constrained to ignore them for various reasons, namely human rights, personal freedom, non-interference, wrongly interpreted religious notions, or fearing flak during democratic elections.

There are a few decisions in life which, once executed, can never be taken back, the most important of which is the number of children a family has. If the new, "innocent," couples cross their limits, their families become burdened with deficits and then their sufferings are certain.

For any government, there cannot be a greater sin and a more unpatriotic act than allowing young couples to form unsustainable miserable families; it amounts to a punishment far worse than a life-sentence of incarceration with hard labour. Members of unsustainable families spend a lot of their time fighting hunger and doing everything to ensure the next meal or food-security. In that process, they lose the happiness and joy of living and invariably lose the opportunity to bring out their talents and individualities, and above all, end their lives creating more deficits for their country and the world.

Wrong Notions of Governments and Responsible People

Most governments and activists think that they can always mitigate the sufferings of such unfortunate unsustainable families with proper aids like free or subsidized food, free education, free health care, free housing, etc. Many governments, like the one in the state of Tamil Nadu in India, are doing much more than this. But they fail to understand the sorrowful psycho-social aspects of these dependent children because the government can never play the roles of a normal father and a devoted mother. So, the unfortunate children may be fed satisfactorily and even educated by governments or service organizations; but their dignity is compromised and their thoughts remain confused and even vengeful for various reasons, like the humiliations and indignities they suffer because of a host of deficiencies and dependence upon others.

Helping people during calamities is a necessity, and people appreciate such services. But "helping" families to descend to the level to seek assistance is a crime. When children with healthy parents are made to live with external assistance for a long time, it certainly affects the pride of sensitive children, because every worthy child wants to be fed and supported with the personal earnings of his/her own parents.

Conclusion

Families are the building blocks of nations and a global community. If humanity strives and helps every family of the world to become a respectable, happy, contented sustainable one, there will be no fresh entrant into the world of crime, no forest destruction or anti-people activities. Then, the existing discontent and dangerous people will gradually lose their support base and go into oblivion through ageing. With time, every ill that promotes GW, too, can be brought down to safe levels or a healthy balance. The creation of unsustainable families will continue to supply youths for all the undesirable activities and give immortality to all the ills, evils, and curses, ranging from poverty and crime to pollution, GW, and CC.

5

Sustainability or Sustainable Living

What is Sustainability or Sustainable Living?

Sustaining something or somebody means: to support, to bear the weight, to keep alive or in existence or to keep going, especially for a long period. Sustainability or sustainable living conditions may be defined as the existence of favourable conditions that assure all people of a decent and comfortable life forever, with all the reasonable necessities. Favourable conditions can be defined as the prevalence of conditions that assure people of the capacity to procure all the necessities with normally accepted efforts and without hurting Nature more than its ability to regenerate and without leaving anything beyond the ability of Nature to neutralize.

Rational Extension

Sustainability has two components—the supporter and the supported or the dependant. Nature is everything for us and Nature supports every life-form—the dependents. We come from Nature and will return some day to it as its elements. During our short life of seventy to one hundred years, Nature alone supports us with its resources. Some of our activities and the ways of living of some of us may appear to be unconnected to Nature. Yet it provides us with our wholesome food, potable water, pure air, living space, and at last, de-pollutes every waste we produce.

So it is crucial that a rational balance be maintained between the positive life-supporting resources of Nature and the beneficiaries.

The beneficiaries include all the life forms, including human beings. Respecting every life form and providing it with its due share of natural resources are of vital importance because every diverse life form has a role in keeping our only host and home healthy and sustainable.

Nature, which we call our planet, is not at all an expandable object as per the requirements of its growing inhabitants. It has a limit, with a fixed amount of life-supporting resources and living space. Vital resources like fertile land and water must rationally be shared by the various terrestrial life forms, including *Homo sapiens.* Unrestricted growth of some species will suck away the rightful resources of some other species and push them to their extinction. Ill health and extinction of some species will trigger a chain reaction that affects other members of their ecosystem, the interconnected ecosystems, and then the whole region. Injury to ecosystems means injury to Nature. Injury to Nature makes life difficult or unsustainable.

Ultimate Balancing Acts

Healthy, sustainable living conditions for humans means that the number of the beneficiary humans must be kept at the right level, or a little lower than the number that Nature's resources can support.

We have more than enough data, space cameras, and computers to analyze the geographical attributes, availability of resources, and climatic conditions of our planet. We know the quantities of resources every person requires and the amounts of the various waste every person produces. From these, we can certainly work out the exact number of people a region or country can support. (See chapter 7)

If present-day humanity has the least sense of responsibility, morality, and concern for the next generation and the desire to perpetuate the human race, every member must take care of every minor thing to hand over a liveable Earth to our children. Human societies across the world keep committing grave, foolish mistakes, day in and day out. They keep bringing out the "prohibited" buried carbon (petroleum and coal) to "sustain" our life, and this must attract our immediate attention. Their many unchecked, ongoing minor, day-to-day acts also harm sustainability or promote pollution and GW.

For instance, we shift millions of tons of sodium chloride (common salt) from oceans for various domestic and industrial purposes. Rising levels of sodium chloride in soil are highly toxic to the plant kingdom. We use tons and tons of microscopic, insoluble particles in consumer goods like toothpastes. They affect the fertility of land by plugging the porous soil. Many commonly used sprays and volatile chemicals create ozone holes. We use huge quantities of many toxic chemicals in our homes, fields, industries, and day-to-day activities, and lots of plastics which too are harmful in many ways.

Ultimate Sustainability-Related Manoeuvrable Spot

Family life is the most economical way of living and families are the ultimate wholesome beneficiaries of Nature. Families have their own supporters (parents) and dependents (children). A country may have surplus resources, yet the breadwinners' abilities and time have limits, so they can wholesomely support just a certain number of children. Competitive living conditions due to limited resources and restricted opportunities further strain breadwinners' abilities and sustainability.

The balancing at family level to ensure sustainability, as per those changing, tougher living conditions (which reflect the severity of unsustainability), decides the wellbeing of the families. The sustainability of a country is influenced by how their families are formed—with or without deficits; and so, that of the globe. Hence, in order to set right the unsustainable equations (population to resources) at regional or national levels, one must go back to families, where alone we can manoeuvre the balancing act.

Changing Trends

The hopeful yesteryears: In the past, sustainability was equated with feeding people sumptuously and providing them with shelter and clothing. Other needs, like water, healthy environment, unpolluted air, employment opportunities, etc., were taken for granted because they were available in plenty and most countries had surplus resources that assured everyone of a hopeful life. Until a century ago, the needs of people were only a few. When the needs or the burden was less, parents were able to support more members. Nature, too, was happily sustaining humans in those days of low population density, because their polluting levels and injurious acts like forest destruction were within Nature's ability to make good.

Positive balance (with far lower population and surplus resources) made life happy, peaceful, and hopeful in every region free from exploitations.

The deterioration toward today: The world experienced food shortages when the population exploded and suffered more when struck by natural disasters. Visionaries equated population explosion with calamity; but critics ridiculed them. During the last century, conditions turned favourable because of the green revolution and large-scale technological advancements, including those related to farming. These made the critics feel triumphant because their ignorance never allowed them to understand the visionaries.

Farm revolutions are still continuing, and now we are in a position to feed even more than the present population of seven billion people. Despite this food-security, we do not enjoy a peaceful and hopeful life because there are also other influencing factors which decide our happiness, hope, peace, and wholesome sustainability.

Unfortunately, food security (including the food aid of poverty alleviation schemes) misguided or empowered too many ignorant families which enlarged their families without right thought or plan and made their families insatiable and unsustainable—with huge deficits at family levels. With time, regional population density exceeded the optimum levels and created regional scarcities/deficits.

Man-Made Fooleries and Authenticity of Visionaries

These deficits or acquired shortages forced the proliferating people of most countries to aggressively encroach upon living space and resources meant for our cohabitants and pushed many species of precious plants and animals to extinction. Even after usurping enormous resources meant for other diverse species, human beings are short of resources, employment opportunities, serene environment, and wholesome food position. (The wholesome food position differs from our technologically-augmented food security). To offset the pressures of the mounting deficits, we sought the "mercy" of the "double-edged" dirty energy and enriched our economies.

And now, because of the growth of the one species (humans) on an enormous scale, all the living beings of our small planet, including humans and the host (planet Earth) which provides us with everything, are threatened with the impact of the huge deficits created by that one species. The impact manifests itself in many ways, including green cover destruction, pollution, GW, and CC. These horrible, apocalyptic signs and symptoms of unsustainability give recognition to the views of those visionaries.

As we have seen, less populous developed countries have also committed the mistake of depending upon an industrial economy driven by polluting energy.

What Does Sustainability Mean for the Future?

The modern concept of sustainability involves the sustainability of everything that controls and comforts life. That means our industrial activities, farming (food source), employment opportunities, healthy environment, and also the whole ecosystem and the whole planet must be sustainable in a wholesome way—totally and individually. (People also call this *green living*.)

Request to the Killer Race

Dear fellow humans, Nature has given you thousands of varieties of food items, including sweet fruits. You can mix, blend, or cook them in any combination to make thousands of varieties of meals. You can endlessly enjoy these varieties of food and drinks; you can enjoy the millions of other gifts of Nature; you can play the games you like; you can enjoy entertainments endlessly; and you can have fun with your dear ones and enjoy the company of dear friends or the other animals and birds. When you love Mother Nature and all her children, you will not suffer boredom at all. What else do you want?

Mother Nature gives all these to you freely. But you are thankless and torture her through your destructive activities (on forests, environment, water bodies, fertile lands, Nature's other children in the form of millions of other species, etc.). Will you ever stab or slash your mother? Will you ever allow someone to apply a red-hot iron anywhere on your mother who feeds you? You are doing more than this to our dear Mother Nature. You devitalize her through a variety of injuries, poison her little by little with pollutants and exterminate her precious other children. When your provider is sick, you cannot think of a hopeful future.

There cannot be any more treacherous, uglier, and more foolish acts than these. Is there any more heinous, unpardonable act?

We do all these suicidal and shameful acts; yet we call ourselves a civilized, dignified, and intelligent race.

What Will the Cohabitants Say About You?

If our cohabitants, including plants, could express their anguish, what would they convey to their "children" about us? "See the most monstrous creatures ever evolved on our small planet. These rascals have plundered everything sacred and precious, grabbed our resources, and aggressed upon our territories, mercilessly have exterminated and still are exterminating many of our relatives, and make life dangerous for all, including themselves. They are gluttonous fools who are not at all satisfied with our Mother's care in the form of abundant gifts, including a variety of energy sources, and have made life unsustainable for all. Then, in order to quench their over-thirst for energy, they went to suck out the filthy poison (petroleum) hidden by our Mother to protect all of us from its harmful effects. Never go near them; and if you do, they will kill you for nothing."

Stop Crime Against the Innocents

We humans talk about humanism, justice for all, equality, transparency, dignity, non-interference, non-aggression, and also about many rights. We have abolished capital punishment in several regions of the world; we treat even the heinous murderer and terrorist with compassion and protect them in safe chambers, wasting huge funds; we use the world court to try and punish mass-murderers.

But, do we care the least for the millions of fragile, innocent, beautiful, precious, and useful (more useful than humans) species? We do just the opposite. While we live an undisciplined, selfish, unsustainable, and foolish life, we will be called rascals, murderers, and plundering monsters.

6

Status of Unsustainability

(Unsustainable Living Condition—ULC)

Where Are We Now?

For the vast majority of mankind, the respectable and hopeful position of surplus resources is history. To make matters worse, those free or almost free resources of yesteryear, like water, fertile lands, pure air, living space, breezes, clean environment, job opportunities, etc., have now become costly commodities. The combination of growing deficits and cost with multiplying needs makes sustaining life more and more difficult with every passing year.

For modern humanity, sustainability is not just feeding people and ensuring shelter and clothing, but sustaining a normally agreeable wholesome, dignified life by fulfilling the normally required many additional needs, including education, health care, safe environment, ample energy, transport facilities, communication gadgets, reasonable industrial activities, infrastructures, and much more. Many families earn enough to satisfy most of these additional needs and enjoy life, but they do so at the heavy cost of dangerous pollution; this apparently happy life is unsustainable.

Pushing Up the Cost of Living

Modern people have muddled up their economy and life-style with their wrong priorities and, as a result of this, prices of many non-vital supplementary or add-on or facilitator-needs like entertainment, communication, travel, physical appearance (with pompous dresses and cosmetics), etc., have multiplied many times more than that of the vital, basic needs, like food.

To make matters worse, modern urban people, unlike their rural siblings, want an uninterrupted flow of energy and transport facilities. If there is any interruption in these, they will starve and ruin their health and economy. Further, modern youth, especially the urbanites, must ensure themselves paid jobs and they must get educated for this, spending many years, huge funds, and their whole youthful energy under unhealthy competition, because a paid job has become a vital necessity for an urbanite living with no direct access to life-supportive basic resources. On the contrary people living in the lap of Nature today, with sufficient resources, can enjoy a life without most of those additional needs.

Today, even to ensure oneself reasonable love, dignity, security, and respect, one has to spend money, time, and energy, and so one has to earn more money to "buy" these. In most developing and poor countries, people buy even "justice" with money; otherwise, "injustice" will ruin their life. Quite often, bureaucratic posts, players of "entertaining" games, skilled labourers, and professionals are auctioned, by which they sell their dignity and freedom to earn more. Often, people buy powerful posts with huge amounts of money and efforts, just to raise their "dignity," power, and sustainability.

More and more people have become dependent on computers, mobile phones, certain machines, entertainments, drugs, gadgets like the pace-maker, etc., and the absence of these terribly affects their normal life (sustainability) or even ends it.

All these bizarre happenings push up the cost of living, too. Modern families easily accumulate more deficits and acquire ULC status very easily. (For more details, see Part II and Chapter 60 of *Book G.*)

Misleading Expressions and Assurances

Despite those huge deficits and threats, we have learnt to live a well-adapted, deficient life (WADL) and not at all a sustainable hopeful life. Sustaining such a deficient life is not at all sustainable living.

Even while burdened with huge debts and shortages, responsible people often reassure the desperate common man with schemes like "sustainable developments," "sustainable economy," and "sustainable living," assured GDP growth, etc. Such assurances are misnomers and misleading. A careful study of their schemes shows that they invariably lead to more deficits and they are implemented with the backing of polluting energy. Such developments in WADL regions may give people comforts and create many jobs but invariably take them a step toward "entrapment." While a country suffers huge deficits of sort, any apparent GDP growth is not growth at all, because such gains are just a fraction of the deficits and cannot clear them.

Instead of misleading the common man, responsible people must recognize and enlighten ordinary people about the all-pervading signs and symptoms of ULC and guide them to end deficits; then the results would be more rewarding.

ULC Is Everywhere; But We Fail to Recognize It

ULC is everywhere and it expresses itself or has "metamorphosed" into uncountable shapes and forms; but we do not connect them to ULC.

The following long list of circumstances in real life will make us realize the ubiquitous and prevailing nature of ULC: Living a life with scanty water, insufficient food, or living with foods created with unnatural means like BT (Bio-technology) or unsustainable, over-intensive agriculture; living at other's mercy or charity or with the freebies of governments for a long time; living in congested, uncomfortable places and unclean environment; hating others for no valid reason; living amidst corruption, crime, and violence; "willingly" joining criminal and terrorist gangs; the necessity of using dangerously congested streets and roads; gulping fast-food in a hurry; running around at top speed to finish the day's "duties"; living a too busy life with no time for family and friends; working hard for a very long time; competing desperately to bring the next product to market; murdering for gain or to end competitions; committing suicide because of unfulfilled needs; rising psychiatric conditions; fast urbanization; presence of war-like conditions; struggling hard to get educated only with the aim of taking a job; migrating desperately; disintegration of joint-families; cheating, hating, and violating peace in the name of religion and God; failing democracies around the world; existence of ungovernable people. There are many more such instances and events we come across daily (especially in developing and poor countries) but they are all nothing but the signs and symptoms of ULC—as we will see soon. ULC exists in developed countries in the form of highly polluting economic activities, from which people are unable to relieve themselves.

Prominent Global Manifestations of ULC

Terrible events such as 9/11, bombings in London, Spain, New Delhi, and Bali, or the regular suicide bombings around the world, cartoon controversy in Scandinavian countries, ethnic cleansing in various regions, unending enmity in Palestine, ungovernable societies in countries like Somalia, violent groups like Maoists and Naxalites in India, Taliban, Al Qaeda, and the many terror groups in Pakistan and Afghanistan, mass uprisings in Arab countries, riots in England, unmanageable Cairo, "civil war" in Syria, recurring boat tragedies of desperate migrants, American "shut-down", harmful Chinese fog, communal violence in India, Pakistan, Sri Lanka and Myanmar, and so on are all manifestations of ULC in the present world; but the global leaders and planners in general and the concerned leaders in particular have not understood them. Without comprehending, they fight all those evils by spending huge funds and manpower. The real causative factor escapes their attention, and in that process they give a "happy, long life" to deficits (ULC) and those horrors.

Enormity of Complications Due To ULC

We must understand that the heinous acts of crime, violence, terrorism, polluting, inciting religious people to go violent, sabotaging democracies, and a variety of similar activities are not carried out for fun or just for vengeance or for nothing. Most often, the perpetrators make such decisions after a lot of conflicting mental struggles and sufferings, frustrations, disappointments, after frequently repeating "to be or not to be," and weighing the pros and cons. Such undignified acts quite often have components resulting from feelings such as competition, envy, jealousy, suspicion, revenge, etc., and even may be done with the "noble" aim of mitigating their family deficits or for being in some job or as a "service" to the society by finishing off the "worthless" great men, or even with the intention of bringing down the status of "proud enemies" to their level. In fact, for millions of people, these anti-environmental, anti-social, and anti-national acts are full time jobs and their families are "sustained" with such "hard earned" income.

It is difficult to suggest any alternative job for such millions of people living in crowded countries with a very high unemployment rate and unhealthy competition.

Warning

Ending deficits by controlling the deficit-causing mechanism is the only solution, failing which, the little peace, happiness, hope, dignity, and freedom we enjoy will be lost.

7

Arithmetic of Sustainability

Wages of Unrestricted Proliferation

As we have seen, sustainability has two components: the supporter and the supported. Our motherly planet, the Earth, supports and sustains all the diverse life forms of millions of species. But the life-supportive resources of Earth have limits. If given opportunities, every one of these millions of species can proliferate to occupy the whole planet. Yet Nature manages them in such a way that the various species are used as controllers and facilitators of other species and thus make life liveable and sustainable for all. If left undisturbed, Nature can protect and sustain every species and take it toward eternity.

Fortunately or unfortunately, humans have learned a few tricks to overcome the restrictive mechanisms of Nature and so have proliferated to outgrow their provisions. This causes deficiencies, leading to poverty, crime, terrorism, pollution, GW, CC, accidents, genocides, suicides, etc. Now, these evils of their own creation try to restrict their numbers and growth. Yet the population grows fast like cancer cells, has extinguished too many other species, and is slowly pushing many innocent races into extinction. Unless the human race understands the limits and corrects the wrongs, more and more people and species will face an inglorious exit.

Understanding Sustainable Limits

Our vital natural resources, like water and usable lands, are of fixed quantities. Similarly, those resources required for a person to sustain a normal life are also of fixed quantities. With these fixed quantities, we can find out the supporting capacity or sustainable limit of a region, a state, a country, or the world by dividing the total available resources with the quantity needed by a single person.

Rough estimates say that the human population crossed those optimum levels a long time ago in most regions. The difference between the optimum and exceeded levels gives us an idea about their deficits.

Fixed Quantities and Our Shrunken Share

Our home, the Earth, has a total surface area of 510,100,500 (about 0.51 billion) square kilometres. Of this total area, land constitutes 29.1 percent or 148,950,800 (about 0.15 billion) square kilometres. Of this land area, vast regions (about one third) are "inaccessible" and inhospitable for most of the life forms. Of the remaining area, we must spare at least one third for forests, water bodies, and for our cohabitants.

Leaving a share for other species is not an act of charity. It is for our own well-being and for clean and sustainable living; all life forms—from invisible microbes like soil bacteria and fungi to slightly larger earthworms and termites to huge animals, birds, and plants—have a role in ensuring the fertility of our soil and a clean environment by converting our filth into clean nutrients for our crops and other plants.

We must use this shrunken area for all our purposes, like living, farming, transportation, other infrastructures, institutions, a healthy environment, and for de-polluting activities.

Unhealthy Course of Mankind

Mankind is a mixture of diverse races with diverse cultures, languages, and traditions, which are mostly related to their own climate and geography. If we want to live a worthy life, we must protect all the diverse races of mankind and their attributes. Unfortunately, the most progressed people of the world, of every country and of the least developed primitive people, are dwindling in numbers. Vast sections of people of poor and developing countries keep exploding fast. They suffer by getting drowned in the deficits of their own creation and thus have ruined their rights and opportunities for a wholesome sustainable living.

These "ignorant" deficit-creating people universalize/globalize unsustainability and deficits in many ways and create hell for everyone else.

Sensible Way of Protecting Diverse Races and Cultures

Every distinct group of the human race in every region must have its own "homeland" to perpetuate its own culture, language, customs, traditions, cuisine, and everything that makes it special. The demographic course of the world is chaotic and tries to harm the above. Harming those through mad proliferation and migration or in the name of cultural integration, multiculturalism, or any other name is a stupid and mad act against the human race as a whole. The right balance between the resources of those diverse countries and their people alone can safeguard their worthy life.

For many reasons, estimating the supporting capacity of the world and planning accordingly does not serve any worthy purpose. Understanding the supporting capacity of each country and its regions or states is far easier and more valuable, because such figures can help us to understand the cause for their sufferings and to plan appropriately. When leaders and planners take those mathematical figures of supporting capacity (the number of people their region or country can hold) as the centre of their planning, every region/people of the world will gain sustainable life with total freedom, dignity, and joy.

Population Density (PD) of a Country

Population density (PD) is the relationship between the total areas in square kilometres of a country to its population and is expressed in number of people per square kilometre. PD does not carry any message with regard to sustainability. But PD in relation to the optimum population density (OPD) or sustainable PD (SPD), conveys the sustainability related message about that country.

Finding the Supporting Capacity of a Country—the Concept of OPD

We have already seen that by dividing the total resources available for human use in the given region by the total needs of one person, we can find the supporting capacity or sustainable limit of that region. (This discussion is based upon very minimal quantities to avoid unnecessary criticism.)

Every human requires food, water, living space, a clean environment, and an area to neutralize their excreta, wastes, and injurious products (depolluting activities), and for the usual institutions and infrastructures. Present-day people need a lot of energy for their day-to-day activities and their requirement of energy must also be made available from renewable or biological sources.

The conversion of all that into natural resources is needed for a person to lead a wholesome sustainable living.

Modern life has detached too many people from Nature. Yet everyone living anywhere is ultimately supported with the products of Nature. For the strict assessment of the supporting capacity of a region, we must compute the various requirements of a person of that region against how much resources are available for them in that region. For many reasons, it is enough if we do the computing with water and fertile land or sufficiently watered fertile land. This calculation is convenient and has a practical value.

The most conservative estimates show that an individual living in a tropical or sub-tropical region with sufficient sunshine and acceptable weather conditions needs at least half a hectare (5000 square meters, or about 1.24 acre) of moderately watered land for all the purposes mentioned. But, people living in areas with water scarcity, extreme weather conditions, poor sunshine, and difficult terrains need more than half a hectare each for a sustainable living.

Every country knows or has the facilities to measure its total area of fertile lands. From that, we must deduct how much of it can be used by people. If we divide the land area thus derived at with a person's need of a half hectare, we can find the number of individuals that the country can support.

Optimum (Sustainable) Population Density (OPD) of a Country

Now we know the number of people the country's resources can support. This number is derived from a restricted fertile land-area of a country; but the total area of that country is far higher than this.

If we divide the number of people (those fertile lands of their country could support) by the total area of that country, we will get the optimum population density (OPD). In other words, it is the average number of people per square kilometre who can live sustainably in that whole country.

An Elaboration

This elaboration is based upon well-populated regions of the present-day world.

Here is an imaginary, sufficiently fertile, small, diverse country with a total area of 300 square kilometres with mixed terrain. About one third of the geographical region is, as in most other countries, mountains, rough terrains, and other inhospitable lands where people cannot live. Another one third contains forests, other green cover, water bodies, etc.

This leaves us with the remaining one third, or one hundred square kilometres of fertile and hospitable lands for human use.

One hectare of this fertile land supports two persons. One square kilometre is 100 hectares and so can support 2 X 100 = 200 people. So 100 square kilometres of this rightful (for human use) area of that country can support 2 X 100 X 100 = 20,000 people.

This country of 300 square kilometres of total land area can wholesomely support or sustain just 20,000 people. Therefore, the OPD of this country is 20,000/300 = 66.66. So such a reasonably blessed country, with mixed terrains and satisfactory climatic conditions, can support about 67 people per one square kilometre. (Optimum total population of that country is OPD X total area of that country = 20,000.)

For various reasons, such as advantageous utilization of resources as families and groups, improved green technologies, livelihood based on water bodies or oceans (like fisheries), and integrated socio-economic life with other jobs, we can allow a few more people to live in the given area without much strain.

So with sufficient lenience, we can fix for a moderately fertile country an OPD of about 100 to 120 per square kilometre. There are very fertile countries/states where 50 percent of their geographical area can be allowed for human use. Such regions could sustain an OPD of about 150 per square kilometre in a wholesome way. But anything more than these levels certainly makes life unsustainable.

Canada and the Scandinavian nations have vast ice-covered regions and get sunshine just for a few months in a year. Countries in the Saharan region and Mongolia and some other regions of the world have vast deserts that do not support human life. The OPD of those disadvantageous countries is just a fraction of that of a fertile tropical region.

Importance of OPD

OPD is synonymous with sustainable population density (SPD), supporting capacity, and also the sustainable limit of that region. It drives home the truth that, with this population and rational planning, they can optimally use their resources and live a respectable sustainable life without apprehension of unemployment and unhealthy competitions. So they need not destroy forests or cause damage to the environment. Now they can recycle their used materials and wastes and convert organic wastes into manure for organic farming and, at last, leave nothing to pollute. Such a sustainable living can give them enough funds, time, and manpower to utilize renewable and natural energy sources, including bio-fuels.

Low Population Density (LPD)

When the population density is lower than OPD, they will have surplus resources and people can enjoy a highly hopeful, well-secured luxurious life.

High Population Density (HPD)

When the population outgrows the optimum level, deficits are inevitable and bring in all the ills, evils, and curses, from poverty and crime to pollution, GW, and CC. We can call this condition High Population Density (HPD) or unsustainable population density or generalized unsustainable living condition (GULC). The curses worsen in direct proportion to the growth of HPD and the duration of HPD. This is a highly ruinous situation and forms the basis for most human sufferings.

In rural regions, HPD evolves following the formation of unsustainable huge families. Migrants from bulging rural regions expand urban population toward HPD. And migrants of poor and developing countries bring about HPD in developed countries.

Understanding Global Ills Through PD/OPD

Amity, peace, happiness, hope, and security of any people or nation have a direct relationship to PD. Today, too many countries suffer too many ills, evils, and curses, causing an unworthy, miserable life with no hope or peace. If the problems of humanity and the world, namely poverty, crime, terrorism, hatred, fanaticism, polluting activities, forest destruction, loss of peace in Palestine, uprisings in Arab countries, ungovernable regions or countries such as Afghanistan and Somalia, migrations, treacheries, etc. are well analyzed in the light of OPD and HPD, they can always find the cause and solution.

Where are We?

There is no doubt that we have gone far beyond OPD into HPD. While we can rationally think of a maximum population of 120 per square kilometre for a normal, vast country, too many regions in Asian, South American, and African countries have five or more times this OPD. When a region has an HPD of five times its OPD, those people need five times the size of their state or country for sustainable healthy living. From such figures, we can understand the enormity of the already accumulated deficits and its consequences in the form of evolved and evolving evils.

8

Why We Failed to Recognize
The End of Sustainability

Understanding Deficits

Until a century ago, a vast majority of people led a nature-based, sustainable rural living. When we live directly out of the resources of Nature, like land and water, we recognize its limits and the strain and shortages related to them. But a life with no direct connection with the life-supportive resources of Nature takes away such wakefulness.

Discoveries Blinded People and Made Them Score "Self Goals"

Shortages are natural when populations cross the supporting capacity (OPD) of their region. Continuance of a life with shortages (above OPD) steadily accumulates more deficits and people cannot live a full and comfortable life beyond certain levels of such deficits. Normally, people get warned when they face deficits and will "shift gears" to adaptation mode, as we discussed. When they are threatened further, people rob the resources meant for other species or migrate to other regions or cities and adapt themselves to a new life.

Starvation is a prominent and foremost sign of deficits, and humanity has been searching for new ways to end it. Green revolution and other farm techniques (like improved dairy farming, fish culture, meat production, etc.) helped people in the recent past to produce more food than they required. So, people failed to mind this sign of unsustainability.

The newer farming technologies and intensive farming required far less manpower than traditional farming and made the huge rural workforce redundant. They too migrated to cities. Migration and urban life needed a lot of energy—the next challenge. The discovery of new energy sources in the form of coal and petroleum met this challenge, too. The beneficiaries of highly polluting, depletable coal do not have an opportunity to see a piece of it at all or how it belches out polluting carbon, because they get energy in the form of very clean, "non-polluting" electricity. How, then, can we expect people to understand the evolving unsustainability and the course toward more pollution?

As we will see, urban living is far more unsustainable than it appears to be; yet new discoveries, inventions, entertainments, opportunities in various newer fields, advancement in education, and the "abundant" energy sources gave an easy and enviable life to those who had left Nature. Many of them utilized the exploding knowledge and took up very successful professions, powerful and well-paid jobs, and profitable businesses. All this made them feel like lords of Nature and blinded them and so they could not see the realities. Most of them felt like living in another civilized world. Under these circumstances, how could they take note of the deficits accumulating at the bottom? To them, ignorance related to Nature was bliss. What will happen when these ignorant, joyous people are given the responsibility to plan for sustainability and to administer their country?

The present state of our planet, with all the harrowing evils and the curses like pollution, GW, and CC, is the result of thrusting the responsibilities upon such well civilized, "irrelevantly" enlightened, highly "suckcessful," great-looking charlatans who keep masquerading as leaders, top politicians, planners, economists, responsible bureaucrats, and those with the responsibility to find solutions to pollution and climate change (CC).

Happy Enslavement Took Away Fear

Now, those living in Nature with deficiencies also get infected with the desire for a great life similar to that lived by the people who left Nature, and they do everything possible to achieve it. Thus, almost the whole of humanity lives a Well Adapted Deficient Life (WADL), and has become dependent on new gadgets, newer technologies, including farm practices, and have become slaves of the great-looking modern living with 24x7 entertainments and, above all, to the polluting energy. The unnaturally-produced surplus food and the unnatural and dangerously polluting petroleum hide their deficits; so they continue WADL without any fear, and even create huge unsustainable families. Thus, humans have accumulated huge deficits and allow the deficits to swell by continuing that life. Growing deficits and HPD further mar sustainability by aiding the evolution of many evils and curses, corresponding to their severity. (Details are in chapters 13 to 24 and also in *Book G*). Yet people do not understand that those evils and curses are created by the deficits.

We cannot expect those "happy slaves" to think about deficits or to sacrifice their comforts for the sake of sustainability.

Great Hope Turned Nightmare for Farmers

Since food was the most needed requirement of mankind until half a century ago, agricultural and other farm products fetched very good prices and gave a wonderful life to the rural population in most countries, so people preferred the life in the lap of Mother Nature. The highly dedicated agro-scientist Norman E. Borlaug's green revolution gave them very high hopes for a wonderful life because they were able to produce three to four times more from the same farms. But it turned out to be an unexpected blow to their hopes. When food supply turned surplus, prices fell drastically and the farmers ran into losses. Too many defeated farm families of poor and developing countries could not buy their other needs, like good shelter and satisfactory medical care, and they were not even able to educate their children.

These rural families had one very definite opportunity to overcome the calamity: to end huge insatiable families (HIFs) and to form a positive equation at family level. The wise among them formed small and manageable families and progressed, but too many continue to form highly deficient families and starve because they have no one to enlighten them. Due to hunger and unquenchable needs members of such families take even hard and risky labour for low wages. They are exploited (like slaves) in villages, cities and in other countries as child labourers, housemaids, and as "contract labourers" in many fields ranging from very tough manual labour to jobs such as paid killers and "proxy accused" (of gangs of ill repute) in judicial courts. Their sweat makes the exploiters rich and "powerful" and creates very wide socio-economic disparities. How can one expect good advice / guidance from the "great" people who enjoy a really great life by exploiting the difficulties of unsustainable poor families (HIF)?

But a Boon to Urbanites and a Booster of Pollution

Because of the great fall in food prices and its easy availability, urbanites were assured of an ample supply of this most important human need. The low price of food has helped non-farming families, especially urbanites, to save huge funds and thereby live a lavish life.

With food security, surplus funds, and evolving vast opportunities, they are able to venture out and invest in newer fields like science, technology, computers, space travel, entertainment, communications, fast travel, atomic science, alternative energy generation, etc. These make modern people prefer urban life and they now dominate vital jobs which decide the course of a country, and even of humanity. Yet they do not seem to understand that all these new jobs are deficit-prone and "sustained" with the help of unsustainable farming and polluting energy in plenty.

I have called the food front an unsustainable food source because, in order to survive with their shrinking lands and vanishing water, modern farmers use new technologies like drip irrigation, too much external inputs like NPK fertilizers and micronutrients, and a variety of toxic chemicals like insecticides and herbicides to protect their crops, rodent killers and anti-fungal chemicals to protect their harvested items, and resort to making these more appealing and durable through chemical-treatments and bio-technologies. If these farmers want to return to sustainable and wholesome organic farming, their expenditure will go up and they will require two or three times more water and land than they use now. But who has such vast areas to satisfy the millions of farmers and where are the huge quantities of water that they require? Wholesome farming remains a huge deficit for the whole human race, not just for the farmers.

High Satisfaction and Complaisance

Almost the whole of humanity lives an apparently satisfactory life; then why must people bother about deficits or unsustainability, pollution or CC?

There is another section of people who live a parasitic life by indulging in corruption, crime, cheating, tax-evasion, and such shameful acts, and even hold important positions in society, politics, and other vital organizations. To most of them, life is pure joy and total entertainment because of easy money, no hard work, and not much suffering due to a deteriorating environment, polluted atmosphere, and erratic climate, because they live in artificially created environments.

It is a horrible fact that even if we are ready to compromise and accept this WADL and HPD, with all their curses, like crime and pollution, life cannot be sustained because already we have accumulated too much deficiencies, filth, and damage, and this deficient state would continue to create more sludge and damage and so would create far worse situations.

Finding a Solution

It is high time we understood how deficiencies are created, who creates them (see the next chapter) and how these grow to threaten humanity with GW and CC. Then we can end them with rational plans.

9

HIF—The Hellish Fountainhead of Unsustainability

Importance of Understanding Family Deficits

We saw in chapter 5 the importance and responsibilities of families. When families are formed with the right thought to avoid deficits, they enjoy a worthy and happy life; but when the breadwinner-dependants ratio goes wrong, deficiencies crop up and, consequently, they suffer poverty and indignities. With time, such families would create some kind of generalized poverty/deficits/unsustainability, or HPD. HPD is a far more horrible condition than HIF (huge insatiable families), complicates and ruins every good thing we cherish and speeds up the evolution of evils and curses which end, for now, with global warming (GW) and climate change (CC).

So understanding the evolution of deficits or unsustainable living conditions (ULC) when starting families is vital to ending all those curses.

Most Ignored Catastrophe

Humanity gave the right attention to conditions like cancers, infectious diseases, oppressive regimes, humiliating people in the name of class, race, or caste, and other sorrowful conditions like leprosy and AIDS. But it failed to recognize a very serious condition which often works silently and damns people to suffer physically, mentally, psychologically, economically, socially, and in every other conceivable way, and makes their lives unworthy and miserable. And even takes away lives prematurely in horrible ways.

This condition/factor behind those curses may not look so dreadful for an onlooker; yet, as we will see soon, it is a hard fact. It is nothing but the unsustainable living conditions (ULC)/deficits/insufficiencies/ deficiencies evolving in families, which are invariably created by those families themselves, in the form of huge insatiable families (HIF), out of ignorance or indifference.

Surprising Facts

The meaning conveyed by the phrase "unsustainable living conditions in families" may appear innocuous and at the most may evoke sympathy. But the real happenings that arise from these conditions are too horrible and undesirable, to the extent to call them a hell.

Huge Insatiable Family (HIF)

Forming Unsustainable Huge Families

Every family, like a mini-government, has the duty and responsibility to plan for deficit-free, content, happy living. Planning at family level is not a sin or a curse, as some groups try to project. Irrespective of the status of a country with regard to prosperity or chaos, peace or uncertainties, worthy or unworthy governance, it is the two-person head of each family (parents) that is responsible for its wellbeing. As we saw earlier, every parent, rather, the new couple, must plan and form their family with a clear understanding of the positive and negative factors which influence their living, in addition to keeping in mind the additional duties "imposed" upon them by modern life.

Living conditions and the other influencing factors differ from region to region and from country to country, and even from time to time. By weighing the favourable conditions against the unfavourable conditions of a region, people can compute the number of children a normal couple can support comfortably in that region. When the new young couples exceed this number, they become unsustainable families with deficits. In other words, the families are too large or huge for those parents to support.

Unsustainable Families Defy Arithmetic, Reason, and Common Sense

It is common sense that, in huge families, the need for food and living space, and funds for education, medical care, travel expenses, gadgets, and other necessities grow in direct proportion to the increasing number of children. Such additional needs, which the breadwinners cannot pay for or provide, have definite quantities and remain as deficits/shortages for that family. It is natural for everyone to expect huge families to suffer in direct proportion to their shortages. But in reality, their sufferings are far more than such expected levels. It happens so because of the complex interactions of many visible and invisible negative factors. While planning, the young planners never give much attention to the "invisible" necessities like happy family-time, parental care, social respect, security, etc; although these also affect their mental, physical, intellectual, social, and economic health—directly and through interactions.

For instance, economic constraints restrict nutritious food and health care. The resultant deficient health and related expenditures worsen the economy, dignity, and social standing further. Failing family time "alienates" children, who often fall into the traps of socio-economic and moral predators and get entangled in sorrowful situations and litigations which demand, further, more time and money, and bring down their economic status and dignity. At last, such viciously spiralling curses complicate every aspect of living and multiply deficits and force them to suffer and spend far more than mathematical or rational expectations.

Studies very clearly assert that it is almost impossible to satisfy (satiate) the physical, mental, psychological, economic, social, and other requirements of dependents once the sustainable limit is crossed. Thus inability to satiate (satisfy) their members is a natural feature of huge families. So, by nature, these huge families are Huge Insatiable Families. For convenience, we can call these unsustainable families (UF); we must remember that the real situation in a UF is far worse than its meaning conveys. Its most appropriate name is Huge Insatiable Family (HIF).

Natural Course of HIF

The natural course of HIFs is inevitable miseries. Such miseries and sufferings are more with more deficits (more dependent children). As we know, deficiencies of vital necessities (poverty/ penury) mean threats to life or inevitable premature death; but basic survival instincts always try to overcome death by trying every possible option. Instincts force them to do something to reduce the insufficiencies so that they can live longer. It is basic knowledge that the options available in this regard are not at all dignified and fall within "beg, borrow, or steal," or "cheat, beat, or kill." These deficiency-reduction or survival options may give them a longer life and even prosperity, but invariably will hurt their conscience and dignity.

As we discussed in chapter four, today's children face a lot of tricky situations, pressures, and challenges from all quarters, like religion, society, politics, peer groups, media, education, etc., where the care, watchfulness, warnings, and support of elders are considered vital. These children need answers for too many questions. Parents with clear planning can help their children in such situations and lead them to success.

An idle mind is the devil's workshop, and wrong contacts can make it an evil factory. Parents can prevent such situations by helping their children find good friends and develop good habits and hobbies by giving them opportunities to play group games, and many more such proactive services which go a long way in making their future bright. But fulfilling such "perceived" responsibilities is not practical with HIF. Thus, when a member is lost to "poaching" or dies because of the wrong path, that family loses even their scanty pride, peace, and hope, and we can describe such a situation as a total ruin. Thus the inherent curses of HIF and these added troubles, losses, and shames make their sufferings multi-dimensional, which affects every aspect of living in many unthinkable ways, and literally makes such a family a hell.

Hell of HIF Makes Life Hellish for Others

If we look at the formative years of neighbouring criminals, thugs, and those like Taliban cadres, Naxals, Al Qaedans, the Detroit bomber

Umar Farouk Abdulmutallab, Idi Amin (a former President of Uganda), Pol Pot (of Khmer Rouge of Cambodia), Hitler, and any such person, we can always find the situation of HIFs, which helped them acquire perverted ideologies and made them hate people with a vengeful mindset. They engage in cheating, crime, violence, terrorism, genocide, etc., and don't mind torturing even innocent children and frail women. These things worsen the socio-economic conditions of their society and country and further worsen deficiencies and sustainability and make life hellish for all.

Even very rich HIFs suffer "invisible" deficiencies and live an unworthy life. Some among the above bad elements like the Detroit bomber, Osama Bin Laden, some of the perpetrators of 9/11, participants of bombing incidents around the world, and many more come from well-to-do HIFs.

Growing Curses

Every sensitive child of any race or culture likes to be fed and supported with the respectable earning of his/her own parents. Every other support, including government aid, is a curse and an indignity for them. When the parents are not in a position to satisfy the needs of their dear children, their helplessness, shame, and guilt hurt, rather wound, the pride and sensitivity of both the parents and children, and this situation terribly affects their mental make-up and life.

One cannot expect such humiliated, disgruntled children with wounded pride to honour and respect an incompetent, irresponsible, and indifferent father (and leaders, too). This strained relationship itself is enough to cause irreparable damage to the peace and happiness of an HIF. The related and resultant indiscipline, miseries, and mental agony are almost never-ending. It is not uncommon to see such youths joining gangs of ill-reputed people, just to irritate that foolish father and the "unfriendly" society. These developments mar their reputation as a family and make them lesser humans in society, which further complicates their well-being and often numbs their "social sense" and national responsibilities.

What can society and the nation expect from them? Yet, with very hard work, self-sacrifices, and perseverance, too many such people have risen to top positions in society, politics, bureaucracy, business, religion, etc. Some of them do great service to humanity; but many others use those opportunities and power to wreak vengeance upon the people or country which humiliated and disregarded them.

. We will discuss here a few aspects of the pain and suffering of HIFs, which invariably facilitate the creation of more deficiencies and miseries.

Obvious First Curse

The moment couples beget more children, straining their ability to support them, they earn deficiencies, inequality, and disparity. The primary deficiency is economic poverty. Poverty itself is a multi-dimensionally painful curse, which one should not wish even for one's enemy. (Details are in chapter 45 of *Book G*).

First Victim of HIF

In order to satisfy the needs of children, every normal father works hard for a long time—even disregarding his own comforts, health, and happiness. The long absence of a father from home invariably gives more "freedom" to his children; and these free children cannot get the timely instructions, warnings, and beneficial ideologies from the experienced father. Such children have more chances to mix and join with undesirable elements like criminals, drug addicts, religious fanatics, and sex offenders.

Despite the self-sacrificial hard work for longer time, a weary, honest father faces indifference, ingratitude, and rebellion from the "beneficiaries" and he feels hurt, demoralized, and weakened. His physical and mental sufferings invariably make him a sick person, physically and mentally. This writer has witnessed the pathetic end of many very responsible and affectionate fathers of huge families. They did not take time even to attend to their illnesses; if they skipped a day's work, their children would starve or would not be able to pay their school fees. The writer sadly remembers the premature death of some such ideal fathers and the pathetic sufferings of their very dear children after their death.

Poor Mothers and Unfortunate Children

The mother, too, has to share most of the sufferings of her desperate husband and takes full responsibility when he is sick or dies. It is not uncommon to see such women taking up very tough manual labour. It is a sad fact that, despite such hard work, their children rarely get a full meal, and such a situation promotes child labour. There are millions of such huge poor families, where all the members, including small children, work yet fail to conquer hunger.

Published interviews or studies of sex workers expose lots of instances where such women reluctantly sell their dignity, body, and health for the well-being of their family members. There are even young girls who turn into sex workers to end the hunger of the many children of their irresponsible parents, and even to support their weary and weak parents.

There are plenty of instances where mothers of huge families in developing and poor countries go to rich countries or distant cities for menial jobs like house-maids and construction workers, leaving behind their children under the care of their weak husbands or other relatives or charity homes. It is not uncommon to hear about their physical, mental, and sexual ill-treatment in distant places. Think of the mind-set and psychological developments of such children who yearn for the unadulterated love of the most affectionate and responsible mother; but see or hear about the sufferings of their weak and sickly mothers.

Can they ever enjoy a happy day in their childhood? Can they form a sustainable family when they grow up? Do you expect them, with mutilated or hardened minds, to become self-sacrificing, patriotic citizens? Don't you think that such youths can easily be recruited by terror groups and anti-social gangs to wreak revenge on the (innocent) society? Will you be angry if such a deprived, starving child or youth destroys virgin forests or steals a loaf of bread to avoid starvation? Today, millions of such youths are just doing the same and later mature into experts in such "jobs." For them, survival by any means is of paramount importance, and pollution, GW, and CC are nonsense.

HIFs are Death-Traps

The sufferings of the children of HIFs are too many and unending, and they start even during their days in the womb. They cannot even expect the "normal," like a toy, the food they desire, timely medical care and immunizations, education, or even affectionate care and guidance from parents. Malnutrition easily makes them victims of even ordinary infectious diseases, which strike them harder and longer and easily take away their lives. These are the children who push up the child mortality rate (CMR) in developing and poor countries. The solution of high CMR is not just food and medicines, but the prevention of the formation of these death-traps (HIF), which gives real freedom and longer life.

Along with the high paternal mortality and CMR in HIFs, the maternal mortality rates (MMR) too are very high because of repeated pregnancies, malnutrition, vitamin deficiencies, anaemia, poor hygiene, hard work, poor care, too much worry, anxieties, and so on. The only way to end or reduce MMR is to avoid pregnancy after the second child.

Thus, HIF proves to be the death trap of every family member: child, mother, and father. Life as an orphan, semi-orphan, or without sufficient love, care, and guidance from parents or a sincere person to trust and love is really a horrible hell which can be prevented only by minimizing the number of children to one or two per family in every crowded country.

Hardened Children

Right now, there are about one billion uncared for or ill-cared for children and youths around the world. Millions of them are left almost abandoned, and there are even instances of parents selling children to feed other members of huge families. Yet governments never interfere and indict those animal-like parents, so they bring out more such "unwanted" children and create huge deficits for them and for their unfortunate countries.

Even if the parents of HIFs are loving and responsible, they cannot satisfy their children and thus fail as parents. These deprived and humiliated children respect and love anyone who is "loving," hospitable, gives the feeling of equality, "respectable," and purposeful. When necessity arises, such grateful children are even ready to sacrifice their lives for these new "families" or "adopted fathers." Vast sections of today's members of violent and fanatic groups like Al Qaeda, Taliban, Naxalites, Lashkar-e-Taiba, Maoists (of India), underworld gangs, members of drug cartels, gambling dens, and so on come from such HIFs.

Their philosophy: Instead of living a miserable life in "hell," in shame, with unfulfilled needs and hunger, it is always better to live an "honourable" and commanding life fighting the powerful, the ungodly, the corrupt and rich enemies, or an enemy-country, or their own unworthy governments who also failed them.

Addicted, Dependent Fathers

Every human expects reward for hard work, or at least gratitude. There are weary, unhappy, desperate fathers who, as we have seen, could never satisfy their families despite hard work. How, then, can they expect love and gratitude? With time, many feel fed-up. I know too many such fathers getting addicted to drink, drugs, gambling, women, and anything or any habit which helps them forget their worries.

There are condemnably parasitic fathers who demand or even forcibly grab the hard-earned money of their wives and children to satisfy their craving and make life more horrible for their dependents.

There are also highly irresponsible and immoral fathers who "escape" from the hell of their own creation (HIF) and their worn-out wives, and settle elsewhere with new, younger wives.

Perils of Old Age

Ignorant parents still believe that they can have better care and attention in their old age if they have more children. But in every crowded society, most such stupid parents suffer loneliness, starvation, and sickness, with no one to care for them, because their children invariably become poorer than they were because of the division of every bit of their wealth. These poor descendants find it difficult to support even their own children and feel their parents as a burden. Again, too many of those children easily find some premise to pass on the responsibilities to other siblings. Disappointments and litigations related to partitioning the meagre family property are enough to create a number of causes to reject the "biased," unjust, and cruel parents. (cf. Chapter 27 of *Book G*).

Condition of the Next Generation

The next generation of HIFs invariably is poorer, even if its members form relatively smaller families, because of division of wealth and possible litigations. But if the next generations also form HIFs, their life becomes too horrible to escape the sure likelihood of premature death and other evils.

Too Late for Parents to Repent

No parent ever wants his children to get involved in any anti-social, anti-national, or other criminal activities. Unfortunately, such activities are full time jobs for millions of youths today. When their parents take note of their children's situations, they feel extremely hurt and plunge into great agony and humiliation. At this point, their regrets or repentance have no value or effect because these do not change the sad situation in any way for the better.

Millions of families sincerely make an effort to form almost sustainable small families. Yet we see and hear about foolish parents around the world who keep on getting children even while the elder children are suffering hunger, destitution, working as child labour, and facing death by starvation or insufficient care, and at the same time, their elder, estranged children are engaged in anti-social activities. Who is there to prevent such ghastly happenings? Misuse of such parents' rights and freedom to take away the dignity, normalcy, equality, rights, and freedom of their own children is something which deserves top attention.

If the world, especially the new young couples, understand that having more children for any reason, for example insensible plans or succumbing "carelessly" like animals to natural instincts, would really degrade them to levels below the animals, the world will be a better place for their children and others.

10

The Long Trails of HIF

Natural and "Infused" Ignorance behind Deficiencies

The pain and sufferings of Huge Insatiable Families (HIF) are so harsh that we compare them to hell and death-traps. We have started grasping the idea that deficiencies of HIFs are the real disease, whose long trail of "symptoms and signs" appears to us as the socio-economic and global ills, evils, and curses—ending with climate change (CC).

These make people raise questions like: Why do people create such horrible death traps/HIFs? How can such a sorrowful situation bring about an apparently unrelated long chain of evils which threaten the whole humanity, all the other life forms, and the health of the planet?

No human wishes to create those situations; yet thousands of families cross their limits every day to become sorrowful hells and many more thousands die prematurely under humiliating circumstances due to that fault. From this we can understand the high degree of ignorance behind those developments.

It is a sorrowful fact that even people in responsible positions swear that poverty and such sufferings are natural to human society. There are religious perverts who relate poverty and other evils to God's wrath and punishment, or God's ways of testing the faith of people. When natural calamities strike naturally or as a "divine" punishment, people do not try to fight against them and often just submit themselves to the will of the supreme power. Because of such natural and "infused" ignorance, too many families do not bother to understand the evolving deficiencies.

Blinding Joy

When young couples have their first child, they get motivated by their precious possession to do more with enthusiasm and purpose. At this stage, every small family with the advantageous equation of two adults to only one child can enjoy sustainable, happy long life even in poor communities and hope for a progressively prosperous future. Growing prosperity, economic security, ample family time, strong attachments, happiness, and hope make every such family a mini-paradise. If the ignorant masses are made to understand the equation that makes hells, they will stop going further to create deficiencies.

Yet ignorant people are often blinded by that joyous life and then they try to create a bigger "joyous" family by adding more "bundles of joy" (children) and turn their paradise into a bundle of misery (hell).

This makes clear the fact that families, anywhere in the world, earn and suffer hell-like conditions only after passing through the wonderful paradise that assures them of respectable living. So deficiency, or poverty, is a foolishly earned situation which comes into reality because of ignorance.

Continuing Ignorant Acts

Studies show that such ignorant or thoughtless acts continue to haunt the whole life of a vast section of people and force them to do more foolish acts in the name of ending deficiencies and tackling the complications or evils of deficiencies. At last, their ill-conceived ideas and acts trap them and the whole of humanity in too many dangerous situations, including pollutions, GW, and CC.

When we look at those new developments, in addition to ignorance, we can find the role of more factors that evolve out of **desperation**; then all these new and old factors join together to pave the catastrophic course.

Panicky reactions: We can imagine life-threatening situations like an attack by a dangerous beast, or being in the middle of an engulfing fire, hurricane, earthquake, or flood. While these threats try to end life immediately, the deficiencies of HIF do it in weeks or in years—depending upon their enormity. No one would ever attempt to face such a life-threatening situation with patience, discipline, decency, or dignity, or in a rational, relaxed way; but invariably would run into desperation and resort to rash acts, which we call panicky reaction.

The role of perverted "ideologies": Humiliations and sufferings related to deficiency/poverty inflict physical, mental, and psychological "wounds," which modify the ideologies or philosophies governing their moral, intellectual, social, economic, and other pursuits, often adversely.

When these elements—from ignorance to perverted ideologies—mix to form an unpredictable cocktail, none can expect a person to behave with honesty, decency, "self-sacrifice," or other virtues. They devise their own mode of action ("self-medication"/treatment regimen) in desperation when they face uncontrollably growing deficits and the evolved and evolving evils. When ethical acts fail, they try to make up for their deficits by using "regimens" involving forest destruction, cheating, crime, violence, etc. These naturally cause far more harm, losses, and damage to others and to the environment than the equivalent of their deficits, and further ruin the sustainability of many innocent families. And then these new unsustainable families also repeat the above "self-medication" (correction and course) and worsen the unsustainable situation in a vicious fashion that brings in more and more of social, economic, moral, religious, political, environmental, and global ills, evils, and curses and worsen GW and CC.

Evolution of Man-Made Evils—The Trail

Consider a rural HIF in poverty with unfulfilled needs. What can we expect those hungry people to do?

Forest destruction: In order to earn something without hurting their neighbours, some of them go to the forest and cut trees with commercial intent. When they are in need of land for cultivation, they clear forests by burning vast regions. They allow their cattle to graze indiscriminately and make lands barren. In these ways, vast areas of forests and green cover are lost every year, which directly aids GW and initiates the other harms related to forest destruction.

Environmental degradation: Overburdened workers of HIFs, including those in cities, with limited resources, energy, and time, bother the least about safe disposal of their wastes, including excreta and other household wastes and chemicals. They scatter them indiscriminately in the neighbourhoods (including bodies of water) and degrade the environment and, in that process, vast areas of land and many venerated ancient rivers and lakes have been turned into filthy, stinking drains or pits.

For want of space, they keep their cattle and fowl close to their residences.

All this preserves and spreads contagious diseases, and encourages animal pathogens to try humans and vice versa.

Crime: When their innocent children suffer hunger and starvation, every parent becomes restless. When acceptable efforts don't work, they try criminal activities like theft. When these are effective, it becomes their preferred option.

Religious fanaticism: Overindulgence in religion is natural in every crowded region. It is a kind of psychological dependence and a source of hope. There are goons among them who exploit the delicate situations of ignorant poor people to earn for themselves a good life. They misinterpret religious texts to suit their needs and in accordance with the temperaments of people. The rascals among them use falsehoods to drag out even unconnected people and accuse them of various imaginary misdeeds. Many such exploiters have risen up to good heights—even to international levels. Desperate people trust them more than they trust well-educated, honest politicians and well-wishers. These preachers often think that they have risen to the high level because of God's blessings, and they consider it a license from God to continue those "nefarious" activities.

Social, economic, and political predations and fraudulences: Poaching and predation go on in every field as an extension of crime and corruption. Cunning and selfish people use all kinds of tricks, including doctored stories, twisted historical facts, and attractive promises to deceive and exploit desperate, innocent youths.

Migration: When conditions go unfavourable in rural regions, the rural folk migrate to cities. Migrations lead to huge consumption of polluting energy, because of the travel and transport industries. Migrations enlarge urban centres which heavily contribute to pollutions, GW, and CC.

Urban crime industry: Persistent unemployment entices some of the migrants and other unemployed youths to join or form criminal gangs in cities and other suitable places. Because of the growing uncertainties and socio-political chaos, even rich and successful people indulge in a variety of frauds, such as tax-evasion, corruption, fraudulent business activities, piracies, faking, drug dealings, etc. In many HPD countries, these activities have grown to levels to rival the national economy and even have the power to change the course of their countries.

International migration: When employment opportunities dry up, competitions soar and other evils threaten, those desperate job-seekers migrate to the rich and lenient nations around the world and thus start highly polluting international migrations. They take the host countries towards the dangerous HPD and augment pollution levels.

Catastrophic Consequences of Multiplying HIFs

There are two very discrete levels of unsustainability with very definite and distinct attributes. The first one is the unsustainability related to family. We have just discussed it and its consequences (trails).

The second one is the unsustainability existing in a country or a vast region like a state or a district. We have already seen it as Generalized Unsustainable Living Conditions (GULC) or High Population Density (HPD). It happens because of the unrestricted proliferation of HIFs. The very certain sufferers of HPD are members of HIFs; but with GULC or HPD, the miseries torture every human of that region, irrespective of rich or poor, planned or unplanned families. All the evils previously discussed take a tempestuous trail with HPD and it further helps the evolution of more horrible evils like terrorism and highly polluting activities. Further, all these effects of deficiencies cross borders to reach other countries through migrants and "proxy pollution" (discussed in later chapters).

We will study HPD and the continuing undesirable trails in the following chapters.

11

Highly Detrimental Population Density

(Generalized Unsustainable Living Conditions—GULC)

HIFs are Lonely Sufferers Until . . .

We have already seen the sufferings of HIFs (Huge Insatiable Families) or unsustainably weak or deficient over-burdened families and their potential to create and worsen socio-economic and other ills. Until an OPD or LPD status is maintained in any country, people enjoy surpluses of life-supporting resources, so unemployment cannot exist if that country is managed sensibly. A well-planned family in an OPD region does not suffer; but agony of modern day HIFs even in an OPD area is inevitable, because despite the earnings of their breadwinners, those families cannot enjoy satiety because of the rising needs of modern day with too many dependents to share their earnings.

With time, the multiplying HIFs raise the population density above the optimum level to cause High Population Density (HPD). With HPD, vast deterioration sets in fast and the happiness, hope, and peace of every citizen, including those of planned small families, become casualties; yet the harsher sufferers are HIFs.

Sustainable Population Density (SPD)

OPD and LPD can be called Sustainable Population Density (SPD) because if every family of SPD countries is sensible enough to form a deficit-free family, it can enjoy a happy, hopeful life forever. Yet, as we saw earlier, SPD does not confer economic freedom on HIFs. However, the members of HIFs cannot blame others for their sufferings, because everyone, including those from HIFs, can find work to earn for their families. Since every able human can find employment, the need for unhealthy competitions, the basic cause for most of the evolving curses, does not occur. But such a sane, happy life goes erratic with HPD, because then it, as a vast region, does not have enough resources or opportunities to satisfy the whole population.

High Population Density (HPD)

When the population of a region or country exceeds its SPD/ OPD, it creates a kind of generalized/national poverty or collective deficits/poverty of that whole region or country. We call this state High Population Density (HPD) or Generalized Unsustainable Living Conditions (GULC). These names or phrases convey the various aspects of it. These mean that people do not have any more free life-supportive resources or employment opportunities because all these have gone into the possession of somebody when their population started crossing OPD/SPD. Now they need more resources and opportunities for the extra population, in direct proportion to the growing HPD or GULC.

So, by default, the given region has under-employed, unemployed, and needy people and their number grows as HPD grows. As all of them cannot find a sustainable job or wealth, they compete with everyone who possesses something or try to grab others' wealth. Such competitions and grab-mania make people panicky and anxious and make them over-reactive to do something to ensure their sustainability. Those who possess enough are also desperate, and anxious to protect what they have. Because of this fear of economic insecurity, people often compete with others and strive to accumulate more than what they require in order to ensure their long-term security. In that process, the deficits swell "artificially" and competitions become highly unhealthy, which in turn, leads to insane and detrimental reactions and initiates a long chain of evils and curses.

Thus, the attributes and the course of HPD are undesirable and dangerous, and the more appropriate name may be Hazardous (Dangerous) Population Density or Detrimental Population Density

(DPD). However to express the mathematical relationship to OPD using the phrase High Population Density (HPD) appears more appropriate.

How Do Countries With HPD Sustain Life?

We just saw that the whole fixed life-supportive natural wealth and the approximately fixed (predictably stable) number of sustainable employment slots of any country go into somebody's possession when the population of the region concerned grows into HPD. Then, every new birth creates deficiencies to be "distributed" among its families and then throughout the country. Under such strained conditions of HPD, if a person or a section of people makes progressive prosperity, it means that the wealth held by somebody has been transferred to them directly or indirectly in respectable or despicable ways. Thus, when someone progresses in an HPD country, some others lose an equivalent quantity of wealth. This is reflected in the studies related to economic progress of any country with static or progressive HPD.

So, if an HPD country makes progress or sustains an acceptable life, it must be due to some of the or all the following:

- They are engaged in some harmful activities which eat into resources meant for other species.
- They utilize the healthy reserves, like forests.
- They are engaged in economic activities with the help of "prohibited energy."
- They are overusing depletable wealth, like minerals, coal, petroleum, etc. (as in mineral exporting and petroleum exporting countries).
- They earn a lot through external trade.
- They earn significantly through migrant workers or expatriates.
- A considerable number of their families have planned well so as to live as small, well sustainable families, and are saving huge funds for dynamic economic activities (as in India and China) and even liberate huge resources which were in their grasp.

HPD and Panic Reaction

In addition to unhealthy competitions for resources and opportunities, people of HPD countries compete with others even for things that facilitate sustainability indirectly, like professional education, special skills, etc. Failures are very common in unhealthy competitions to find a sustainable life. The failed people must find ways to prolong life by mitigating deficiencies. Now their options have shrunk to the undesirable end of the spectrum and they are forced to try "jobs" involving crime, corruption, immorality, etc. Thus, non-respectable jobs become their saviours and add a few more links that at last connect HIF and HPD with CC. Even criminals and terrorists face tough competition with one another.

These new jobs are not self-sustaining, but are parasitic. They hurt and devitalize those who try to live a respectable life through honest means, and honest families also turn desperate and panic to protect their wealth from the "parasites." When they are driven to the wall, even these dispossessed decent people may become parasites with a vengeance. Lenience, carelessness, and negligence (of parasites and those who possess) would cause unexpected, huge damage and losses. Every person living in a highly deficient (HPD) poor and developing country can see and hear such happenings every day. All this worsens living conditions far faster than the mathematical equivalent of the deficits (as happened to HIFs) and further facilitate the creation of more deficits and evils.

Contrasting Outcome of Deficits of HIF and HPD

HIFs, as small coherent units, struggle to minimize their deficits and, in that process, create a few evils for society. HPD regions do the same as a vast but incoherent community or country. Eventually, for various reasons discussed later, the struggles and evils-creation of HPD proceeds in cyclonic proportions to create more numbers of harsher evils than the former.

HIFs are strained families, yet, they cherish virtues like mutual love and care, so the noble principle of "one for all and all for one" prevails and this prevents competition and corrupt acts within. So their time, energy, and earnings are not at all wasted. Every family member spontaneously comes forward, without grumbling, to share the sufferings and sorrows of other members at difficult times and is even prepared to make compromises and sacrifices. These palliate their miseries faster and reinforce their resolve to live. Often such sufferings and sacrifices strengthen their intimacy, which even makes them "joyous." Such intimacy and love give them a purpose to live and boost their morale to fight the challenges as a highly charged, united force.

Healthy practice of worthy religion also plays a highly beneficial role in such families. Trust in God keeps alive a family's hopes during trying times. Further, such dampening of desperation prevents psychological breakdown and even overcomes suicidal tendencies; but, practicing religion-based unworthy ideologies harms those who practice them, and also harms their neighbours, their countries, and even the world.

Unlike HIF, a region or a country with HPD is a mixture of a variety of people with diverse and divergent attributes. To them, their own interests are more important than those of others. They prefer to compete and try to grab as much as possible to strengthen their long-term economic security; but they hate to share with others, even their surplus wealth. People bound to one another ideologically may help each other to some extent; but total agreement (as exists in families) is unusual. While religion has had positive effects in troubled families, it often causes more harm in an HPD society, because the wily among them try to exploit religious sentiments in too many ways. As we look around, we can see that the diversities or multiplicities of culture, race, religion, language, etc. of HPD societies are all misused by desperate, immoral elements to create more division and chaos.

So the living conditions always worsen faster with more diversity until HPD conditions exist and create many additional evils, like hatred, racial and religious intolerance, treacherous acts, etc., and thrust more burdens upon meek and patriotic people.

Thus, unlike the harmony prevailing in HIFs, HPD conditions create disharmony and worsen the already troubled situations.

Viciously Spiralling Reactions

Since unhealthy competition, crime, hatred, corruption, grabbing-sprees, and antisocial and anti-national acts are integral parts of HPD society, the entire population, consisting of diverse families—HIFs and planned small families, the rich or the poor, the powerful and the meek, the employed or the unemployed—are pulled into the chaotic whirlwinds of HPD to suffer. These work in vicious ways to worsen the region's sorrows far more than the proportion of deficiencies.

For instance, perhaps a poor, needy family requires wealth equivalent to about one hundred dollars to tide them over a difficult time. When its members try to compensate deficits by cutting forest trees, they cause damage to the tune of more than that amount and initiate much harm related to loss of forest. Similarly, plundering parasites like criminals and corrupt goons often grab and accumulate far more wealth (enough to support their families for generations) than they require. Thus, the greed of one family ruins many innocent families and makes their lives unsustainable.

In order to be somebody and to earn a livelihood, another wicked person may spread lies and doctor information with the intention of creating hatred and division in the society which take away their peace, harmony, and trust, and can even lead to communal wars. In these ways, the lives of millions of hard-working, innocent families around the world, which live an almost carbon-friendly or sustainable life, are pushed into highly deficient, carbon-unfriendly, unsustainable life. Such losses even force many innocent victims to commit suicide or to starve to a premature "natural" death. Today many people live a highly "suckcessful" life through such parasitic living and even rise to great heights in various fields like trade, politics, bureaucracy, religion, service organizations, and even in bodies which can influence policies. Can you imagine the fate of such HPD countries with these "respectable" people?

Evolution of Adversities with Rising PD

Assume that we are dealing with a small country having resources and employment opportunities to comfortably sustain one million people.

Wonderful Life with LPD

If they just have a population of about 800,000, everyone has access to vast resources and job opportunities which take away the cause for unhealthy competition and its harmful course. They have ample free time, energy, and resources to neutralize pollution and to create renewable energy and to clean up environmental damage.

The talented among them and those who desire and opt for special jobs or professions do so out of choice, because people need not compete with the aim of earning through it. When people do their work out of craving (as it was happening in our district about fifty years ago), they do their jobs with involvement and dedication, so they do not feel bored and even long hours of work do not tire them easily. The country gets the best service from dedicated people. Thus LPD conditions augment the advantages further.

The favourable features of LPD provide a calm, clean, peaceful, friendly, happy, and sustainable life to the whole population. They have no reason for belligerence and hatred or to cheat others, but have a lot of opportunities to compliment and congratulate each other and to enjoy festivals and celebrations together. So, love, mutually helping tendencies, and respect for others become innate virtues that make life wholesome and purposeful. What more can one dream of? We can expect such a life only if the population density is kept within OPD.

Ordinary Life with OPD

When the population density of our hypothetical country equals OPD or is maintained at around one million, their life can go on smoothly, almost like that with LPD. But since the huge reserves of LPD are absent, they must plan everything carefully and spread their population in such a way to utilize their resources and job opportunities in the most advantageous and balanced ways.

Strained Life with HPD

Imagine that their population is one million and one (1,000,001). Now everyone of that country must sacrifice one millionth of their wealth or comforts for the extra person. It just goes unnoticed.

With a population of one million and ten thousand (1,010,000), everyone has to sacrifice about one hundredth of his/her comforts or wealth. This too may not have a visible impact, because people spontaneously adapt to a deficiency of such a small amount.

When a population is one million and one hundred thousand (10 percent above OPD), everyone will have to sacrifice about one tenth of their comforts. Even here adaptations and comforting entertainments may blind people to the multiplying population and growing deficits. Yet all the ills and evils discussed earlier sneak into their societies because of the evolving practical difficulties with shortages. And then, with growing obvious deficits and corresponding unemployment, all those evils and curses make their presence stark and curse them in vicious fashion. In order to sustain such a deficient state, people seek the services of the powerful monsters—petroleum and coal.

The Complicating Course

The complicating course of HPD and related sufferings varies from people to people. These are influenced and modified by factors such as socio-economic and religio-political philosophies, literacy, etc. As we will see, its harsh course harms the most patriotic and meek people and invariably favours the crooked and unethical brutes. The activities of these immoral crooks worsen living conditions further and make them more unsustainable.

For a convenient elaboration, consider that the above county has a population of 1.5 million.

Theoretically 500,000 of them must go into extinction to give a normal life to any 1,000,000 people. Or, for a uniform and equitable living, each one of them must sacrifice about one third of his/her comforts and wealth. By doing so, all of them will die prematurely because of partial starvation.

But in normal practice, none of this happens. With HPD, unhealthy competitions set in. Some try to beat competitions by doing hard work. Some try to get jobs by earning good qualifications through tough education and by developing skills. The innocent poor people take up even risky works for low wages, just to protect their dependents. The lazy, the immoral, the cunning, and the brutal people try easy ways through corruption, deceit, crime (including murder for gain), violence, terrorism, etc., and grab the hard-earned wealth of the hard-working patriots and decent citizens. No meek and patriotic people can withstand the treacheries and intimidations of unpatriotic, immoral rascals, and will invariably spend their days in sorrow and get "freedom" from those miseries through premature death.

Any HPD community consists of diverse people, ranging from the poor and the honest enduring miseries and starvation to the enormously rich people enjoying power and lavish comforts.

Yet, one cannot blame the brutal rascals for this degradation, because they are the creation of HPD. The poor succumbs to exploitations because of poverty that creates the brutal rich and hence the power of ending these sorrows is in the hands of the same poor who have created HIFs and HPD. When such pathetic families strictly adapt sustainable families (preventing HIF) sorrows face natural death. (For more, see chapter 63, "Letter to the Poor," *Book G*.)

Today, we do not see such a sad transformation to the extent it should happen in proportion to deficits because farm revolutions, advantageous technologies and gadgets, entertainments, medical facilities, and above all, the huge helping hand of coal and petroleum have prevented the catastrophic harms of HPD. Unfortunately, these "palliative" factors are highly unsustainable and they hide the surging deficits and create more evils and curses like pollution.

Warning

HPD and its progenitors, HIFs, are the highly deficient factors behind all the ills, evils, and curses humanity and the world suffer today. It is most unfortunate that too many countries and regions suffer unbearable socio-economic ills and other evils and curses with an HPD of double and triple the OPD, or even more. Nothing is done to reverse it, so living conditions worsen with every passing day and the pent-up or suppressed "feeling" of people explodes in many regions and countries in various forms—hating others easily, readiness for physical violence and readiness to violate law, resulting in mass uprising, violent protests and other unruly activities.

If humanity desires to live forever on our small planet, every fast-breeding region and family must be enlightened on the deficits they create, their consequences, and the way to end it by forming sustainable small families.

Real Story of People Who Experienced HPD and OPD

European HPD and Horrible Butchery

Europe can never support a PD vis-à-vis a fertile tropical country. But for various reasons, they enjoyed longevity earlier than others. Longevity pushed their population to cross OPD even before the nineteenth century. They suffered ills and evils like unemployment, high competition, hatred, belligerence, enmities, unending wars, etc. which culminated in two world wars.

Until World War II, huge numbers of Europe's healthy, enterprising, adventurous, and courageous youths "escaped" from the crowd and ventured on voyages in uncharted oceans to find advantageous trade, employment, and new places to live. Despite those large-scale migrations, the pressure of HPD was so great that it dragged them into many regional wars and eventually the two world wars. They massacred their own brilliant and patriotic youths in millions. The side effects of war, like disease, poverty, and starvation, destroyed millions of children and civilian people. Such large-scale pathetic deaths brought down their population density to LPD levels, with all the advantages for a wonderful life.

European LPD and the EU

LPD spontaneously ended their belligerent mindset and made them cherish a hopeful, friendly, and liberal attitude. Even the UK and Germany, which were deadly enemies during those wars, started to love, respect, and help each other. The result is a friendly European Union (EU). The peace, hope, and trust of LPD gave importance to humane values and virtues like equality, human rights, dignified existence, transparency, non-exploitation, upholding democracy, helping others, etc.

At the end of World War II, Europe and Japan were in very bad shape, with flattened infrastructures and factories, huge war debts, huge loss of youth, etc. Unity, hard work, and the absence of wars enabled their progress. They progressed so fast that they were able to donate huge sums of money and technology to many Asian and African countries which never suffered any war damage but enjoyed the best infrastructures, education facilities, and administrative set-up which were left behind by colonial powers.

Reversal of Migrations

HPD drove away large numbers of Europeans from their motherlands. They imposed their rule and colonized countries which had been suffering from misrule, disunity, superstitions, class exploitation, inhuman practices, and above all, LPD due to very low life expectancy as the result of exploitation by their own people and mass killer diseases. Most of the colonial governments entirely changed the faces of their colonies with benevolent revolutions in education, administrative machinery, science, technology, infrastructures, democratization of institutions, medical facilities, justice systems, implementation of rule of law, and much more. When the colonizers quitted the colonies after World War II, the new independent countries could have utilized those facilities to build happy, peaceful, and hopeful nations. But with all these facilities and a growing life expectancy, they proliferated far faster than their developmental achievements. HPD was the consequence, which really marred their freedom and the worthy life they deserved.

These countries which had been taking European migrants till World War II suffer all the evils of HPD—like pre-World War II Europe—and so their people are migrating to those developed countries with a comfortable population density. Conditions are so bad in most of these free countries they force even the descendants of their freedom fighters, religious heads, politicians, and bureaucrats to quit their countries and migrate to white men's countries. Their grandparents fought with these same white men and forced them to quit; but now the most unthinkable shame is happening because of HPD.

Unfortunately, the Western countries have not understood sustainability, LPD, or OPD in the right sense, and do many imprudent acts which take them again toward HPD. The signs and symptoms of HPD are very obvious in many European towns and cities. Will they wake up and stop the course toward HPD? And will the other "independent" HPD countries of Asia, Africa and South America wake up to end HPD and its sorrows and shames?

Importance of Understanding the Evolution and Courses of the Curses

We have seen the horrible consequences of HPD, horrible to the extent they force people to commit heinous crimes, and powerful enough to chase people from their motherlands. But that is not all; HPD turns further more catastrophic to force people to commit many more harmful and suicidal acts, like polluting the atmosphere and destroying forests and thereby causing GW and CC. We will discuss these in the coming chapters.

12

Understanding the
Warning-Signals of Deficits

Threats from Right and Left and from Above and Below

Deficits of diverse nature multiply fast—in numbers and in quantities—with the onset of HPD. Since the concept of deficits is unfamiliar, people do not think in terms of it; but all of us feel their effects or see the "signs and symptoms" of deficits like poverty, crime, violence, hatred, terrorism, demographic reversals, pollution, GW, and CC. If we look at these carefully, we can understand that these act like Nature's devices to end deficits. Since Nature cannot create more resources to mitigate deficits, it tries to mitigate deficits by pruning the deficit creators. If we continue to feign ignorance, Nature may come out with far more horrible ways to end deficits. So understanding deficits can pave the way for humans to escape from Nature's horrible pruning.

At present, Nature uses many methods to eliminate the creators of deficits. For instance, GW and CC cause torrential rains which wash away upland human settlements towards oceans. The rising sea levels and unusually huge waves try to engulf populations in low-lying areas. And hurricanes, floods, landslides, droughts, and other GW-induced calamities try to finish off the others. Every day, such inglorious elimination of human population is going on in front of us; but we never relate these to the deficits we create.

Other than these, Nature forces deficit-creating humans to assist it in that "noble" job of deficit-reduction by eliminating their own race through crime (including murder), violence, terrorism, wars, pollutants, and many more such acts.

We have innumerable instances. If we have "seeing eyes," we can see. Do we want any more warning signals?

Ubiquitous "Signals" of Deficit-Reduction

We know that anyone with deficits has to resort to "beg, borrow, or steal" or "cheat, beat, or kill" in order to sustain living or to reduce deficits. These are shameful situations and no one desires to do these; yet, as we will see, almost the whole of humanity is involved in such shames. So the ubiquitous presence of such shames proves or "signals" the prevalence of deficits.

Begging: It is a common sight in poor and developing countries, but others, including many people of very rich countries, try to do it in sophisticated ways in the names of social, cultural, political, environmental and religious services and activities. People do not even spare God in seeking alms. It is very common in crowded countries to see huge crowds of desperate and needy people flocking to "powerful" religious places (gods) and god-men with many "requests" or quid-pro-quos.

Borrowing: The fossil energy we use is equivalent to a borrowed resource. Living on borrowed wealth is a shame and is unsustainable. We have already accumulated this carbon-debt in the form of accumulated pollution. Like insensitive creatures, we continue to borrow it in larger quantities and enlarge our debt burden. Now, this debt (pollution) hurts us directly and through GW and CC. If we want to live with "dignity" and freedom from those hurts and threats, we must repay the debt to the "lender" by acts like reburying (paying back to the depths) the accumulated carbon.

Stealing: Forest destruction, occupying the habitats (land and space) of other species and usurping their resources like land, water, etc., are nothing but stealing.

Cheating, beating, and killing: Humans mercilessly kill and hunt animals and indirectly ruin their lives in many ways. We have already driven many precious species to extinction without any regrets. Without even the least sense of responsibility, we destroy forests which help us to sustain life. We do these cruel acts in plenty against fellow humans, too.

Dangerous Insensitivities

Some of the fertile regions of the world have reached a dangerous population density of four or more times above OPD. That means they now need a geographical area and energy equivalent to many times the present area in order to live a sustainable living. But how many responsible people are realizing it?

Now we just have a few countries, such as the USA, Australia, and Canada, hovering around OPD. Wise use of this situation will benefit mankind as described in chapters 21 and 22. But they, too, are doing a lot of insensible acts to create HPD.

Psycho-Social-Political Response to Chronic Deficits

The effects of deficiency do not just stop with those of physical shortages of food or comforts; but invisibly torture them with worries, anxieties, hopelessness, and indignities. More than this, the sight of the sufferings of dear ones hurts people severely. All these influence the "philosophies" of grown up people and the personalities of children, which easily make them accept anti-social and violent ideologies to end their deficits. Widely prevalent corruption, crime, nepotism, greed, exploitation, misrule, etc. are the products of this, which further angers the victims and those in need, and literally moulds many of them into "explosives."

When those disgruntled, furious youths are brainwashed by the ideologies of malicious and ambitious hate mongers, they willingly do horrible acts like 9/11 or 26/11 of Mumbai, or bombings and suicide-bombings as are happening now in crowded countries. Already, vast regions of the world are in the hands of wrongly indoctrinated people. They keep doing enough destructive activities to give sleepless nights to peace-loving people and governments. Yet, the perpetrators as well as the victims (including leaders and planners) have not understood the role of unsustainable conditions or deficits. The situations are worsening, and for many reasons, even youths from huge rich families join "powerful" malicious groups and ordinary people "explode" or "implode."

Will Stabilization of Population Help?

Stabilization of population means an attempt to sustain life at this unsustainable HPD. With stabilized population at this level, the present level of deficit-reducing activities, like parasitic jobs, forest destruction, and harmful polluting activities, will continue and will create new peaks every day. So, GW and CC too would worsen with time.

The Way Out

Only when we regain OPD, or preferably LPD, will we be able to stop every harmful and polluting activity, which will give way to healing and recovery.

An understanding of the sequential evolution and course of the curses (see next chapter) and the approximate relationship of it to changing HPD would give us an idea about our position with regard to OPD.

13

The Sequential Evolution of Calamitous Curses

Orderly Evolution of "Disorderly" Curses

People all over the world enjoyed hopeful, sustainable living until a particular time in the past, which differs from region to region. Out of ignorance, people made their lives unsustainable (along with its curses). As we have seen, Europeans brought about HPD and its consequent evils more than two centuries ago, but the people of my district in South India started experiencing those evils only after the middle of last century (in my life time). Close observation and experiences very clearly show that the evolution of evils and their course follow a certain definite order or sequence in accordance with increasing HPD/deficits/ unsustainability.

Poverty of the Past and Present

Poverty is the foremost manifestation of deficiency, unsustainability, or shortages, and is synonymous with them. People of pre-modern days suffered poverty for various reasons, like exploitation, natural calamities, mass killer diseases, or wars; and not due to insufficiency of vital resources. In those regions, which were free from exploitation, even bigger families enjoyed a happy life because more hands meant more work and more opportunities to utilize and convert those vast surpluses of resources into wealth. Those people never needed "civilized" people's necessities, like costly education, polluting travels, pricey energy, special toiletries, expensive gadgets, etc. So people strived to form huge families; but the high mortality rate acted against them.

With time, humanity started enjoying longevity. Different people started enjoying it at different times. The developed countries that developed modern medicine and liberated themselves from religious and political exploitation experienced longevity more than two centuries ago. Their population grew fast to reach HPD, and as we have discussed, they suffered its evil consequences far ahead of others.

Small groups of primitive people suffer high mortality even today. Yet the vast majority of people now enjoy thrice or more times longer life-expectancy than those of the last quarter of the nineteenth century. So, more and more regions crossed OPD around the middle of the last century and depleted all the reserves of resources. Absence of surplus resources curtailed the advantages of huge families, and from then on, huge families mean **inevitable poverty**.

Sequential Arrival of Evils

The idea of sequential evolution of man-made ills, evils, and curses along with the growth of HPD has already been highlighted. This orderly evolution of evils takes place with rising HPD because the already evolved evils and certain desperate conditions of increased deficiencies (with the further rise of HPD) combine to form the right "recipe" to create the next evil. Deficit is the primary or universal ingredient of every "recipe" of evil in the society. When the number of the evolved evils multiplies and when HPD goes further up to create more deficits, all these combine to create the next harsher evil. In other words, the evolved evils combine and complicate the deficient society to create the new evil.

For instance, terrorism is an evil that evolved much later than poverty. For the right recipe of terrorism or if terrorism is to develop in a society, there must have been many previously evolved "ingredients" like poverty, unemployment, corruption, and ungovernable conditions and newly-developing, desperate situations which create immoral rascals who must create dangerous ideologies to motivate people to terrorism. The evolution of terrorism waits until the arrival of these ingredients.

For these reasons, we cannot find people for terrorism in a wholesomely sustainable region. Similarly, every evil has a story in its birth.

Common Sequence of Evolution

As has been said, **poverty** is the simplest form of deficiency in a family (HIF). When HIFs multiply, HPD/GULC arrives. The early sign of HPD is **unemployment**.

Already too many needy families exist in that HPD society, and unemployment denies them the opportunity to come up. Thus, it worsens poverty and lowers the threshold level to reach poverty or unsustainable conditions.

Poverty and unemployment work together to bring **unhealthy competition** for the available scanty resources and jobs.

Some sections of needy people in rural regions compensate for the shortages by plundering forests and over-using green cover. Thus **forest/ green cover destruction**, which favours GW, comes into existence.

When dignified efforts under tough competition fail to end starvation, some among them try **crime** (like theft), and the cunning among them choose **corruption** in order to compensate for their shortages. Thus, the community adds a few more evils to their deficient region. Corruption also includes corrupt ways of getting jobs like bribery, nepotism, etc. Corrupt practices deny jobs to eligible youths and bring in unworthy people to vital posts and worsen administration, development, and progress. Thus, many well-educated, sensitive youths fume because of the injustice and wait for better days or for opportunities to take revenge on the society and the system.

When life is tough in rural regions, with shortages and evolved evils, people **migrate** toward cities and migration becomes an inevitable reality. Their travel strengthens the transport industry and the process of **urbanization and industrialization**, all of which favour **pollution and GW**.

Quite often, the victims of these evils and the fuming youths who lose their rightful opportunities to corruption prefer an uneventful life in poverty; but some of them turn violent to fight corrupt and exploiting people. Thus, **violence** is added to the other evils. To some, these evolved evils, like crime and violent grabbing, are full time "employment" and they make good their deficits through parasitic life.

All this further strains sustainability and makes people more desperate and restive. Immoral opportunists in religion, region, society, and politics pose as saviours and exploit the desperate people and transfer their deficits up to those frantic people by indulging in **fanatical and sectarian idealizing and activities**.

The combination of corrupt and incompetent leadership and developments like **violence** and sectarian thoughts **make governance difficult or impossible**.

The most immoral among them create very dangerous, perverted ideologies which teach hatred and intolerance. They "brainwash" desperate, innocent youth and those fuming youths and utilize them to fulfil their greed and ambitions through **terrorism.**

By now, deficits soar in rural and urban regions and these are compensated for with more industrial activities, with the help of huge quantities of polluting energy. Thus, **uncontrollable pollution** becomes another permanent feature with HPD.

Thus, evolution of newer evils happens along with the growth of deficits. All these complicate life further and also initiate and worsen **GW and CC**.

Understanding the Evolution and Course

Now we have a list of anthropogenic evils. (We will have detailed discussions in the coming chapters about those with consequences.) If people keenly observe fast growing communities for a long time or if they study different communities in different stages of the described course (HPD), they can understand such an order in their evolution.

Facets of Deterioration I Witnessed

Lessons to be Learned

During my boyhood days in the 1950s, we enjoyed wholesome, sustainable living in our village. But now, conditions have deteriorated to hopelessness. More or less the same is the fate of this region or our district.

In contrast, we read about and even witness families, communities, and countries like Singapore and China that suffered chaos in the 1950s, but now have a fairly hopeful life.

Most of the regions and countries which suffer chaos and ungovernable conditions today enjoyed a far better life when China and Singapore suffered. Understanding these opposite courses in the light of the prevalence of HIFs and degree of HPD can certainly help the modern planners to come out with failure-proof, predictable policies.

Beautiful Scenes Which Changed Fast

Before the 1950s: Alexander Humphrey Minchin is the father of mass irrigation of my district, Kanyakumari, at the southernmost tip of India. He was a highly courageous, immensely benevolent, and brilliant British engineer. This white man, a compatriot of the colonizers, risked his life to build the biggest dam across the largest river of the district and an extensive irrigation system in the year 1906. The assured irrigation facilities changed the face of our district. Our grandparents worked in great enthusiasm and hope and converted the barren tracts into rice-paddies using the water. It ensured to them full employment and food security and brightened up their lives.

The scenes of the 1950s still run in my mind like a 3-D film. My village of that time was sparsely populated and every family had more than the required fertile lands to sustain a contented life. Water was surplus and our men worked in joy and hope in our rice-paddies. We also had dry land crops like coconut, palmyrah, mango, cashew, and many others, including oil-seed trees which lighted our homes. We, as children, used the vast vacant lands to play different games and even used the perennial bodies of water for playing games. Every elder loved every child of every home and even guided us in the games and narrated stories and historical events.

The families of my village were closely related, and Christians and Hindus were in equal numbers. There were Muslims in neighbouring villages. The village folks enjoyed all the festivals of every religion and there was no hatred or animosity among them. Because of the food security and the best allopathic medical facilities established by Christian missionaries in the middle of nineteenth century, the death rate came down dramatically from our grandparents' time and population was steadily increasing. As a child, I envied huge families because they had enough children to play any game at any time they liked.

1960s: Our village had a missionary school (established around 1820) where we had schooling for five years. For middle-level schooling, we walked about three kilometres to a bigger missionary school in a nearby village. A few of our good friends who were with us in the primary school and playgrounds were missing in the latter school and they did not even come regularly to the playgrounds. When I visited them, to my surprise and sorrow, I found them engaged in small jobs as child labourers and with the responsibility to look after their younger and new-born siblings. All of those children were from huge families with too many children, which I had envied just a decade before.
During the last years of the 1960s, the irrigation water became erratic and strained agricultural activities.

1970s: Witnessed more poverty: In the year 1974, I completed my medical studies in the state capital Madras (now Chennai), and had plans to go abroad for higher studies, as most of the young medics desired. In those days, I happened to go as a medical officer to another village, where I presently live. It was a very beautiful, big village with a sparse population. The people were very affectionate and courteous. They loved me very much and took me like a family member of theirs and entrusted their healthcare to me. After a few years, I intended to go back to Chennai for post-graduation study or to go abroad. But the elders entreated me quite affectionately never to leave them. I felt that they really needed my services as a doctor and so I adopted this lovely village, which was fast growing into a small town, as my new home; but I never knew that this place was destined to grow faster and wealthier because of new rubber plantations.

This place is suitable for profitable rubber plantations and has pleasant weather. However, I saw poverty in the huge families, as I had seen in my village. The sorrows of poverty were such that it was inhumane to sit idle when ignorant families kept earning poverty by adding more children than they could afford to provide for. So as a service, I used every opportunity to suggest to eligible couples that they restrict the number of children to two and to bigger families that they stop with what they had. I took special care to instruct those parents coming with malnourished children and those coming for second and subsequent childbirths.

The miseries of poverty touched me; yet all I could do was give them free treatment and some small help. The government, too, had a lot of schemes to end poverty. Despite all these, huge families suffered in too many ways.

By the latter half of the 1970s, the children of the 1950s (of the former village) got married and formed their own families and divided their family property, like rice-paddies and ancestral houses, among them. The share of the descendants of huge families was too small to support them. Even with assured irrigation, these fragments of lands could not support a family; with erratic irrigation, their sufferings were inevitable. Thus poverty afflicted too many of those new families in too many ways and also brought about social and economic disparities where equality prevailed until recently.

In those days, the prominent man-made socioeconomic ill of these regions was poverty, along with disparities and inequalities of their own creation. These naturally helped the evolution of evils like crime and corruption. Disparities and inequalities, along with their associated feelings, like low self-esteem, jealousy, and envy, created a kind of "incompatibility" even among siblings, their families, and other close relatives.

Toward the end of the 1970s, I wanted to bring out a booklet on contrasting family histories (socio-economic), which could enlighten the reader on the evolution and end of poverty. Such tell-tale stories could have warned innocent peoples of the necessity to form small, manageable families and the governments to form rational policies to end poverty and other evolving curses.

1980s: More Evils: I charted out the detailed histories of a sufficient number of families; but because of the busy practice I could not complete it. Even if I had finished it, it would have become almost irrelevant; by that time, newer, more prominent and more horrible evils like crime, open hatred, intolerance, and violence appeared to make the previous evils less prominent.

Our district was one of the most literate in India at that time; its literacy level was comparable to the literacy levels of Western countries. Despite prosperous plantations and education, the district witnessed the appearances of those evils by 1980, along with the growth of population. During early 1980s, the district as a whole felt some kind of premonition because of few hate-mongering religio-political leaders.

As we all know, ideologies in general and religious ideologies in particular (especially in crowded communities) play a definite role in shaping the mind-set and life of people. Followers of religions with too many superstitions, costly rites, and exploitable practices and traditions suffered and lagged behind and augmented socio-economic disparities, already initiated by HIFs and the division of family wealth. The immoral, exploiting leaders used such disparities, outright falsehoods, and twisted historical events to "poison" and divide people and to create animosities and murderous hatred. At last, those harsh effects of HPD defeated every rational thought and the benefits of education and family ties, and exploded in communal violence in the year 1982, which resulted in many deaths and a huge loss of property.

By retrospective thinking, I can assert that our district had crossed OPD levels even before 1970, but we never felt it. Since those days, a small number of people had been migrating from their villages, seeking jobs in cities; but the number of such people swelled with years and reached new heights after those violent incidents. They invariably reached the state capital and helped the growth of urban centres.

Open laboratories: All those circumstances acted like open social laboratories, from which I have learnt how HIFs, HPD, disparities, faulty religious ideologies, greed, etc. played their parts in creating unliveable conditions and calamities. So, the scope of the book widened.

By the mid-1980s, I went again to Chennai for post-graduate studies (after appointing responsible doctors to continue services without interruption). Chennai too had grown a great deal during the previous decade and there was too much crowding and filth, and people in general were too busy and anxious with the parallel growth of anti-social activities.

Since the 1990s, the world witnessed more and more international terrorism, the stark worsening of pollution, and then the growing awareness about global warming (GW) and climate change (CC).

Later, since the turn of **new millennium**, horrible incidents like 9/11, bombings around the globe, suicide bombings, and events in Darfur, Somalia, Iraq, Afghanistan, and more such calamities shook the world.

Now in country after country, enlightened youths keep rising up against their indifferent, long-standing leaders. All these circumstances perplex keen observers, but for me these happenings are a repetition of what I had been witnessing for years on a smaller scale.

A Sad Course and the Aggravators

Back to my childhood village: irrigation water stopped coming in the early 1990s and so paddy cultivation became history. The HPD conditions and failing farming activities raised unemployment and other evils to new heights. More than 60 percent of the descendants of original families of 1950s had migrated out. Even then, the HPD conditions prevailed, with all those curses. The mistake that condemned them to all those evils is the unchecked proliferation of population through HIFs into the early 1980s.

Now, this adopted, naturally-blessed village too has grown into a crowded town because of proliferation and inward migrations. While my childhood village simulated poor and developing countries with too many outwardly migrating people, the adopted one acted like developed rich countries and attracted migrants.

We now have in our HPD district people of a wide range of castes, races, religious adherence, political activists, and followers of different cultures. In the mid-1970s, people celebrated and enjoyed festivals together without any discrimination. But now, because of the HPD conditions, these diverse people prefer to differ with one another in whatever way possible and thus this multicultural paradise turned into a chaotic, unpredictable society. They often use their social, cultural, and religious differences and festivals to gather people to exhibit their strength, which also helps them to demand economic and political concessions from government; because in a democracy, these numbers "count."

Thus, despite wonderful achievements in diverse fields, mankind is bogged down with uncertainties, selfishness, enmities and outright threats due to pollution, GW and CC because mankind has outgrown the fixed resources Nature has earmarked for it.

We Don't Have Time to Remain Complacent

Thus, from poverty, we have come a long distance to suffer GW and CC. I have incorporated all these systematic evolution of evils in my earlier book, ***Give Yourself a Sane Happy World: Sans Poverty, Crime and Violence***, published in India in February 2007, and then in London by the end of 2008 with a few additions. The aim of that book was to end all the man-made evils by reversing the way they evolved. Since that book is more generalized and huge in size, and since the prominent curse of today is GW and CC, I have written this book specifically to enlighten the world of the true "biology" and "biography" of GW and CC, so that rational policies can be made to mitigate / end those in the most rational and predictable way.

I have often quoted points from the first book and pointed out areas about which more information is available. I refer to the first book as ***Book G*** (available at amazon.com and net).

Now we will have a fairly detailed study about the evolved evils and their vicious impact upon other evils, including pollution, GW and CC.

14

Aspects of Poverty

We have already seen some aspects of poverty: its birth, the harsh sufferings of its victims, and how centuries-old poverty differs from the poverty of today. We need a correct understanding of modern poverty in order to end it resolutely, because ending poverty plays a very crucial role in ending the evils, including terrorism, pollution, GW, and CC, which evolved later than this.

This chapter describes more aspects of it, especially the modern complicated situations which easily bring about poverty.

Multiplying Needs Promote Poverty

In the past, the needs of ordinary families were limited to food, clothing, and shelter. But today, the needs of families have multiplied and some of them differ from region to region and with their economic activities and their distance from Nature. For instance, education, polluting energy, and continuous transport of food are indispensable for a respectable urban, "civilized" life, but people living near Nature with surplus resources can enjoy a moderate life without them.

Thus, civilized people, who have gone far from Nature, have made some of the newly-added needs indispensable or really vital, because their insufficiency may endanger their lives. Further the worsening of socio-economic and political situations adds newer needs to the list and pushes up the cost of living. (Part II of *Book G*).

Trends of Soaring Needs

When LPD prevailed and surplus resources were available, people never spent anything to find a job, and they never had to spend huge sums for education with the sole aim of getting employment. They never needed huge polluting factories, costly gadgets, fast-moving vehicles, and huge amounts of energy to speed up travel and economic activities.

But education has become a necessity with HPD and urbanization, because life is too competitive and opportunities are scarce. As unemployment soars and competition is tough, then in addition to education, they may require special skills too, to acquire a job. Further, special equipment, machines, and speeding vehicles have become necessities to face competition.

With crowding and urbanization, people build crowded and multi-story residences where air remains stagnant. In tropical countries, the air inside houses gets dangerously warmed up because of the weather and the heat emitted from kitchen and humans. The moisture of respiration, perspiration, cooking fumes, together with other gases or sprays make the air noxious. These can sicken and make residents prone to infections or even kill people. In such closed spaces, when someone with respiratory infection sneezes or coughs, the microbes easily infect others and hike their medical bills. In order to circulate air and regulate ambient temperature, they have to buy gadgets like fans and AC machines. Absence of these gadgets threatens life directly and through infection. So those costly gadgets are in no way less important for life in crowded towns. And to run them, they must continuously buy energy in the form of electricity or some polluting, costly fuel.

Congested and competitive urban life curses people with a lot of mental, physical, and metabolic disorders and now pollution attacks every human system to cause conditions from simple skin inflammation to dangerous cancers of internal organs hiking medical bills. All these incur huge spending in many ways.

Again, to protect precious savings, costly equipment, and people from criminals, families must spend considerably for safety-gadgets and special guards.

In crowded, poor and developing countries with rampant corruption, crime, violence, injustice, high cost of living, ungovernable conditions, etc., one has to buy even dignity, love, sex, justice, job opportunities, and safety for a price.

Further, to get refreshed from the monotony of jobs, anxieties, tension, and unfriendly surroundings, people must buy entertainment, "happy" holidays, and other activities which try to reset the body, mind, and soul to continue a normal life.

For modern youth, computers, mobile phones, fashionable dress, and costly toiletries have become necessities to face the "competition" to attract partners and "friends," and even to climb up the social and professional ladders.

Poverty Promoting Factors

For many reasons like those described, modern families easily fall into poverty and their sufferings further multiply when their region crosses OPD.

HPD viciously complicates poverty because of the additional challenges, like unhealthy competition, corruption, crime, injustice, insecurity, etc.

Today, when we talk about poverty, the deficiencies of these newer needs relevant to them must be taken into consideration.

Consequences of Poverty

When poverty threatens people, they cannot make provisions for environmental care, pollution clearing, costly renewable energy, forest protection, and such responsible jobs, but often do the opposite, harmful acts.

When poor families have more children, their next generation invariably becomes poorer because of a shrunken inheritance. Too many very rich families of the past, including aristocrats, have become pathetically poor because of too many children (HIFs), and have become unequal even with average families. Disparities breed envy, jealousy, and hatred, and create enmities.

When life becomes horrible in a community, some of its members migrate away, leaving their dear ones, and live a "rootless life." Migrations initiate the travel industry and alter the demographic pattern of host regions.

Poverty forces every nation to spend considerably for its alleviation. These unending services prevent the nation's progress and affect its development.

Additionally, all these consequential adverse situations further complicate people's lives and make everyone prone to poverty.

Expose the Ultimate Authors of Poverty

The unending sufferings, shameful situations, and indignities of poverty are too horrible and pathetic to bear and so must be prevented at all cost. (For more, see chapter 45 of *Book G*). People often blame exploitation and other socio-economic evils for poverty, inequality, and disparities. This is true to some extent, yet the poor families themselves are the ultimate authors of the situations and so they alone can prevent them, by forming sustainable families. (*Book G*, chapter 63). Today, poverty eradication schemes like Millennium Development Goals (MDG) show success only in regions which adopt a small and sustainable family norm.

Major Truths About Modern Poverty

The present-day world must understand the following facts, which would help a desperate humanity to end poverty in the most rational way.

♦ Modern humans need far more costly items than people needed a century ago. This intensifies poverty and makes people prone to poverty.

♦ HPD has wiped out reserves of resources and opportunities, which makes poverty eradication a tougher job.

♦ The power of ending poverty lies entirely with the poor families.

15

Unemployment and Unworthy Employment

Wholesome Employment

The position of wholesome employment in a country reflects its robust economy, which ensures worthy and respectable life to its citizens. All three are almost synonymous. Wholesome employment position means that every healthy adult of that country must be able to get decent/ acceptable employment with which he must earn enough to support a normal family by working seven to eight hours a day for about five to six days a week.

Onset of Unemployment

When a country enjoys OPD and has worthy policies and plans to engage their people optimally in various sectors and also has the provisions to give workers of every sector an equitable remuneration, the question of unemployment, poverty, disparities, and inequalities does not occur. This statement also expresses the fact that, even if a country has an optimal population, it can be beset with unemployment and related curses if it does not have worthy policies (for instance, the USA).

However, unemployment is an unavoidable curse of HPD. Further, if the country's policies fail to meet the cited requirements, the unemployment rate shoots up and too many go underemployed (for example, Greece).

Contrasts and Limits

Today, unemployment is a very common curse of too many countries—invariably due to HPD and also due to the violation of the described conditions. At times, contrasting situations happen. For instance, developed countries with a low percentage of HIFs and favourable population density suffer unemployment and recession, but Gulf countries with a too high percentage of HIFs and HPD are able to employ larger numbers of migrant workers than their total population.

Western countries enjoyed full employment until recently, but now suffer unemployment despite OPD-like conditions because of certain thoughtless acts (explained in chapter 30, "Economy") and also because of wrong policies, rather absurd "magnanimities" (explained in chapters 20 to 23) which take them toward HPD. Yet they continue to "import" migrant workers in too many sectors (for causes explained in chapter 16). The Gulf countries in general enjoy a robust economy because they overuse their depletable wealth and heavily depend upon external markets (see chapter 11). Both these situations—Western and Gulf economy—are unsustainable. The structure of Western economy is faulty and unsustainable, so even if they give comfortable employment to all, it is an unsustainable condition. Both cheat themselves and give undue hope to their own ordinary people and also to the desperate "would-be migrants" around the world.

Moronic Criminals

Quite often, insensible, directionless leaders blabber that they have great plans to create vast employment opportunities for their needy people; but how many have achieved this? Everyone must understand that, in any country, every department or business or profession has a particular limit of supporting employees; employing people beyond that level will make that department loss-making or that business unprofitable, or the income of those professionals will come down below sustainable levels. (See chapter 13, "Employment," in *Book G*). So responsible leaders must avoid giving such hope. This amounts to cheating and is a crime.

Primacy of the Farming Industry

Farming creates real wealth from the bounties of Nature. If farming activities are done by respecting Nature's plans (integrated organic farming), harvests can be repeated again and again without depleting Nature's resources. It is this farming industry that energizes every person to do his work. And it is the most permanent and viable industry, needed until the last human exists on earth. But today, because of irrational policies, its share to GDP (gross domestic product) has become just a fraction and so is its employable limit.

We must understand that almost every other industry, including money-spinning economic activities, is "carbon negative" and so are parasitic or injurious as far as Nature is concerned. But integrated farming never leaves any pollution, does not cause chemical or physical injury to Nature, and never promotes anything that aids GW and CC.

If the world intents to achieve a sustainable economic activity (including employment), every effort must be taken to maintain a healthy equation between wholesome farming and other economic activities. In other words, every other economic activity must be built on the broad-based, strong foundation of this wealth-creating, energy-providing, indestructible, Nature-based economy. A country that plans in such a way will never face a chaotic economic situation.

Weakened Foundation Industry

But in the name of civilization, urbanization, respectable living, and profits, farming has been weakened to the extent it needs to be propped up with subsidies. There are regions where it is neglected so much that many food-producing farming families are driven to starvation, premature death, debt, humiliation, and suicide.

It is an uncomfortable truth that worthy planning is impossible with rising HPD; sorrowfully, it is this sort of suffering rural farming families bring about HPD through their HIFs. Ending deficits and starvation in every farming family is a crucial necessity for the health of every nation.

Importance of Strengthening the Agri-Industry

Instead of offering subsidies if the governments fix the right (equitable) price for agricultural produce, help the farming families to prevent HIFs and slowly wean unsustainable farming in favour of integrated organic farming, then, farming families would gain freedom, dignity, and hope.

Too many "powerful" economies suffer economic turmoil because they do not have a strong and sustainable support base. On the other hand, those countries, including poor and developing ones, where more than 50 percent of their families sustain themselves with farming activities (like India), do not face humiliating economic chaos (except when monsoons fail). We now have a greater scope of strengthening farming economy further than this (as described below) and when this happens, the buying power of this 50 percent of the population is sufficient to support the other sectors or at least can prevent economic crisis.

Possible Great Future

If the villagers plan sustainable small families, they make available a lot of resources, like land and water, and can go for sustainable (organic) farming, which will employ more people profitably. In addition to the creation of enough grains, pulses, fruits, vegetables, industrial raw materials like cotton, timber, and rubber, beverages like tea, coffee, and cocoa, and medicinal plants, they can do bio-fuel related farming. This can further be supported with poultry, dairy, fresh water fisheries, etc. Rural income can further be boosted with involvement in renewable energy creation from wind, sunlight, medium streams, tidal waves, and bio-fuel factories.

Rural life near Nature is the most economic way of living. When the huge funds spent for dirty energy are slowly diverted for these, they can easily gain economic freedom. Then, every other freedom will follow naturally, to give them a joyous, fully-sustainable, respectable, and non-polluting life.

Modern Economies Build Unsustainability upon Unsustainability

Since Nature-based life is the most wholesome and the most economical, people who migrate away after ruining it can never think of such a life in cities. Urban economies are supported with dirty energy, rural marketing, and rural raw materials and so are not really sustainable. So encouraging urban growth or attempting to strengthen urban economy beyond the healthy limit weakens the sustainability of the whole country.

Yet despite the vast growth of urban population (a bad sign), too many ill-informed leaders and other public personalities, as mentioned previously, often assure people of creating more jobs through sustainable developments and sustainable economic activities. At present, almost all such "progress" happens with very high levels of residual pollution. Any economic act or development that pollutes more than it can neutralize is not a sustainable one. Trying to sustain something (development or economic activity) through unsustainable means is an oxymoron. Instead of engaging in such foolish "developments," if they end the situation (HPD) behind these, everything would turn out fine in the most natural way.

Devitalizing Newer Jobs

When a population grows, they require more and more people to do the various jobs—from farming to bureaucratic activities. Until they remain within OPD, these jobs would mutually benefit everyone. But with HPD, those complementary arrangements turn into competitions and then unhealthy competitions ensue. The unhealthy competitions further create unworthy parasitic "jobs," like corruption, crime, and other evils, which make the process of employment disorderly and ruin the economy and sustainability.

In HPD countries, the shrewd among the unworthy parasites amass huge wealth and enjoy lavish living. Some of their "organizations" have grown to employ thousands of people and they have international connections. Even vast regions of many crowded countries are under such "differently employed" people's care. These dangerous "employment bureaus" and "job-creating" organizations will remain in one form or the other until HPD prevails or HPD-like situations are created due to wrong policies. Since these go against sustainability, they favour GW and CC in some way or the other.

16

Unhealthy Competitions and Challenges

Healthy Competitions and Challenges are Healthy Necessities

Reasonable competitions and challenges stimulate people to think deeply, to plan seriously, to search for new and advantageous things, to innovate, to do things meticulously, and to bother about the future and long-term security. Thus, challenges activate and exercise all the natural faculties, socio-economic abilities, and political rights, and make people alert to possible failures, falls, threats, or harms. The absence of competitions just does the opposite and (as we see around the wealthy world and in rich families) makes people dull, un-industrious, and even makes them indifferent to matters concerning freedom and life and death.

Unhealthy Competitions

Yet, too much of it in the form of unhealthy competitions and challenges is undesirable and may act almost like threats. Threats naturally evoke survival instincts and often make people overreact. When people face unhealthy competitions (threats), they either fight for survival or try to fly away to escape from the difficult situation. Both these, fight and flight, are emergency functions and are harmful to all involved (the aggressor and the aggressed upon) in many ways and take away noble traits like peace, happiness, humanism, self-sacrificial tendencies, and even can make people antisocial and anti-national when their honour and life are at stake.

Cyclical Shrewdness and Indifference

There are uncountable instances of happenings around the world and in history where we can see how people handle very tough situations or challenges with all-out efforts, and also the opposite, of enjoying lavish comforts in the most irresponsible way. When people suffer deficiencies and humiliation and face tough competition and challenges in life, they work hard to overcome those difficulties or even may try to end them through criminal ways, and when these survival efforts fail, people do not mind even quitting their motherlands and proceeding to unknown and unfamiliar remote corners of the world.

In practice, those who enjoy success by any means in highly competitive societies try invariably to accumulate as much wealth as possible in order to give their children the best possible life, and with the "noble" intention that their children must never face the difficult and humiliating situations they faced. Hence, these children enjoy all lavish comforts and are over-protected by their parents, so they face no challenges.

Affluence, comfort, and security invariably take away the motivation or stimulus to achieve. There are too many such children who even hate education and refuse to learn life-supportive skills and bother the least to understand the prevailing socio-economic and other unfavourable conditions, or even are oblivious of the need for some employment, because they have huge wealth to enjoy. Quite often, such pampered children waste their wealth and life, often on lavish gambling, unfaithful friends, drugs, sex, etc., and lose their comforts and security. There are too many instances where such indifferent, pampered people have accumulated huge debt and suffered indignities and shame. Invariably the challenges of suffering and poverty in their later days stimulate their affected children to achieve and to excel like their grandparents—thus go a kind of cyclical change.

Today, too many people of many western countries while away their precious days indifferently because they never experience the challenges their parents faced during the World War days and later in rebuilding their war-ravaged countries. Hence, they, including those in vital and responsible positions as leaders, policy makers, celebrities, and service organizations, are complaisant and commit vital mistakes like those affluent boys. On the other hand, youths of poor and developing countries use every opportunity and try to imbibe the best knowledge and skill because of constant challenges in every field, so when they migrate to Western countries they easily excel over their less motivated counterparts in the host countries.

Well Known Historical Example

We have seen how Europe suffered and faced unhealthy challenges and competitions of HPD until World War II. They risked dangerous voyages, endured restless labours, and fought socio-economic ills, evils, and too many wars. These came to an end with World War II. Yet the memories of the harsh life kept that generation alert to every threat. When they felt communism as a threat, they went even to the extent to stockpile atomic and hydrogen bombs with the capacity to exterminate the whole human race.

But the following generations, which enjoy the fruits of the sacrifices of their ancestors, do not have any worthy challenges or competition. So they fail to recognize even harsher threats than those of pre-World War II and communism. Often they fail even to point out the wrongs around because they don't want to draw "criticism," but make themselves "irrationally humane gentlemen," which gives wrong signals to the malicious detractors. They are not even able to understand the significance of nationhood/motherland/homeland or to visualize the consequences of their irrational and uncalled-for benevolence and its possible effects upon their own children despite the many open threats to their life, honour, economy, and freedom.

Price of HPD and Unhealthy Competitions

At present, the people of poor and developing countries are losing peace, trust, hope, and happiness because of HPD, and suffer like pre-war Europeans—with hatred, enmities, unending violence, and cruel deaths. Again, the HPD-driven unhealthy challenges, trade practices, and other happenings make people and governments restless, anxious, and tense, and make life horrible with mental and physical diseases and socio-economic and political disorders. At last, the self-destructive pollution has come to stay permanently, like the sword of Damocles.

If people around the world learn the significance of HPD and LPD from European sufferings, recovery, affluence, indifference, and the return again to chaos, they can end their own curses without bloodshed and brutality and prevent/arrest their course toward greater pollution, GW, and CC.

Leaves No One Unhurt

The world must understand that unhealthy competition and challenges are early signs of HPD, which affect the whole community. If they are alert and realistic to prevent it, they can easily march toward contented, sustainable living. But every delay begets evils like crime, violence, terrorism, or ungovernable conditions; then their life turns more miserable and the recovery time stretches longer.

People in influential positions must understand that no one can think of a peaceful, worthy life with unhealthy challenges and competition. Even those who have vast wealth are not at all free from challenges. The world is in dire straits, and those (individuals or countries) with sufficient wealth or good income must keep in their mind that somebody is around to grab what they possess, so other than working hard to earn, they must be on their toes to protect what they have. Those who failed to protect their wealth, those who lost to competition and those who earned their own poverty must struggle hard; even then they may be forced to choose some not-so-good "job" like crime, corruption, violence, terrorism, or begging as their breadwinning profession. Even these harsh professionals are not free from competitions and challenges, and even the strongest and most violent leader among them lives with fear for his life.

Inescapable and Unending Sufferings

Even peace-loving, patriotic people suffer in too many ways. In fact, they are the worst victims in any HPD country. For instance, a decent family spends all its possessions to give the best (costly) education to their bright boys and girls with the full hope that they will support the family by getting the right job. But when they do not get a job because of corruption and nepotism, what will be the feelings of the children who have sacrificed their fun, play, and entertainment of youthful days to have that successful education, and what about the parents who spent their whole resources with trust and hope, and now stand as paupers? What can we expect them to do?

Similarly, in order to beat challenges and competition, too many well-meaning people invest their whole wealth in decent businesses, small factories, or minor trade activities. Most of the honest people fail because of the criminals in society, politics, bureaucracies, trade unions, or among the workers which are nothing but unhealthy challenges of HPD.

Ultimately, unhealthy competition and its outcome do more harm to those countries and the world than what is normally expected; and promote and toughen every evil, including polluting activities, GW, and CC, as we will see in the following chapters.

17

Blood-Sucking Professions in HPD Regions

Limitations of Employability

Modern society needs a variety of services (jobs) for smooth going. When we look at jobs from a sustainability point of view, we find jobs which are carbon-friendly and those which are pollution causing. For a sustainable and efficient going of the society and to avoid pollution, a rational proportion and relationship must be maintained among them. Every job has some kind of mutually beneficial or mutually dependent relationship with other jobs and people. Thus, the number of employees required by any occupation depends upon its beneficiaries (purpose). There is an upper limit to the number of employees a particular job or profession can sustainably support. Depending upon the changing trends of population density, economic activities, and the health of society, those numbers can vary considerably from time to time.

As we saw earlier, an orderly and mutually supportive employment is possible only if people enjoy an orderly society within OPD. When this smooth going is threatened by HPD or foolish policies, there come too many parasitic, blood-sucking jobs that deteriorate the health of countries, including wealthy countries, make life more unsustainable, and hike the levels of carbon-unfriendly jobs disproportionately.

Evolution of Diverse Jobs

When people live near Nature as compact communities and within OPD, they get most of their requirements through comprehensive farming and live as mutually helpful people. Since they know each other, they hesitate to indulge in unacceptable activities, and since they have full employment, the need for those unacceptable activities ("jobs") like crime, terrorism, cheating, etc. does not arise. But, a variety of new jobs, including these unacceptable, exotic "jobs" evolve when their population exceeds OPD, and the numbers and varieties swell fast with urbanization. Readers must carefully follow the sorrowful following course to understand that every new job which evolves after that initial wholesomeness (OPD) is carbon-emitting and goes against sustainability.

When people migrate from villages due to growing HPD, the travel and transport industries become necessities and employ people to operate transport vehicles and to man the related manufacturing industries.

With crowding and urbanization, they require more administrators, coordinators, political activists, police officers, and employees for energy creation and distribution, etc.

These people require more infrastructures and residential blocks, which multiply jobs related to construction: engineers, masons, and related workers.

When HPD rises and unemployment soars, jobs are earned under unhealthy competition and an unhealthy social order. These generate unacceptable "jobs" related to crime, corruption, terrorism, gambling, drug trafficking, faking, and many more.

When corruption, crime, and violence multiply, they require more police officers, more judicial courts, and more people to deal with legal matters.

To compete for employment, the newer generation needs more education and skills, so schools and technical institutes multiply and then need more teachers.

When people work under unhealthy competitions, they must produce quality products in larger volumes in shorter time. Then they must market them aggressively by taking them to the customers in the shortest possible time. To achieve these ends, they need more factories, related tools, and equipment, faster transport and communication facilities, and workers for research, manufacture, and related activities.

Wars are common with crowding, so they require soldiers and related industries, and workers to manufacture war machines like rifles, canons, fighter tanks, frigates, fighter planes, etc.

To market them, many business establishments arise and employ people.

Restless, competitive and anxious life, pollution, and urban living easily sicken people. They require more hospitals, medics and paramedics, and people for related research and manufacture.

The tedious, tense, and monotonous life makes people weary and bored. They require quality entertainers to forget their worries and to refresh their minds.

The hopelessness of HPD forces many people to get some kind of hope and solace through their trust in God. Thus, religions employ a lot of people for religious affairs, including stark cheating and exploitation in the name of God.

Modern people want to look attractive for many reasons, so the beauty industry employs more and more people.

Other than this, modern living offers too many jobs, related to media, computers, communication, space explorations, etc.

These jobs may appear too many to choose from, but depending upon HPD, too many job-seekers will never get the job close to their heart or never get a job at all, and so must find some other way to earn their livelihood.

Flourishing Detrimental Jobs

Healthy adaptation in such circumstances has limits. With partial employment, they can carry on with life to some extent. Since chronic under-employment and unemployment are life-threatening, many among them may choose parasitic jobs out of desperation or compulsion.

For a society which enters HPD conditions afresh, choosing crime, terrorism, and other anti-social activities as their "profession" may appear humiliating, but as we see in crowded countries, with rising HPD and with the passage of time, more and more people choose such shameful "professions." It is not uncommon to see in crowded countries corrupt men, tax evaders, rowdies, other criminals, and those cheating and terrorizing people in the name of religion, politics, culture, etc. roaming around like respectable people.

Exotic Adaptation

Because of the unchecked growth of HPD, millions of people around the world have chosen or were tricked into "parasitic professions" like theft, extortion, kidnapping, murdering for gain, terrorism, drug dealing, distilling, cheating people using religious and political ideologies, destroying forests, etc., as full time or major professions.

The frustrating social, economic, mental, and moral conditions like disparities, poverty despite hard work, unemployment despite willingness to work, offensive affluence enjoyed by "unworthy people," pervasive corruption, nepotism, and crime in the society, the pathetic suffering of family members, hunger of children; such inevitable, sad situations often harden people's minds or justify such acts. For others, these are compensatory acts or opportunities to avenge the "cruel" society which made their lives unhappy. Illiterate fanatical barbarians even believe that hurting and dispossessing "irreligious" people is a way of serving the Almighty.

With time, all these dangerous people become accustomed or fully adapted to their way of living and even develop their skills to professional grade.

Ambitious Parasites and Disproportionate Losses

Today, so many ambitious parasites have amassed huge wealth, and they and their family members have risen to enviable heights in politics, bureaucracy, religion, society, business, and even in judiciary and police departments by using their money power, influence, or muscle power. Invariably, they continue to accumulate wealth far beyond their necessities and enjoy "invincibility."

For the "suckcess" and growth of one brutal rascal, many families would have lost a lot and even many lives would have been extinguished. Countries of such bad people fall to ruin because of the growth of criminals and because of the devitalisation or destruction of many humble, patriotic, and honest families.

These Look like Horrible Ills, but are Signs and Symptoms of . . .

Now we have named many newer jobs. Can we find one fully sustainable, carbon-friendly job among them?

The presence of a few like them is enough to frighten a peace-loving society and they further cause heavy losses in many ways. Our responsible leaders had been doing all to end those dangerous "jobs," but these evils have all along been resisting eradication because our policy makers never understood that these "plundering jobs" became a necessity for them in order to minimize their deficits. And thus these are signs and symptoms of a hidden, humble disease—HIF/ deficits/ unsustainable conditions. At last this real disease remained untouched to worsen HPD, which generates more and more polluting and evil jobs.

Will the world wake up to this fact?

18

Urbanization

(Cities behave like furnaces that warm the globe)

Contrasting Process of Urbanization

Once serene villages of poor and developing countries have lost their sustainable life because of HIFs and HPD (overcrowding) and are now beset with every known evil. Normal life is impossible and people are squeezed out of these villages or they escape as migrants. Their most common destinations are the urban centres. Unending migrations enlarge urban centres and create complications there, too.

While the cities of poor countries grow because of inevitable immigrations from villages, those of developed rich countries attract workers because of their huge industrial and other non-farming activities and opportunities.

Killing the Perennial "Enricher" to Buy Threat/Danger

Wholesomely sustainable, integrated natural farming is nothing short of the proverbial golden egg-laying fowl that enriches its master's life day after day without leaving him a dependent. The failure to understand this fact and the desire of modern man to enjoy wholesale urban living reveal their ignorance and remind us of the fool who wanted to get "all" its eggs by killing it. Natural sustainable farming and a wholesome and healthy rural life are almost dead and the highly unsustainable and harmful urbanization flourishes along with the many curses associated with crowding.

Agricultural activities fix carbon dioxide and use all the polluting wastes to create food and other materials for us and sustain our life, but urban life and their economic activities just do the opposite and contribute heavily to GW and threaten our existence through CC.

Highly Deficient and Precarious Urban Living

Every non-farming family depends upon farmers for their ultimate survival and they earn life-giving food in an indirect way by finding some other jobs, most of which use polluting energy in plenty. Urbanites rarely understand the defects and deficits of urban life and the faulty economic structure of modern life where the contribution of the vital agriculture industry to GDP stands stunted. People can enjoy urban life as long as everything goes smoothly; but understand the difficulties and the importance of farming and food when its availability is threatened at times like riots, transport strikes, wars, and economic chaos.

Through and Through, a Polluting Existence

Urban life harms Nature in many ways. It releases carbon dioxide fixed in the farms as food and uses a lot of polluting energy to run homes, factories, and vehicles. Other than releasing huge quantities of greenhouse gases, these activities directly heat the atmosphere. Thus urban centres literally act like furnaces that heat the globe.

Other than polluting energy, everything—like cement, iron, and other metals and materials—used in plenty for urban "developments," are manufactured and brought to cities at the very high "cost" of pollution.

Additional Wrongs Squeeze Out More Villagers

Farmers give life and energize the whole of humanity with the fuel called food. It is with this energy alone that people all over the world work in every sector and build their respective national economies. Farming is more valuable than any other vocation. Yet the well-organized, highly influential, and well-educated urbanites act in many irrational and selfish ways, which makes sustainable organic agriculture a dying industry. In most countries, farming has lost the support it needs and so the weak agro-industry is forced to adopt unsustainable, carbon-unfriendly farming methods.

To make things worse, vast sections of farmers in poor and developing countries create their own hells in the form of HIFs, which create very high levels of HPD in villages with unhealthy competitions among them. They competitively do intensive farming with their larger families and larger population. In order to earn the maximum from their shrinking lands, they choose the most profitable crop of that time. When most of them try that "costly" crop, they produce more than the market needs. Their profits plummet because of the glut or they suffer losses, which further ruin their village economy and trap them in debts, sickness, and related curses. These further force many to abandon farming and to proceed toward cities. Thus, unchecked urbanization is a sign of growing unsustainable conditions in rural regions.

Significance to GW and CC

Rural poverty favours forest and green-cover destruction, and so GW. Growing urban centres, too, heat up the atmosphere, and this double whammy favours a faster march toward CC.

Making Furnaces Called Cities

For ages, urban centres developed around some perennial water source, like rivers or lakes. Water makes the land fertile and feeds them and also enriches green tracks and forests. But as towns and cities grow, people clear the areas of thick vegetation and forests. The civilized urbanites divert most of the water for domestic, industrial, construction, and such purposes and destroy the green covers that had been absorbing carbon dioxide and light and the heat of the sun. Thus green cover destruction promotes GW directly and indirectly.

With time, these urbanites encroach upon bodies of water and fertile lands and convert them into residential areas, offices, paved roads, etc., which prevent the harvesting of rain water and obliterate water bodies. Now, for their survival, they divert water from every possible source and make other water-dependent areas barren, and thereby promote GW.

Accumulations of human waste and other toxic materials ruin the remaining bodies of water and fertile lands, kill vegetation, and promote GW.

When the number of families multiplies, they need more travel and transport facilities, more industries, and more of the polluting energy that promotes GW.

Their domestic activities and metabolism too create an abundance of carbon dioxide and a variety of other pollutants and heat.

The greenhouse gases and heat liberated from machines, vehicles, industries, energy-creation, and home activities are added to the warming effects of vanishing green cover and the vast light and heat reflected by concrete pavements and buildings. These combine to make cities real furnaces which heat up the atmosphere. Rough estimates say that the heat emanating from a unit area of a crowded city is more than ten thousand times of the heat emitted by a similar area of forest. That means a city must raise new vast forests of about ten thousand times its area to neutralize its GW effects. But is it possible? Have we got land and water to do that?

And so they remain as huge deficits.

Ultimately, vast cities are far worse than vast deserts; deserts just reflect heat and light but cities do many times more harm. Cities can influence atmospheric temperatures and affect air movements far more severely than deserts, and change, to that extent, the weather and climate.

Filthy Peripheries Act like "Repositories" of Disease

Until a few decades ago, every category of migrant people, from illiterate labourers to highly skilled professionals, found satisfactory work in the newly developing industries, other evolving jobs, and construction activities. These employment opportunities have their limits, and when jobs dwindled, those migrants competed with similar people by offering themselves for lower wages, which lowered their standard of living. Those of the lower strata are the most affected. Such inevitabilities forced them to settle down in the filthy shanties or slums of cities. With time, slums expanded recklessly in all the poor and developing countries. Their highly contaminated, unhygienic environment and poor toilet facilities are real threats to everybody's well-being. For an extra income, they keep fowl and other animals in close proximity. These conditions turn slums into repositories of every known contagious disease and infesting parasite which devitalizes those unfortunate people and, at times, turns pandemic.

With growing unemployment, poverty, diseases, and disparities, it is natural that all the socioeconomic ills and evils we discussed elsewhere proliferate and turn many urban centres into war zones and dirty hells which directly and indirectly promote GW.

Rise of the Inconsequential

We just saw how the competitive agro-activities caused gluts and losses. Their loss is gain for the urbanites. Now an average urbanite spends lesser amounts for the most vital food than what he spends for entertainment or toiletries. So they save huge sums to the extent to create funny jobs, like "money managers." Greed turns many "managers" into manipulators of the economy. The huge, "lopsided" savings and speculative trading, and irresponsible and often foolish "auctioning" in bourses and markets often inflates values of every saleable item, including common commodities like food grains. At last, the sufferers are the ordinary people, including farmers who may not be able to buy enough of the food they produce.

Sensible governments must control such undue monetary advantages of a section of people, speculative activities, and other inflation-causing activities. But at times, even responsible people have described such "rising wealth" as great progress and as robust growth of economy. It is common sense that such artificial pricing has to come down at some point and cause difficulties. During such tough times, instead of rebuking those irresponsible people, many governments come forward to compensate such losses (like bank losses, crashing stock markets) and remain as pathetic spectators when those immoral parasites scoop their "bonuses" (for making huge losses); but how many governments compensate appropriately the losses suffered by poor farmers during calamities?

Thus the carbon-fixing, life-giving industry suffers and loses whatever sustainability it enjoyed. Such sorrowful living conditions force farmers to go for further, even more unnatural farming (like BT), artificially boosted farming (like using growth factors), indiscriminate use of pesticides and other harmful chemicals. These just repeat the cycle through gluts and cause health hazards for humans and the natural species of crops, and degrade farmlands.

Handle Wealth with Clear Guidelines

Modern governments must be watchful and prevent the mirage of economic growth due to preventable inflation. With computer facilities, governments can manage their "money" with very few "money managers." It just requires clear-cut laws and very clear and rational guidelines regarding the various fees, interests, and other rates. But too many ill-informed, half-baked economists, bureaucrats, and politicians succumb to the "attractive" dealings, predictions, and promises of greedy parasites and kill their economy, as happened to many top and medium economies around the globe. Sickness of leading economies affects other countries and their trade partners, especially the poor countries, and, at last, favours factors which promote GW.

If those huge savings are rationally used or "ploughed back" to support healthy farming activities, bio-fuel farming, and other greening activities, the rural economy gets invigorated to employ more people. Such a situation will reduce migrations from villages, control urbanization, and form a wide (economic) base to support urban economy and the national economy.

Woes of Urban Living

Compared with the few advantages of urban living, its inconsistencies, desperations, and anxieties are too many; because urban life is not at all self-sustainable. The social security schemes of western countries shield many of their people from these deficiencies. The economic security, respect, and affluence of well-employed and well-placed responsible urbanites and business class make them love urban life.

Life is not just economic security. Life in a village is well rooted and widely branched. It is enriched with deeply entrenched traditions and colourful with functions, festivals, and other celebrations, but urban life is monotonous, materialistic, and frustrating.

Youthful days with "sufficiency" (because parents provide) may pass quickly without any hitch in cities, but their evening years are painful in many ways. The unused abilities of "retired" people and idle urbanites go highly against carbon balance. On the other hand, in a well-developed, sustainable rural community, every person can use his talents and energy in some useful and carbon-friendly way so long as his health permits and can enjoy life with people, pets, and "rewarding" crops and so must be promoted.

Yet Urban Life Goes On

Scientific and technological developments create a variety of jobs to suit various tastes and temperaments. Further, urban facilities, easy access to various services, entertainments, presence of vast peer groups, busy schedules, desire to achieve in a competitive environment, etc., keep people engaged. These circumstances give them some purpose in living and hope in these uncertain days, and are better than the dull and hopeless life in HPD villages. But, if planned sensibly toward OPD, the carbon-friendly village life can be made more purposeful and interesting than urban life.

When Urban Centres Reach High Levels of HPD/GULC

The unchecked proliferation of population in the HPD villages of poor and developing countries at last "saturates" urban centres and curses them with all the associated ills. HPD in rural as well as urban regions means that the whole country has used up all its "springs of life" and suffers as an HPD country. An HPD nation can never enjoy a worthy, healthy life, but always suffers degradation of values and virtues at every level and at every area.

So what can we expect them to do?

People "escaped" from their dear villages when HPD "tortured" them, and now the whole nation suffers HPD and initiates international migrations. Conditions are horrible in many countries, so migrants risk even illegal routes, where many die pathetically.

Balancing Urban and Rural Populations

For too many reasons, like efficient administration, manufacturing activities, businesses, and other facilities, our urban centres have to stay firm. Urban life is supported with cheap rural supplies of raw materials, food items, and rural markets. If this mutual dependence is to be healthy and sustainable and the national economy to be stable and resilient, the rural people must be freed from debilitating HIFs, and the rural economy must be strengthened to support more people, as discussed elsewhere.

Curse of Great Countries

Today, most industrialized, developed countries are burdened with a very high proportion of urban population, and too many developing countries are following them. Every great country which wants to live a respectable and hopeful life forever must end economic dependence, instability, and vulnerabilities to external chaos by ending deficits at every level and by doing all it can to promote wholesome rural living.

Present-day developing and poor countries and huge countries like China and India have not yet reached sorrowful levels of urbanization. Instead of allowing the sorrowful days to arrive, the developing countries must consciously prevent irrational urban growth in order to enjoy a stable economy and to prevent future shocks, uncontrollable pollution, and GW.

19

Violence, Terrorism, and Ungovernable Conditions

A No-Man's Desire

Every child is born absolutely innocent. Parents of every background and from every culture and religion wish and do everything in their capacity to give their children a happy, long life as respectable and useful citizens.

Then why do we have hardened terrorists who put others' and their own lives in jeopardy?

How do people develop the hatred and vehemence to kill even innocent children and women?

Why do we have people who hate others to such an extent that they choose to eliminate them by ending their own lives as "human bombs"?

It is the poor and desperate people who need orderly democracy most. Then why do such people over-work to make their communities ungovernable and disrupt their democratic institutions?

Costly Failures Help the Growth of Evils

We had been blaming the unfavourable society, unreliable economy, poverty, unemployment, fanatic religious leaders, impotent political leaders, corrupt officials, cultural incompatibilities, etc., for the evolution of terrorism. No doubt, every one of these has its role (as an ingredient of the recipe we discussed), but its root (or major ingredient) lies elsewhere. Detailed studies reveal that the point of origin of all those incriminating factors, as well as this evil of terrorism, is one and the same. Since the world fought these evils without understanding their real "manufacturer," those evils have grown in volume and dimensions. Today, to millions of youth, terrorism is a livelihood, honour, and pride. Many terror groups have organized themselves with "military discipline" and have specialized in a variety of destructive acts and are holding vast regions in many poor and developing countries under their sway and even show their presence in developed rich countries.

Unthinkable Background

People doubt if I say that the ultimate causative factor is the deficits developing through HIFs. We have already discussed the visible and invisible deficiencies of HIFs, their growth (HPD), and the consequences. Deficiencies or shortages must weaken the victims and make them less efficient. That is how ordinary people and responsible leaders look at marginalized and underprivileged humans. But it is from these "weak" backgrounds that people who terrorize the mighty, shake governments, and make regions and countries ungovernable come.

If we analyse past history, we can say with certainty that violence, terrorism, and chaotic, ungovernable conditions spring up in any region after the firm footing of their older "siblings," like poverty, unemployment, crime, corruption, etc. That means the deficits in those regions had been growing steadily over a long period and all those evils had interacted to create terrorists. This can be proved by counting HIFs in such societies and by understanding the degree of HPD. It gives a wholesome idea about the cause for the troubled conditions in countries like Somalia and Afghanistan and such regions of Sudan, Pakistan, India, Thailand, The Philippines, and certain South American and other countries.

Aspects of Terrorism

Violence, terrorism, and confrontational attitudes are not at all new phenomena. They appear in various forms whenever there is anxiety about security and the future. When someone mentions the term *terrorism,* we just imagine the physical form of it; but "seeing eyes" can spot terrorists in every walk of life and even among well-read, "responsible" people in the intellectual, social, economic, political, religious, cultural, and moral spheres. For instance, wily people (whose minds are as vehement as that of the worst terrorists) have subjugated vast sections of people with their cunning intellectual power without shedding even a drop of blood. Such "invisible" terror activities are going on even today, in countries ranging from the most poor to the richest, and their cause ranges from "noble" to the wicked.

Historical Events

Our world was a divided one until a few decades ago, in the name of capitalism and communism. Each of them believed that the other ideology and its proponents were threats, and so opposed its spread, even with terror tactics. In that process, they were about to scorch all of humanity with powerful bombs. The crisis ended when Russia and China experienced declining numbers of their HIFs.

Again we saw the belligerent conditions of HPD in Europe before World War II, and the end of it with OPD. But now those anxieties, distrust, hatred, belligerence, terrorism, and wars have become part of every society or country that has too many HIFs.

Changing Ideologies and Binding Factors

Even today socio-political and economic ideologies are used in some regions to attract youths toward terrorism; but nowadays "religionists" commit the worst blasphemy by misguiding their own desperate youths into terrorism. Religion is just faith, so the perpetrators use it in whichever way they like, especially by misinterpreting religious texts in their favour.

Ordinary people of HPD regions give too much importance to religion and fear to question religious utterances, which emboldens the crooks. The crooks cunningly use God and "safety" and "honour" of God and religion to recruit youths, to indoctrinate them, to mould them into determined terrorists, and also to create support bases in the form of sympathizers, donors, informers, safe-homes, etc. They fail to understand that the act of mortal humans protecting their immortal and almighty God amounts to ridiculing and shaming their religion.

Quite often, these violent people call their violent acts a freedom struggle—to get freedom from corrupt regimes, directionless leaders, exploiters, poverty, unemployment, injustice, etc.

Some "Signs and Symptoms" of Unsustainability Today

The Taliban in Afghanistan serves as an example. They do not respect the laws of their land because their HPD motherland could not give them a sustainable living. Hunger, crime, injustice, marginalization, humiliation, frustration, and desperation often cause deep wounds and permanent scars in their minds and hardened them to perpetrate violence in the most inhuman ways, by even publicly torturing their own respectable, well-educated people, frail women, and innocent schoolchildren. They are angry because their prominent people, governments, education, "orderly" society, etc. could not give them dignity and contentment. They feel a kind of pride, strength and purpose in life by joining such violent and trusted peer groups, and by doing so, they get an opportunity to wreak revenge upon the mighty people or government which failed them.

Often such youth are misguided to hate even distant orderly societies like Western countries and other socio-cultural, political, and even religious ideologies. These angry youths readily extend their wholehearted support even to international terrorism by collaborating with organizations like Al Qaeda, so that they could harm more people who enjoy a better life and bring down the status of those "proud" people to their levels.

Why the Illiterate Poor Fall Prey to Religious Indoctrination

It is appropriate here to understand why they give such importance to religion—to the extent of sacrificing their own lives. Life in the lower strata of HPD countries is horrible with poverty, starvation, diseases, enmities, crime, violence, and rampant premature deaths. For them, seeing the next morning itself is a miracle and people in general attribute their existence (a miracle) to their merciful God, and so are extremely grateful. That is why they come forward to do anything they think pleases their God and vehemently oppose everything and everybody who insult God or religion, or those who appear to be rivals and threats to their religion; because they cannot think of a life without their benevolent Almighty.

Terrorism a Tool to Safeguard "Springs of Life"

Scarcities of resources and employment opportunities are common evils in crowded regions. Violence and terrorism can even be considered as an attempt to safeguard whatever is left, because even educated urbanites engage in violence when necessity arises. It is not uncommon to see educated leaders and cadres of religious and political parties engaging in violent protests and scuffles even in cosmopolitan cities like Mumbai, when job seeking, desperate youth of other states enter their territories. Naxals and Maoists of India, with hard-line political ideologies, profess to protect their fertile lands and forest wealth from the plundering rich people like mining companies and industrialists.

(Observations, unbiased studies, and past experiences very clearly say that fertile land gives a far better sustainable living to ordinary people than any industry in its place.)

HIF, HPD, and Democracy

Democracy is the best form of government, and ordinary people expect better tomorrows through the government they elect and trust. But if living conditions worsen, what will they do?

Examination of political situations shows that democracy faces a catch-22 situation quite often in every developing and poor country. The growing deficits of HIFs and HPD torture people with poverty, unhealthy competition, crime, etc. For them, the only solution is the policy which prevents the formation of HIFs. Whenever sensible governments and patriotic people advocated planned, small families, foolish people and moronic activists took it as an impingement upon their fundamental and reproductive rights and destabilized that government. Governments avoid such policies, which naturally worsen living conditions and prompt voters to dump those worthless, incompetent governments.

When corruption, crime, violence, terrorism, suspicions, etc. become rampant, wholesome governance and democracy fail. If there is stability in crowded regions, it is invariably maintained by fake-democracy or by someone who is very tough—a tyrant. Western democracies have been striving to make every country a democracy. Their efforts often failed because they never bothered to address the demolishing factors. At last, with pleasing names like "right to democracy" and "fundamental rights," the conditions worsened with far higher HPD. Instead of trying to implant or impose democracy, if those well-wishers use the stability created by "undesirable" leaders or governments as in Myanmar, Zimbabwe, Somalia, Afghanistan, Iraq, North Korea and such countries to stop the growth of deficits by preventing HIFs, democracy establishes itself in the most natural way.

Even Ordinary People can Turn Violent

Witnessing the pains of starvation, exploitation, injustice, discrimination, and victimization of dear ones and friends hurts every normal human. When such brutalities are unending, even well-bred people can turn violent to wreak vengeance and to ensure justice and security. The recent mass uprisings in Arab countries are examples.

Often the intelligent and courageous sufferers of the curses of HPD think it is better to fight the unworthy leaders, the corrupt rich, the mighty, and the haughty, and die "respectably," rather than to die a pathetic death in indignity, like rats and flies, through starvation, exploitation, and other effects of HPD.

Even Violent Groups are not Free from Unhealthy Competition

We can see unhealthy competition and brutal massacres even within and between violent groups which profess similar ideologies. When they have powerful enemies, like rich countries and powerful governments, they join together for action; but when the enemy becomes irrelevant and when their support bases weaken, the rival factions or other groups try to weaken and eliminate their competing groups. Today, too many such people, ranging from ordinary street thugs and underworld criminal gangs to well-known terrorists, die because of rivalries rather than in police or military action.

Successful groups organize systematically, with too many departments or "ministries" with specific duties, like idealizing youths to join, convincing ordinary people to support them, finding the right donors to ensure a free flow of funds, strengthening security by stockpiling weapons, training of cadre, spying, doing all to maintain supremacy over other groups, etc. They always need a "worthy enemy" to motivate their people, so they always magnify the "treacheries" of the enemy, use false stories, twist historical events, or drag their God in to create a huge enemy. To prepare innocent, poor youths for the ultimate sacrifice, they even promise or assure great life in heaven with every good thing they can think of.

Silent Terrorists

Crooks with their selfish motives sabotage economic, social, religious, intellectual, environmental, and moral spheres. They are not at all less heinous than the worst terrorists and come from almost the same background and perpetrate "terrorism" silently. In fact, these silent terrorists do more harm to a country than poor, open terrorists, by engaging themselves in black deeds like fomenting social disorders and religious discords, manufacturing fake medicines, adulterated food, fake equipment, and pirated goods, counterfeiting currencies, forest destruction, illegal mining, drug dealing, gambling, smuggling, corruption, etc. Such individual black economies ruin a national economy.

Often, such "suckcessful" silent terrorists buy respect, socio-political positions, including ministerial posts which give them protection and dignity and even a patriotic halo.

Terrorists in the Garb of People's Representatives and Leaders

Ordinary people trust these charlatans more faithfully than a well-read, simple, and honest politician or leader who could not remove their sorrows for the reasons discussed above and does not give false promises. Considerable numbers of such undesirable people are regularly elected as people's representatives in almost all the crowded democracies because of their "philanthropies" and intimacy with ordinary people, and often rise to powerful positions, including the office of head of state. What can we expect from them?

As we see around the world, such worthless leaders thrive by misguiding people with boastful promises and through populist schemes. They use too many tricks to earn trust and respect, usually through their "love," "concern," "patriotic" talks, and by professing their faith in their dear God and their determination to annihilate their "enemies."

Harsher Sufferers

Everyone thinks that terrorists, who claim to fight for their people or country, are great threats to a nation's enemies; no doubt, but the harsher sufferers and losers are their own people, who lose their wealth, peace, happiness, and progress. When the terror groups lose credibility, they use violent means to extract money and other facilities from their own innocent, law-abiding people; because those terrorists are not trained in any other job or are too lazy to do hard work.

Possible Strategic Errors

The world must remember that none of those terrorists or criminals was born with those traits, but with a lot of material deficiencies and a lot of "evils" to fight against. The world "encouraged" these situations by failing to stop the further generation of deficiencies. Religious and other ideologies do not create terrorists; but terrorists hijack those as tools to succeed in their efforts. Religion is a very strong binding force with the power to keep together vastly different people (of social status, races, linguistic groups, and nationalities) under one umbrella as mutually helpful and even self-sacrificial brothers.

Fighting criminals and terrorists alone will never end these menaces. By fighting, we may neutralize a few of them, but the deficiencies of

HIFs and HPD and the bereavement on the terrorists' side will generate more, and more determined terrorists.

It is very difficult to fight such groups in their domains, because they easily merge with ordinary people and evade confrontations, but terrorists can attack others easily because they know their geography more than others. Because of the difficult living conditions of those regions, too many ordinary people support such groups.

Soft Targets Boost Terrorism

We must also understand that violence, terrorism, and such rude acts are opportunities to "explode" pent-up frustrations, anger, shame, envy, and vengeful feelings. They can use this explosive force only against a "soft" enemy, like impotent governments, weak minorities, unarmed rich people, and countries which observe humane principles (like Western countries) because a strong and brutal enemy would hunt them to extinction. That is why terror groups cannot flourish in countries like China or under tyrannical rulers like Stalin, Idi Amin, Sadam Hussein, or Robert Mugabe.

The successful "explosions" against "powerful," soft enemies, like Western countries, give them some kind of pride, elation, and the feeling of invincibility, which encourages them toward more actions and the courage to widen the fight against more enemies.

Until (soft) people are there to be identified as easier targets or nasty enemies to be eliminated, their fighting spirits remain high. For instance, "American Satan" (as many terror groups address the USA) is an inspiration to many groups around the world for many reasons, like their (the Western countries) imprudent dealings (Cover Story "Frontline" October 19, 2012). Because of them, the terror groups fight even other innocent people remotely "connected" to them or identifiable with Western countries (like the slain governor, minister, and blaspheme victims of Pakistan).

Best Strategy Ends Terrorism

Experiences and observations very clearly say that the best way to defeat such fierce terrorists is to ignore and isolate them and their related people or even countries completely. Then they cannot make propaganda, raise funds, and recruit cadres in the name of such enemies. Absence of enemies will take away the purpose of being a "freedom fighter," and with time, they will have opportunities to introspect and "implode" (fight their own rivals and unworthy people or express disapproval through mass defiance or rebellion). Unlike in "explosions," where casualties and damages are heavy and fighting continues endlessly, in implosions, the loss of life and wealth will be minimal and a time will come sooner for ending brutalities because the victims are their own people.

Again, with introspection, they understand the significance of HIFs, HPD, and the huge deficits behind their hopeless disorderly life and correct it with patriotic enthusiasm. Ending these evils is of vital importance to humanity because these promote too many acts which facilitate forest destruction, pollution, GW, and CC.

20

Migrations—General Aspects

Pathetic Side of Migration

We have already seen that when a rural population crossed OPD to create HPD, people migrated out and expanded urban settlements. Every responsible person must understand that migrating away from life-giving Nature, leaving behind the most intimate relatives and well acclimatized regions, is a heart-rending decision. Yet when deficits accumulate and threaten people with unemployment and starvation, the excess population has to quit the region where their forefathers lived for generations and toiled with the noble aim of giving them a happy life.

Unquenchable Heavy Cost of Migration

We may look at migrants as persons or families seeking a hopeful life somewhere, but we must also understand that each one of them carries a huge vacuum or deficiency. By vacuum, we mean that each one of them lacks considerable quantities of basic necessities like food, water, living space, infrastructures, and a worthy job, and the new place must provide all these in order to prevent the evolution of evils like crime and violence.

With migration, travel and transport industries evolve and so new a vacuum evolves for huge quantities of energy, which Nature does not possess. New urban settlements demand more energy, also. To fulfil this deficit, humanity is forced to bring out filthy energy from the depths of Earth. By doing so, they add another curse and a deficit. The curse is pollution and the deficit is the lack of funds or facilities needed to neutralize pollution and to substitute the filthy energy with "sustainable energy."

Happy Home and Unhappy Distance

As discussed in chapter 4, a well-planned home gives the most harmonious life. Life in harmony as a family or community is the most advantageous, economical, pleasing, and desirable reality. Such a harmony or uniformity gets diluted with every outward move and no one would like to "suffer" life in unfamiliar, contrasting regions for a long time. From this, we can assess the power of the huge deficits which chase people as migrants.

Happy Homeland/Nation

A country or motherland or homeland is a person's extended home, and is built with the same aim as a home is built. Every region has its own language, literature, festivals, functions, games, economic activities, food habits, and religious and social traditions, developed by its own people, to suit their geography, seasons, and climate. Other than these man-made features, their region has its own enchanting geographical gifts and beauties, specific plants, animals, birds, etc., which people consider as their own and thus become their natural custodians. It is the duty and responsibility of every human to protect all this—culture, environment, flora and fauna—forever and ever, for the sake of their own children, to preserve their identity and to make the world a diverse, enchanting place.

Nature, too, has given adaptive features like dark skin to withstand a hot, tropical climate, pale skin for those near poles, good lung-power to those living at high altitude, etc. If people live a planned, sustainable life, their happy homeland gives them a wonderful life, but crossing their limit to form HIFs and HPD will certainly take away the great joy of living and even chase people to alien lands as discontent migrants.

Pain of Distance

As we saw, harmony, familiarities, mutual concern, cooperation, and the benefits of natural adaptations get diluted as one migrates away from home. The more the distance, the greater is the unfamiliarity, and so are the negative aspects and the feeling of being odd, "orphaned," and insecure. Such segregations even make the person concerned an object of curiosity because of his contrasting features and culture.

Migration is a curse to the migrant as well as to the hosts in every respect—personal, family related, social, economic, demographic, and environmental—and always works toward more pollution, GW, and CC. It is most unfortunate that a vast majority of global populations have created HPD, which squeezes them out of their birthplaces. The condition of many people is so desperate that they do not mind even going to regions with a contrasting, harsh climate, unknown languages, incompatible culture, different traditions, and a religion they hate.

Deficit-Ending Journey Ends with More Deficits

We just saw the way migrants add an additional burden to the deficits with which they departed from villages. But they do not realize it because of the glitter of new life, like "respectable," clean jobs, facilities within short distances, unending entertainments, and the other circumstances discussed earlier. Further, they make urban living more advantageous and attractive to the extent they condemn village life as nasty and tedious. People migrating to realize "sustainable living" invariably get trapped with more problems, which worsens their unsustainability.

Sad Consequences of Migration

- Initiates activities which **favour GW and CC:** Migrants initiate transport, travel, and related industries, urbanization, new carbon-unfriendly jobs and industrialism.
- **Splits families:** People around the world find fault with modernization, degradation of ethical values, and even the Western cultures for the vanishing of good old joint-families and the evolution of nuclear families. But studies very clearly say that when the number of family members grows beyond the capacity of their family resources or other economic activities like a family business which supported them, they are forced to seek alternative

opportunities. So they split because of their own over-growth (cf. chapter 51 of *Book G*).

♦ **Dangerous freedom:** While people, especially youths, live as joint families or in compact villages, there are a lot of experienced and interested people to watch, warn, guide, and correct their every wrong move, be it personal, social, or those related to job, sex, marriage, or family. This naturally prevents many costly mistakes at the right time and saves them from many sorrows. But when a person migrates to a town, he is free from the eyes of his dear people. These "lonely" and free youths have a lot of opportunities to go wrong—to try sex, crime, gambling, drugs, etc. Almost all the HIV positive youths I have encountered are such temporary or permanent migrants.

♦ **Undoes demographic equilibrium** and even drives races to slavery and extinction: Historically, immigrations of strange people with strange ideologies and culture have devastated regions in many ways. Their physical (social) growth and their intellectual, economic, and cultural invasions have slowly and steadily ended the peace, happiness, independence, and even existence of many hosts (Cover Story "Outlook" August 13, 2012). Even today, many people speak the language imposed by migrants, follow harmful religious rites and customs introduced by cunning newcomers, and have forgotten their own great culture and traditions. The most common victims are unwary, progressed, liberal people and those at the other extreme. At present, we do not even have the traces of many such people who once dominated many regions with an enviable life. Since people never learn from others' mistakes or from history, similar silent invasions, ideological plundering, "psychological terrorism," political castrations, and exterminations continue unabated. (See chapters 42 and 59 of *Book G*.)

From Bad to Worse through Migrations

For many reasons, even responsible people who experienced the sorrows of migrations never understood the cause, cost, and curse of migrations. So, the villages which experienced the exodus of people a few decades ago still continue to have HIFs and HPD. So the cities of developing and poor countries are overflowing with desperate humans and they overstrain infrastructures, cause water shortage, extend filthy slums, compete for dwindling job opportunities, and at last help the growth of the under-world of crime, gambling, drug trade, sex industry, etc.

Conditions are so bad that many of them are mercilessly exploited, brutalized, and ill-treated in cities. Often, such innocent migrants are thrashed and chased away by organized urban gangs and even local political parties of many cities like Abuja, Mumbai, Karachi, Dhaka, Cairo, Manila, Mogadishu, and every other crowded city of poor and developing countries. Yet those new migrants cannot go back to their villages because the conditions there are worsening, too.

Everyone Suffers

In crowded countries, unhealthy competition, unemployment, and other evils of HPD affect people of every category, from top businesses to the small vendors, highly specialized professionals to illiterate unskilled labourers, and the very rich to the very poor. Sorrowfully, even employed people face undue demands, strains, anxiety, and tension. What can they do now?

Background of International Migrations

Rural as well as urban regions in almost all poor and developing countries suffer HPD. This means the whole country has strayed into a highly catastrophic danger-zone of uncertainties and inevitable sufferings. HPD of the whole country means that they have exhausted their eternal "springs of life." By "eternal spring," we mean a unit of resource or a job opportunity that can comfortably support a family. With HPD, all "springs" go into the hands of somebody and are in use; and those countries need more springs to support the excessive families. But no country can create any resource or more job opportunities in a sustainable way.

Now, unhealthy competitions curse the whole nation with corruption, crime, violence, terrorism, and ungovernable conditions, and even sicken democracy and institutions like the judiciary, bureaucracy, politics, and religion, and viciously complicate life. It is under these circumstances that people of all categories scramble to move away from their own countries to any country where they can find any job or a place to settle.

International Migrations

International migrations further promote pollution, and their most preferred destinations are the highly polluting huge cities in Western countries or the rich Gulf countries. We know that urban centres act like furnaces to heat up the atmosphere, so migrants enlarge the "furnaces" of distant countries. Thus, when migrants move from a rural or a relatively rural background to cities, their contribution to pollution multiplies. International migrations shift their deficiencies, polluting activities, and even vices like hatred, fundamentalism, and terrorism to the host nations. All these add together with many other factors to make the Western countries super polluters

Why Do Migrants Prefer Western Countries?

Most Western countries maintain a kind of "LPD" status which ensures orderly life, relative peace, job opportunities, and above all, a cordial mindset. They value human rights, fundamental rights, democratic principles, equality, transparency, and such humane virtues. Their efforts to end disparities, discrimination, racism, and their attempts to naturalize migrants are really exemplary, which make migrants feel safe and hopeful. (Unfortunately, many migrants fail to appreciate such noble attitudes, which they cannot expect even in their motherlands.)

The economy of most of developed countries is industry-dependent. In order to maintain their superiority, they must do a lot of innovation, carry out inventions, manufacture faster, and create research activities, which generate more jobs that suit a vast spectrum of people, including migrants.

Some Intricacies of International Migration

Many Western countries think that absorbing or naturalizing migrants with incompatible cultural backgrounds is a humane duty, and talk about equality and multicultural societies. These are praiseworthy, humane deeds. Yet such notions are highly ill-conceived because culture and various customs are specific to a particular region, and cannot be practiced satisfactorily in any other region, and so such attempts create more disharmonies and even develop suspicion and hatred in the minds of migrants.

As we have seen, every human has many duties to protect every wonderful gift his nation possesses. A migrant who is indifferent to such basic thinking can never make himself a worthy citizen in any other land. For these and many other reasons, aiding or encouraging migration and implanting migrants, who cannot adapt in unrelated regions is a highly undesirable and even immoral act. If any broad-minded person, celebrity, or country is interested in or in sympathy with any people or culture, the broad-minded person, celebrity, or country concerned must help those disadvantaged people to protect their race and culture in their original region and not in other countries. Besides, if those enthusiasts teach migrants their faults, like HIFs and HPD, and help them to return as contented people, it would do more good for them and their people than irrational benevolence. Such contented people patriotically preserve their identities and their natural gifts and contribute to global diversity. Imprudent benevolence invariably creates more ills for both, as we will see soon. Already, millions of people suffer because of such "hospitality."

Historical Proofs for the Relationship between HPD and Migrations

As we discussed, Europeans migrated out in huge numbers to LPD regions when they suffered HPD. European migrations ended with the cruel death of millions of Europeans during the world wars which brought down their population to LPD in the most violent and stupidest way. Unfortunately the Europeans have not learned any lessons from that worst tragedy in human history. And so they attract diverse migrants from regions/ countries crossing OPD to HPD. These inward migrations take EU again toward HPD which can be inferred from deterioration of the health of economy, declining peace and happiness, uncertainties of employment, chaotic streets and the feeling of hopelessness, especially among the youth who lean right. The pent up frustration of youths explodes at times in many violent ways and murderous attacks as in the Norway massacre and the repeated shootings in USA. The desperation caused by HPD in Greece is so horrible which force them to sell their islands, beaches, palaces and even embassy ("New Indian Express" April 22, 2013, p12).

Lesson to the World

We have seen repeatedly the effects of HPD and now its power to chase away people from their own homelands. Rejecting one's motherland is not a simple or trivial affair, and must be taken as the mother of all shames. So every country which suffers the shame of being rejected by its own people must correct their population density.

People in developed countries must understand that they can enjoy a respectable life with hope, security, and true freedom only until they maintain LPD or LPD-like status and so must strictly prevent every foolery which takes them again toward HPD. The much sought-after LPD countries must maintain that status, not only for the sake of their wellbeing but also for the sake of global progress and global union as global villages, as we will discuss soon.

21

Migration and Mutual Emancipation

Handle the Golden Egg-Layer with Care

Many regions in the world, like developed countries and oil-rich Gulf countries, enjoy a favourable population density or employment opportunities or both, which give them LPD-like status. Hence, they attract and support millions of migrant workers. Small countries like Singapore, South Korea, and Taiwan, and to some extent vast China, are worrying because of the falling fertility rate (number of births per woman), below replacement levels of population. So they too will start attracting migrants. The world must consider such host countries as precious "golden egg-layers" (not as gold mines) and must handle their fortunes with wisdom to avoid the fate of the fabled bird. If the crowded countries use those "springs of life" (golden eggs) with wisdom, both guests and hosts will benefit, and wholesome progress will gradually remove disparities and other global ills and bring diverse countries together to form the well-integrated and most desired respectable global village. But irrational and ill-conceived deeds bring curses to both.

Answering an Enigma

It is a sad reality that despite stabilizing or falling populations, progressive countries like China, the USA, and EU suffer unacceptable levels of unemployment and other evils. This makes pundits question the wisdom of family planning programs to stabilize the populations of crowded countries. Ending this doubt is a necessity to embolden patriotic leaders to form rational and predictable sustainability-related policies for their suffering masses.

We have already studied the significance of OPD or LPD, and the very harsh effects of HPD. Now, if we apply that knowledge, we will understand that despite population stabilization or even shrinkage, those countries like China have not come near OPD and still suffer very high HPD/GULC, and the Western countries are returning to HPD-like conditions through their imprudent acts, further discussed in the previous chapter. In addition, most developed countries suffer highly irrational and detrimental population distribution, with a very high percentage of unsustainable urban population. So until they reach real LPD and correct the irrational population distribution, unemployment and other ills like crime and pollution will remain as problems for them to solve.

They enjoy prosperity and their youth population declines. These youths prefer "easier jobs," and the unemployment rate remains high for easier jobs, but tough and demanding jobs have fewer seekers and so attract migrant workers.

Flow of Migrants

Diversities and uneven population-densities prevailing in India can be compared with those of the world; and can be studied easily. Most northern states of India have an unacceptably high percentage of HIFs and HPD and continue to create more HIFs; they suffer very high levels of poverty, unemployment, unhealthy competition, and related curses. In contrast, southern-most states, especially Kerala and the southern district of Tamil Nadu (Kanyakumari), have contained such chaos by adopting small families for more than two decades, so HIFs are rare. This stabilizes their population and they are moving toward OPD. Because of a planned life of small, contented families, these southern families send their youths for higher education and "dignified" jobs elsewhere in the country or abroad, so migrants from northern states are moving in for tougher jobs. (About 250,000 such workers are in Kerala at present; they send Rs 175000 million to their poor families in North India. "Dinamalar" Feb.17, 2013, p14, "Times of India" Feb.18, 2013)

Too many modern youths of already developed countries have gone a step further and they do not even like to suffer the "pains" of tough education, like medical studies, to gain tougher skills and to do tedious jobs. So, developed countries attract workers of all categories.

Burden of Progressive Countries

HPD correction (as in China) or decline in population (like Japan and Western countries) always starts with a fall in the numbers of children and youth, so they always have a relatively high proportion of ageing population. This disproportionately high ageing population normally remains until their children reach old age. It takes the time of about two generations; by then population falls steeply.

It is the duty of every family and nation to care for those who have sweated to build their nation. Since the proportion of supporting (working) population shrinks, progressive countries face economic difficulties that will persist until their populations stabilize at real OPD or LPD levels (with the right distribution). To maintain this OPD/LPD, their families must come forward to accept at least the ideal family size of two adults plus two children, or the right size that maintains their population at a stable level.

The woes of these countries multiply further because of the reluctance of a vast section of the "pampered" generations to do tougher jobs or to work for longer hours. The really hard working, patriotic work force feels the burden of a disproportionately high ageing, dependent population.

Mutual Mitigation of Burdens

Thus, while developed and progressive countries suffer a shortage of workers of all categories, most developing and poor countries, plagued with unemployment, unhealthy competition, and other evils, are in a position to offer millions of vibrant workers who are ready to go to any corner of the earth which offers satisfactory jobs. Prudent utilization of these mutual needs benefits both the parties.

Make the World Smile

LPD and rational distribution of population give the most sustainable happy life, so every country must work toward it. If host countries plan wisely and their people choose to live a responsible life with normal planned families, they can end their problems within a few decades and realize the above state. During this transition period, they must do all they can to treat their migrant workers with respect and send them happily back to their own dear countries at the right time, and fill the vacancies left behind with new migrants—as is practiced in countries like Dubai. We can call this a benevolent "migrants rotation" policy, which benefits more migrants and at the same time does not disturb the healthy population densities of the host country. As we will see, such rational arrangements speed up humanity's progress toward a global village. But indiscriminate offers of permanent residence to migrants will do the opposite, by creating HPD-like conditions and its evils in host countries and also more enmities and hatred around the world for those hosts.

While using the employment opportunities of host countries, crowded countries must attempt to correct their own HPD by preventing HIFs—as was successfully done in the state of Kerala in India. The progressed countries and world bodies must also do all they can to enlighten these HPD countries and their migrant workers on the burdens of HIFs, HPD, and related evils. Then, by the time a few batches of migrant workers return home, their motherlands would have progressed a lot and the former migrants can enjoy a great life with their own grateful people in a more contented environment and with a lot of friends around the world. By now, the age disparities of those host nations would narrow or normalize.

Need of the Hour

I have been stressing the concept of "global village" repeatedly because such a coming together is the least deficiency-causing, most economical and desirable life for humanity and will speed up the eradication of all the evils and curses we know, including GW and CC. Globalization and the global village must happen naturally on equal terms. Disparities make coming together difficult and chaotic. Mixing diverse discontented people in the name of a global village, globalization, humanism, naturalization, or other sweet terms would cause more disruptions and chaos—as is happening now (for instance, the riots in England). Yet coming together would happen spontaneously and smoothly when every country ends HIFs and HPD.

22

Sweet are the (Prudent) Uses of Adverse Migration

Do Not Waste a Great Opportunity to Unite the World

Sweet are the uses of adversity. It happens quite often when adverse conditions are used with prudence and with rational foresighted plans. We just saw how the adversities of contrasting countries can turn sweet and even can create a sweeter global village—if the globe is prudent.

Yet, because of ignorance, country after country commits mistakes and makes life miserable for mankind. Already a lot of highly damaging demographic, social, cultural, environmental, economic, pollution-related, and political changes have taken place around the world, especially in many host countries and the "fertile" regions of migrants' own countries because of rampant and desperate migrations. Too many regions and cities (like Buenos Aires, *Time,* Jan. 11, 2011: 11) look like mini battle zones and take away the hope, peace, and dignity of both the migrants and hosts.

Severity of Mismanagement

I can quote innumerable instances of such deterioration. But, to prevent diversion from our major aim, I would like to pen just one instance. Western countries helped Pakistan, a country with very high levels of HIFs and HPD, with huge donations and aid during natural calamities and during wars. Millions of Pakistani migrant families are living a far better life in Western countries with many rights they cannot even think of in their homeland. Yet no Westerner can walk on the streets of Pakistan without fear. And the participation of a small section of Pakistani migrants in anti-West activities is well-known.

It happens because of the highest order of stupidity on the part of Western countries and the highest order of ignorance on the part of those beneficiary migrants.

Where to Apply Prudence

We now know that even if all the rich people and rich countries of the world transfer all their wealth in favour of the needy masses around the world, they cannot satisfy all their needs. Yet if we judiciously use those little surpluses or spare "life-springs" of developed countries and other rich nations, vast sections of needy families around the globe will earn a contented, happy life.

But now, because of imprudence, the opposite is happening. Many peaceful, contented regions are turning into chaotic hells. If the world is at all interested in ending man-made curses including GW and CC, everything must be done to prevent such harms.

Best Use of Spare Springs

By a "spring of life," we mean a unit of basic resources, employment, or a combination of these that supports a normal family comfortably for a very long time or endlessly. The total springs of a nation is an almost permanent gift of that nation and can support that number of normal families. (This is just another description of OPD.) Migrants leave their countries because they have exhausted their springs and a host nation receives migrants because they have got spare springs.

Those HPD countries enjoyed surplus springs in the past. This knowledge must warn the host nations that they too can reach a harsh HPD status if they allow their population to swell by permanently settling migrants. Then where would these hosts go?

Surplus resources and opportunities (springs) must be used judiciously to benefit as many migrants as possible; but at the same time, it must retain its "freedom" to return to the owners if necessity arises.

When a spare spring of a host nation is given permanently to a migrant (that means when migrants are permanently settled as families), only one family is benefited by a unit of resource and if that family fails to plan sensibly and has too many descendants (as they had been doing in their countries), their next generation will demand more of those vital springs and quickly exhaust them to create unemployment, unhealthy competition, and other evils in the host nation (a cause for discontentment among such people).

But, if the hosts allow the migrants to use the springs to gain contentment and then help them return to their own countries, such prudent, yet "harsh-looking" acts work wonders for the migrants, the migrants' countries, and the hosts. When one migrant returns home, he leaves a spring free so another migrant can utilize it to gain a dignified life. By such rolling of the beneficiaries, more poor families earn a dignified life around the globe and remain grateful and happy. The hosts earn many friendly, grateful people around the world—which includes those contented migrants, their family members, friends, and relatives. For this to happen, the migrant users must be made to understand that they are just temporary owners—as is happening with Dubai-type migrations.

When migrants cannot claim permanent ownership, they utilize the opportunities to the best of their abilities to gain economic freedom and return home in the shortest possible time to enjoy the success with their own family members and friends. By such actions, the springs act like un-depletable, eternal life-givers—as we are going to see.

We call such rolling of ownership "migrant rotation."

Evolving "Spring Fields"

Now, other than the developed and rich countries, as we saw elsewhere, many other disciplined countries and many regions within developing countries are slowly coming up with free springs because of population stabilization or reduction. And so they, too, can do the previously described benevolent acts of emancipation.

Committed Mistakes

Migrations have entirely changed the face of vast numbers of villages, regions, and even countries. There are people who accuse the settlers of new continents as usurpers but fail to read their own histories. In too many regions around the old world, the people who live there now are not the original people.

If we trace back to find the fate of the original people, we will understand the sad extinctions of too many great cultures and civilizations because of immigration or invasion by aliens. It is another sorrowful fact that, in most of the instances, the victims are enlightened, hospitable, civilized people with morality. They succumbed because dignity prevented them from doing inhumane acts while the undisciplined barbarians and treacherous people (migrants/winners) did all kinds of ugly acts and never felt sorry for the sufferings of the decent hosts.

Desire of the Globalists

We don't want any more such victors or victims; but want every race to live on our beautiful planet forever and ever with their dignified culture, agreeable traditions, and the humane customs they enjoy.

Sane patriots from any part of the world wish for every people in every country in any part of the world to conserve everything which constitutes their nation and makes them special. When a globalist from India or China visits England, he would like to see in England, the English people (race), with their own culture, customs, cuisine, and the beautiful faces of English children and everything which characterizes England. Similarly, when enlightened Europeans or Africans visit India or China or Japan, they would like to see everything Indian or Chinese or Japanese, and the faces of respective races, and not European or African people or culture. So striving to protect one's own race, culture, and other features is not at all racism, as some ill-informed morons and those with vested interests complain, but it is the moral duty and responsibility of every citizen of every culture and country. And it is the duty of those complainants, too, to protect their way of life in their motherland—not in alien countries. Then global diversities would thrive forever to greet the visitors and future generations with something new and special, and make life joyful, explorative, fun-filled, proud, and worthy for all.

Yet I would like people to free themselves from faulty, unfriendly, hurting, and exploitative ideologies, as Europeans did in the sixteenth century (liberating people from religious bondage). Now, knowledge flows freely, and with modern facilities, including social networking, every people can easily do such work of liberating people (as is happening in Arab countries). But, instead of cleaning their ignoble culture and traditions, many people are contaminating the liberated regions with primitive, superstitious and inhumane ideologies. It is wrong and will take the world again into the dark ages. The liberated (from economic, social, religious, political, and other bondage) people around the world must also be cautious and avoid every foolery which takes them back toward the dark days and to HPD.

Why do I Refer to Europe Repeatedly?

There are uncountable historical and current happenings to illustrate the ravages of population pressure, migrations, and related events. But I repeatedly use the historical happenings in Europe because European history is well known to many, and every other country has got some gratifying relationship with Europe. They and other developed countries now have a definite role to play in unifying the world.

Build a Global Village

Humanity suffers division, enmities, and other curses because of huge man-made deficiencies. If we end these deficiencies by preventing HIFs, the disruptive traits like suspicion, belligerence, and hatred will vanish naturally and give way to a friendly coming together—as happened in post-World War II Europe.

If everyone is deficient, no one can help the other. As we saw, the wholesale transfer of the whole wealth of rich nations would not fill the huge vacuum of accumulated deficits. So, before every "free" country falls into a deficient state of HPD, we must sensibly use the free "springs" of developed and other rich countries to extricate the needy countries from those sorrowful situations.

"Bitter are Results of the Imprudent Management of Adversities"

People migrate with the ambition of earning a respectable life and long-term security for their families. The fulfilment of this noble ambition depends upon many factors, as we will see.

Observations and studies very clearly show that single migrants have vast advantages to earn and save far more than the migrants who live in host countries with their families. The policies of the host countries influence the attitude and earning capacity of migrants. For instance, the Gulf countries like Dubai strictly prohibit migrants from political activities, do not allow migrant labourers taking families to their countries, and never allow migrant workers to settle in their countries. So, without any distraction, a migrant earns his desired wealth in the shortest possible time and returns home early. No one feels hurt because of those restrictions.

At last, the overwhelming majority of the workers returning from Gulf countries give a very high opinion of Dubai and other Emirates; but those migrants living in developed countries with all the rights and freedoms of the citizens often complain about their hosts and even indulge in unacceptable activities. Such complaints and curses are greater when they have permanently settled. Such complaints are greater from those with contrasting religious and cultural leanings than from those who are racially different. Utilizing every healthy advantage is prudence and the opposite is foolery.

Huge Earning Capacity/Advantages of Single Migrants

Single migrants enjoy many advantages which justify popularizing it as the best policy.

Advantages over the natives: Compared to a native worker of any country—be it a developed Western country or an oil-rich Gulf nation—a single migrant worker can earn much more than the native worker of the same category for the following reasons:

Motivation: A migrant is highly motivated to work hard and for a longer time. He learns skills quickly with extra care and works without hesitation. He does not even bother about entertainment, because earning more than what he has expected is pure joy and working for more time with such happiness never tires him easily.

All round savings: A native worker has a lot of people, like family members, kin, and friends, to whom he is obliged in several ways. He may have to spend part of his time, energy, and money for family matters and cultural, religious, political, and social functions and celebrations, and so on. But migrants literally have no or few such people and can work for more time without distractions. A migrant can stay at or near the work site and so saves time and energy to do more work. This saves the transport costs, too. Migrants hate idling because they have almost nothing to do in the social, political, and cultural sphere. Too much rest and leisure hurt them more than over-work because wasting time delays fulfilling their expectations and re-joining their dear family and people.

Comforts Take Away Advantages of Migrants

An ordinary person's earning capacity is highly hampered in crowded countries because of unhealthy competition, corruption, crime, and such evils. The normal earning of a migrant in a Western country is not less than five times the normal savings he can make in his native land, and when he makes use of his opportunities advantageously, he can make it twenty or more times.

This means that one single migrant who supported a compact family in a frugal way with his income in his native land can now lavishly support dozens of people with the earnings in Western countries. Millions of such migrant workers' families lead joyous lives in third world countries and enjoy their festivals, other celebrations, and all the cultural, social, religious, and other functions and activities with a sense of gratitude to the host countries which make that possible.

But when the migrant takes his family to the Western country as its citizen, he loses all the above homeland joys and loses the advantages of earning he enjoyed as a single migrant. Now, with that limited income and with the high cost of living, these migrant families suffer deficiencies which bring unexpected sorrows and pull down their standard of living. If they had been with their people of similar socio-economic status, such sufferings never hurt much. But when they live among comfortable aliens, it hurts them terribly and makes them feel belittled, cheated, and marginalized.

Again, as free citizens, when migrant families involve themselves in social, religious, cultural, political, and such activities, these further eat into their time, energy, and earnings and make them poorer to that extent. When poverty/deficiencies threaten, they demand their rights, privileges, and benefits as a citizen. These make both the migrant and the hosts unhappy, unlike what happens with "migrant rotation."

Usually, first-generation workers have strong motivation to do more work, which is good for the migrants and the hosts. But from the second-generation onward, they live as carbon-guzzling urbanites with eroded motivation. Again, too many of them fail to use a "spring of life" rationally, with right plans to prevent deficiencies (HIFs and unnecessary religious and cultural activities, which made them poor in their countries), so remain poor, disgruntled, frustrated, angry people. Such desperate people often protest and fret and fume with irrational suspicions even when noble attempts are made to integrate, or for unintended "hurts"—as we see frequently (like the cartoon controversy, the head scarf issue, etc.). All these issues go against sustainability and favour GW and CC.

The West Managed HPD, but Mismanages LPD

When Europe had HPD, the challenges of deficiencies and unhealthy competition made them a shrewd and over-working, industrious people. They could make inventions, innovations, and bring about the industrial revolution, and their migrants courageously ventured on uncharted oceans at great risk to colonize and conquer vast regions around the globe—the first globalization. All these have reversed since the end of

World War II because the stimuli are gone when they start enjoying unchallenged life with LPD.

Further, their visible prosperity and well-secured life made Europeans too complacent, even in vital matters concerning socio-economic and national security and freedom. Too many adults just want a "free and liberal" life and are reluctant to raise responsible families—which is pathological. As we saw, most of their youth prefer a very easy life. Then how can their nations have strong pillars? They have to borrow "pillars" to support their economy and even security (as President Obama is doing).

These give undue advantages to migrants, who happily do more of their hard work and make the masters lazy, obese, "illiterate," ill-informed, and even addicts to many vices and an easy life. Such realities embolden ill-willed among the migrants to harm the host countries. Out of such grave ignorance related to various aspects of their life and homeland, they continue to allow indiscriminate immigration and naturalize too many highly "incompatible" migrants and give them all the rights, including political rights—even to those who never sought them and also to people who openly hated and cursed them.

The West did all this as a humanitarian, noble duty. But it is this benevolent act which did terrible harm to the ordinary "beneficiary" migrants, as discussed below.

Permanent Residence to Migrants Harms Both

Takes away the enormous advantages (earning) of the single migrants (explained above).

Makes migrants socio-cultural orphans: A person's natural homeland gives him the most harmonious life with a lot of common racial, social, cultural, religious, and other features, functions, and celebrations which keep him a busy social animal and in the best spirits. All these have connection to his geography, climate, literature, and history. Since he has his own people (race) and other features around him, he never feels odd or "orphaned." Hence, the "new citizens" (ex-migrants) remain as islands of contrasts and objects of curiosity and disharmony among contrasting aliens (hosts), which creates ill effects upon the migrants and on the hosts.

Denies migrants the opportunities to celebrate success: When the migrant's kin enjoy economic security and other comforts because of his sacrifices, they naturally respect him as the most esteemed member of the family. Such a status gives the migrant the most pleasing contentment, self-esteem, and social importance that make him feel like a great achiever. Most of these go away with citizenship.

Denies migrants the opportunity to serve their people: When migrants return with economic prosperity, foreign experiences, vast knowledge about the reason for the progress of hosts, and with new global friends, he can share his knowledge and experience with his countrymen to improve their living conditions. But the opportunity to do such services is lost when he is granted citizenship abroad.

Western countries lose bosom friends and deny the world the opportunity to come together: When migrant-rotation is practiced, present-day migrant workers, the past (returned) beneficiaries, and all their family members and relatives feel grateful and friendly to the host (Western) nation and uphold their pride and even love to receive people from those host countries. Millions of grateful friends of Western countries multiply with time in every corner of the world. These grateful friends in millions also help their countrymen understand and love the host nations. Such understanding, goodwill, and coming together of millions of families of the world could have averted many harsh happenings around the world. But Western countries acted exactly like Don Quixote by permanently settling millions of families and have earned innumerable enemies around the world and blighted this great opportunity of forming a global village.

Prevents the normal duties: Everyone is indebted in many ways to many people in their life. It is a natural duty of everyone to look after their ageing parents as they looked after them as children. Further, worthy teachers and educational institutions, good friends, well-wishing relatives and neighbours, honest religious persons and institutions, benevolent governments/motherland, etc. play a role in shaping a person

155

and his prospects. It is an unwritten law and moral duty of the benefited people to pay back in the form of some service and with gratitude. Only then can those institutions survive to serve more, and those noble people enjoy "job satisfaction" which motivates and encourages them to do more. How can a "fortunate" migrant held up abroad do that?

Denies migrants the opportunity to reap the benefits of his sacrifices: As grandparents and ageing weaklings, benevolent, successful migrants (who are back home) can spend their last days in the best possible ways, with their dear people around. It is also an opportunity for their relatives to pay back.

Prevents national duties: Migrants, too, have their own distinct culture, languages, literature, food habits, geographical beauties, and economic activities in their motherland. It is everybody's duty to protect and develop everything that constitutes their nation and everything that distinguishes them from others and was handed down to them by their forefathers.

Denies opportunities to work to regain real freedom and pride: People migrate carrying with them the "personal and family deficiencies" caused by HPD. Thus, they relieve their nation of its national burden in some small measure and lessen unhealthy competition. They further contribute to national income and return with considerable positive features and balance and even may be in a position to teach and employ desperate people. They, as enlightened, experienced, contented, and patriotic citizens, have the duty to help and take part in such acts that wipe out their nation's sorrows and make it free, sustainable, and proud.

Pains of Single Migrant

The inevitability of living as a single appears to be very harsh. But people must understand that living with never-ending wants creates many harsher heartburns, quarrels, and even separations in families. A hopeless and anxious life as a family takes away most of the pleasures of it. To the vast majority of people, sacrificing some pleasures for the sake of an assured hopeful, respectable, and sustainable living is a preferred choice. Often the persons who fail to sacrifice something in their youthful days for a better future become worthless, disrespectful objects of families and even society, and often end their lives as highly pathetic, uncared for, unwanted creatures—often prematurely.

Temporary separation is the inevitable price people have to pay for creating an unsustainable community with huge deficits. With the correction of deficits, such sorrows end naturally.

23

Don't Kill Peace-Making
Through Migrations

Painful Curses of the Third World are Global Problems

Belligerence, hatred, enmities, and wars have become day-to-day affairs in crowded poor and developing countries and even between neighbouring, crowded unsustainable countries. Most of them are not even on talking terms to exchange their views and grievances, so the stand-off protracts and denies them progress, peace, and hope. These are the people who often destroy forests and contribute a lot to "proxy pollution" and favour GW and CC. Therefore unrests of any kind in any region must be taken as global problems.

Noble Job of Peace-Making

Helping rivals or enemies to reconcile and to make peace is a very noble job. People with bad reputations and in bad socio-economic conditions cannot do that. So peace-makers/peace brokers must be contented people with an unbiased, balanced mind, and above all, they must be trusted by every group involved. Developed countries had been doing such noble jobs for decades and have prevented many wars and saved millions of lives and precious natural wealth from destruction. The peace-making efforts of some small Scandinavian countries are really superb. It is the LPD-like state which gave them such a respectable status; because when they suffered HPD before World War II, they did the opposite and fought each other. But their wonderful status of being mediators is eroded for many reasons related to their short-sighted magnanimity, changing population density and its effects—invariably through proliferating migrants, continuing inflow of migrants, and migrant-related ill feelings.

It is the crowded countries which often need peace-makers; but unfortunately it is through their migrants and their religio-political hate merchants that peace-brokering countries are losing their praiseworthy status. If those peace-makers and the responsible people around the world fail to understand this aspect of deterioration, our world will lose many mediators.

At the End of World War II

As mentioned elsewhere, the poor and developing countries of today have gained freedom and appreciable peace and have been enjoying encouraging opportunities. While Europe and Japan were flattened with bombs, none of the belligerent countries of today suffered such damage, but enjoyed an advantageous LPD, peace, surplus resources, access to vast knowledge and technology, and the administrative facilities and infrastructures left behind by the colonized countries.

World Today

With those advantages, those countries must have worked hard with patriotic spirit to prove their worth and must have earned economic freedom and a contented, sustainable life. But they are suffering every known evil and curse, which they did not have, even during alien rule. Now, many regions have deteriorated to levels which require external economic help and the services of peace-makers.

In contrast, war-torn Europe and Japan worked hard to gain a respectable life, which has enabled them to support many needy countries economically and with technology. They now host/ employ millions of hopeless, desperate people from crowded countries and protect victims of wars and political plots. Because of such population shifts (including those in the Gulf countries), many poor and developing countries feel considerable relief from unhealthy competition, poverty, and other evils, and many enjoy reasonable "economic freedom" because of the remittance of their expatriate workers.

Countries Waste Magnificent Opportunities

They literally squandered away their wonderful opportunities because they never had a clear idea about the factors which ensure sustainability and economic independence. As a result, they lavishly used their fertile power. Thus they proliferated without any plan, and outgrew their resources; this cursed them with sorrows, including hatred and protracted wars.

Thus, they have made the noble, peace-making and other services of the Western countries a necessity. If the world cooperates with peace-makers, does all to preserve every region's advantageous LPD status and utilise emancipation efforts (like "migrant rotation"), our world can earn peace early.

Killing the Peace-Making Mission

The economic freedom and hopeful life (conferred by LPD) gave those peace-makers the impartial, liberal, and benevolent mind-set, and they voluntarily helped needy people. They visited war-torn regions, met opposing groups, and even invited them to their countries for face-to-face talks by offering comfortable platforms.

In that process, they have saved the lives of many political and religious leaders of belligerent countries. It is unfortunate that many such protected leaders later turned against those benevolent nations when they regained power in their countries. Many of the benefited migrants also behave in highly damaging ways, by misusing the freedom and fundamental rights they enjoyed in their host countries. Because of such unbecoming attitudes and acts of the benefited people, many peace-making and liberal countries are losing their own peace and respectable status and many of their towns turn into mini war zones.

At last, blind hospitality and related acts, like thoughtlessly settling incompatible and openly belligerent migrants, take away the LPD-like status of many developed countries and create enemies. In addition to this, the senseless interference and involvements of certain developed countries in other countries bring further disrepute and more enemies around the world.

Twin Brother of Migration is Anti-National Terrorism

As explained earlier, migration and terrorism evolve almost for the same reasons and almost at the same level of HPD. To escape from those unbearable evils pertaining to that HPD, migrants flee to some other country and make good their deficiencies; those left behind continue to suffer corruption, crime, nepotism, etc., which takes away their faith in their leaders and the system. Some among them turn violent, create war-like situations, and "destroy" their own responsible people, institutions, and everything which failed them. When wrongly indoctrinated, they would torture even innocent people. Such acts of terrorism may fulfil some of their needs and dampen their anger, but multiply their total deficits, worsen their sustainability, and create more curses.

We know that "fight" (terrorism and wars) and "flight" (migrations) are emergency functions to escape from a danger or dangerous place. Allowing these to continue would cause irreparable damage. If their own leaders and the responsible people of the world understand this, they can make worthy policies. And if needed, meanwhile, they can utilize the services of peace-makers. Now it is time for peace-makers to teach the warring groups the importance of OPD.

Wrong Signals

As we have seen, most Western host countries are moving toward HPD because of migrants—high fertility and continuous inflow. The wrong signals are obvious in the form of rising crime, unemployment, riots, and terrorism, which have triggered the rise of right wing groups. If rational thoughts and acts fail to prevail, the world may lose sincere peace brokers and then the belligerent groups would cause more damage to each other.

International Hatred Weakens Peace-Makers

To make matters worse, many moronic and selfish third world leaders make Western and neighbouring countries scapegoats in order to hide their own fooleries. Quite often they even blame the former colonial countries for their ills. Their fanatical religious leaders and terror groups also use issues like "ill-treatment" meted to migrants and ridiculing their religions (like the cartoon controversy, the head scarf issue, "sacrilege" of gods and temples) to misguide their people against Western countries. But the same cunning people never reveal the huge donations and benefits their countries receive from the same "enemy" countries, or the hospitality their migrants enjoy in those countries. At last, even a peace-maker of Western countries cannot walk on the streets of beneficiary countries. Many migrants enter host countries with such a poisoned mind-set and often behave accordingly, which resulted in 9/11, 7/7, repeated bombings, street protests, and venomous teachings in religious places and through media.

The Fooleries of the West Kill Global Peace and Global Union

Despite the shames and damage that they have already suffered, the West continues to create enemies for themselves and their innocent children. People with vested interests from around the world have dragged thoughtless Western countries into many costly conflicts in various regions, bleeding them terribly, devitalizing their economy, eroding their honour, and demoralizing their innocent people.

Such malignant stupidities of the West not only ruin their peace and progress but also affect international peace and amity.

Indifference Can Bring Back the Dark Days

Religion-related treacheries, cruelties, exploitation, conflicts, and enmities have been torturing peace-loving people of the world in the worst possible way and have extinguished millions of precious lives. Cruel and immoral religious leaders obstructed enlightenment and kept the world in darkness and backwardness for too long. Europeans gained religious freedom in the sixteenth century, after shedding rivers of blood. Such freedom from religious madness is in no way less important than the political, social, or economic freedom, for which leaders like Abraham Lincoln, Mahatma Gandhi, Martin Luther King, and Nelson Mandela fought. Yet millions of people of these enlightened days suffer religion-based tyrannies, and onlookers stand helpless. Europe progressed fast in various fields, like democracy, human rights, science, medicine, technology, etc., because of hard-earned religious freedom. Other counties could have learned a lot from these, but how many have learned?

Today, vast regions of the world remain backward because of faulty religious ideologies, superstitions, and imprudent and costly religious practices. Even their educated people and leaders keep committing such shameful acts. Their migrants in liberal countries could have learned the importance of religious freedom. But many of them continue to be in the same debilitating culture and even contaminate liberated Western countries. Further, many fanatics enslave their migrants and natives with wrong teachings and keep religion-based hatred, violence, and other wrongs flourishing. If others interfere, it will backfire on them; hence the actual victims themselves and their enlightened leaders must come forward to fight to gain freedom from "religious" marauders.

While things stand in such a pathetic state in many countries because of religion, many of those liberated Western countries do the opposite and are importing rabid and silent fundamentalists of a wide spectrum into their countries, and slowly and steadily taking their countries to the pre-sixteenth century religion-based slavery and retardation.

Looming Dangers

The disgruntled youth of many peace-making countries are turning right and are being accused of being neo-Nazis, xenophobes, racists, and hate mongers.

Can a country holding racists and xenophobes go for peace-making?

Mathematical projections say that by the time present-day children of many developed countries become parents, they will face unhealthy competition in many fields, including politics (democratic elections), and when they become grandparents, they will start losing their freedom, peace, and even existence. (Chapter 59 of *Book G*; graph on page 477). The *Economist* (May 8, 2010:13) says that the USA has twelve million illegal migrants (not including legal migrants). By the middle of this century, white Anglos will be another minority in the USA. *Time* (May 24, 2010:25) reports, "There are regions in Western countries with up to 31 percent of non-white migrants."

These events naturally force even the hosts to migrate out; this has already started. But where will they go? The hybrid citizens, who are the cause for this HPD, have their own countries to go to.

Imprudent Migrants and Moronic Hosts

Other than HPD, factors like faulty religious, cultural, economic, and even political ideologies and practices complicate life and force people to migrate. In such situations, every worthy migrant must try to learn from the progressed hosts; but most of the "citizened" migrants prefer to differ with them regarding social, cultural, and religious matters, and continue those faulty habits and customs which packed them off as migrants. Hence, many migrants remain dissimilar, despite the efforts toward integration, and resist cordial relationships with hosts as well as with migrants from other parts of the world.

In practice, even to sustain a conversation of a few minutes, we need an understandable language, common interests, sharable knowledge, and as many other things in common as possible. Then how can we expect the least unity in the above situation? "Isolated" new citizens always prefer to organize their own people and try to spend their days as different people and often try to impress others with their contrasting, harmful practices and even "contaminate" host countries as described. In such situations, it is impossible to form a "harmonious" multicultural society; in practice, integration attempts often raise suspicions and anger and cause more disharmony, more suspicion, and more hatred.

Diversities which Divide

Diversities are appreciated when people are contented and there is no apparent threat to their sustainable living; but it always creates divisions and wrong reactions under HPD. Even minor differences and misunderstandings are magnified by those with vested interests to create enmities and disharmony. It is a sorrowful situation that even highly educated, well-settled, "civilized" people are not free from such shame—such is the power of HPD over education.

Every different racial, religious, and cultural group has a different appearance, physical features, colour, habits, traditions, practices, religious marks and expressions, food habits, etc. These differences naturally make others, especially children and youth, curious, which makes them ask questions and even pass innocuous comments. This is natural and normal. A child who is not curious enough to raise such a question is not a normal child at all. But there are many who feel embarrassed at this and take those questions as unpardonable insults. In mixed countries like India, Sri Lanka, Nigeria, Indonesia, and Pakistan, people frequently face such problems, which later lead to crime and violence, and even murders, for the sake of God and "blasphemy." There are well-read and well-reared people among them who respect diversity yet are made helpless.

Do Not Create Enemies for Your Children

Today, millions of children of migrant families get a liberal education in Western schools along with the native children. Children and even youth are not clever enough to talk in a polished way, suppress curiosities, and hide what they think and feel, so they face the situation discussed above. These enquiries and innocent comments often create "deep wounds" in the minds of innocent "victims." With time, and as adults, such "mental wounds" can create negative attitudes and hatred, and could wreak havoc—as we see often in Western cities and daily in almost every poor and developing country with a mixed population.

For the above reasons, innocent children and youth often find themselves in a catch-22 situation. When native children exclude migrant children to avoid rub, it will be taken as discrimination, exclusion, and even as racism. And if they mingle with the migrants cordially, their friendly, "uncomfortable" questions make them racists and xenophobes. The migrants, who exaggerate such trivial happenings to dangerous proportions, take even worse forms of discrimination, abuse, and exploitation as normal in their own countries.

Today, thousands of Western youths are punished and even jailed for matters related to "discrimination" and "xenophobia," and experienced adults who express their views are condemned as fanatic right wingers. Creating such an un-harmonious society fails everybody.

Unhealthy Global Developments

Many countries want to assert their "power." Many disorderly countries acquire nuclear facilities. Many countries form regional and international blocks with vague agendas and motives and try to take advantage of the vacuum created by the imprudence of Western countries. There are even countries and blocks to back rogue "nuclear" powers. The power of the UN is vanishing.

These emerging powers or blocks bother the least about global curses like terrorism, pollution, GW, and CC, and are not at all able to do anything worthwhile for their own people. Most of such people feel great by criticizing and ridiculing the Western powers; but contribute nothing for humanity or their own people.

Repetitions of Laboratory Findings

The last few chapters may raise concerns about biased writing. My studies, observations, and involvements in the open laboratories of human societies have given me more than enough knowledge related to hatred, terrorism, migrations, etc. I know too many instances of very tragic ends of really patriotic and benevolent people, how their exit affected people in need, how the situation was exploited by unworthy people and how this degraded society. Those tragedies are evolving on a larger scale in too many orderly societies and countries around the world. The suggestions with regard to ending terrorism, wise management of migrants, the necessity to protect the peace-making status of developed countries, etc. have been taken from real life events. (ref. chapters 33, 42 & 59 of *Book—G*).

Peace-makers are also humans, with all the weaknesses. They enjoy such a position because of their sustainable living conditions and contentment. Every country of the world can earn such a position by striving to form LPD. Now, the situation is fluid and unpredictable, and if we fail to act sensibly to protect everyone who has gained real freedom and do all to lead others toward it through sustainable living conditions (not "sustainable" developments), time may turn harsh and take away even the existing opportunities.

24

Pollution

Natural Mechanisms Prevent Pollution

Nature gives us food and a variety of useful items like firewood, building materials, a wide range of oils (including potential bio-diesel), and industrial raw materials through the plant kingdom. Mankind and other animals use the products of the plant kingdom and create a lot of polluting filth. If all the filth, like excreta, kitchen wastes, animal carcasses and human corpses, accumulate around us as non-degradable filth, living becomes difficult or impossible for the very animals which create the filth. Fortunately, Nature uses its physical energy, chemical interactions, bacteria, fungi, and a variety of small creatures like earthworms to convert all these wastes and excreta into food for the plants. Thus, a lot of "unseen" and inconsequential living beings work day and night to remove all this toward zero pollution and to ensure our wholesomely sustainable living (green living). Those benevolent creatures are members of certain interdependent ecosystems. The health of all those interdependent species is vital for the healthy and sustainable existence of life on our small and beautiful planet.

Nature intended humans, like all other animals, to live a contented, sustainable living within its means. But we hoodwinked Nature's controlling mechanisms and violated many red-lines. Now, overgrown humans demand enormous quantities of resources and energy, which Nature does not possess. In order to fulfil the extra energy, we bring out the "buried demon" of fossil fuels that pollute and harm all life-forms. We grab the resources meant for other living beings, including the benevolent ones, and destroy forests. In that process, we massacre many species and create more pollution and destroy more than Nature's mechanisms can rectify.

Foolish Violation of Life-Saving Mechanisms

It is basic common sense that the right balance must be maintained between polluting humans and de-polluting agents like plants and micro-organisms for healthy, green, sustainable living. This means that sufficient space and resources like water must be spared for those benevolent creatures and forests and they must be free from injurious, man-made toxic pollution like chemicals, radiation, etc.

But we, the "most intelligent" species, have failed even to mind this very basic beneficial equation of life and death. Billions of people pollute their environment and bodies of water with their excreta and other personal wastes, which act like "weapons of mass destruction" and take its toll; yet they continue. Now, despite awareness about the dangerously accumulated greenhouse gases and the dangers of coal and petroleum, we create situations which demand more of them and keep accumulating them to dangerous levels, which in turn, digs graves for all living beings.

Nature Gave Us Green Environment to Live Well but We Attempt Suicide

A clean and healthy environment is the requirement of all living beings, including plants and microscopic organisms. When we mention a healthy environment, it must include clean atmosphere, clean water, and a clean upper layer of soil. All of these influence our healthy existence and activities because they are what we breathe, drink, and eat.

Experts say that our planet took millions of years to make conditions suitable for human living, with the right composition of gases in the air, the right kind of water with no toxic chemicals, pollution-free fertile upper soil to grow our crops, and the right atmospheric conditions to create the right climate and seasons. For example, the upper layers of soil had been washed with rain water for millions of years to free them from the toxic minerals and chemicals still found in the deep soil. Over many millennia, Nature carefully buried the excessive atmospheric carbon deep into the bowels of the Earth as coal, petroleum, etc. in order to set an atmosphere that maintain a tolerable range of temperature so that life can exist without any hitch.

But we have turned foolish to the extent that we over-work to bring all those buried life-threatening materials, like petroleum, coal, gases, toxic minerals, etc., and do many patently foolish acts to undo the wisdom of Nature; we are suicidal.

Humans are Digging Graves for All Living Beings

Every addition of harmful material or chemical which cannot be recycled or detoxified by Nature interferes with the various functions of Nature and its de-polluting mechanisms. They, in turn, harm every life form and affect the health of our planet through global warming (GW), which leads to climate change (CC).

Modern man creates millions of tons of injurious chemicals as solids, liquids, and gases, and in addition, digs out varieties of harmful minerals and petroleum from vast land areas. All of this directly puts those lands out of "service," and the harmful chemicals contaminate and harm all the elements of Nature and threaten the remaining life forms, including the perpetrating human species.

Why and How Humans do Suicidal Acts

The highly polluting "furnaces" of urban centres and the many newly evolved "carbon-unfriendly" polluting jobs are part of modern life. Civilized humanity demands, rather depends upon, huge quantities of filthy energy. In order to wean away these huge dependent populations from it, we must find equal amount of non-polluting or renewable energy, which is unthinkable, so that huge quantity remains as deficits (to be fulfilled), and the quantity grows every day.

The green revolution has made food plenty and cheap. Humans need far less land for cultivation than they require for natural, organic farming. With the strength of this cheap food, people proliferated further, with "great hope," and converted those redundant fertile lands (formerly carbon-fixing) into carbon-unfriendly polluting areas. Such extensions of non-farming activities further worsen the above situation. This functional conversion of land from carbon-fixing crop land into carbon-emitting regions is more than a double harm from the global warming point of view.

Not only do these industrial activities contribute to pollution, but every human, ranging from white-collar workers, manual labourers, to their idle family members, become passive polluters. Every human who is not in a position to neutralize or help to neutralize his/her wastes, including exhaled carbon dioxide (through equivalent number of trees or farming), and other pollution like chemicals and plastics, is a polluter.

Western "Progress" Toward Highly Polluting Economy

It is basic knowledge that countries with Low Population Density (LPD) naturally enjoy surplus resources and opportunities and so must be able to enjoy fully sustainable living conditions. And they should never suffer socioeconomic ills and cannot have reasons to pollute. Rational thinking says that Western countries must enjoy a fully sustainable and pollution-free life. But, because of faulty population distribution and faulty economic structures, they are forced to pollute heavily and are not able to reduce it. (See details in chapter 31, "Economy.")

Western countries took to industrialization far ahead of others. So they were in an advantageous position with a better research back-up. They could utilize the global markets because of their pioneer status and contacts around the world. So their industry-based urban economy grew fast. These required more urban industrial workers.

By the mechanization of agriculture, they "freed" people from a farm-based life, who then went to fill urban opportunities. This resulted in a highly unhealthy distribution of population, with too many polluting urbanites against too few engaged in healthy farming. Now, their mechanized (polluting) farming has become unsustainable because of too much input and energy needs and often needs external markets.

People started loving urban life because of their new-found freedom from unpredictable and "dirty" agricultural pursuits, newer industrial and other developments, better facilities and entertainment (see more in chapter 18, "Urbanization"). Now, the urban population of many Western countries and even some developing countries has gone up to 80 to 90 percent of the total.

When such a vast majority is engaged in manufacturing and service sectors, they need a very huge market. Since their rural population and economy shrunk to a very small fraction, they cannot provide enough market for their industrial products, so they required huge external markets. In order to sustain such a dependent economy, they must maintain their superiority in quality, innovations, productions, and marketing, with proper research and other facilities. For this, they needed migrants, ranging from highly skilled professionals to unskilled labourers, which further enlarges their urban population and increases their levels of inevitable pollution.

Thus, industrialized countries do not manufacture for themselves alone, but for many other countries, mostly poor and developing countries. That means the latter countries indirectly contribute to the pollution of industrialized countries (proxy pollution). Considerable numbers of their industrial workers include people from many other countries.

Entrapped High Polluters

It is a sorrowful state that developed countries know that they are top polluters, yet are not able to reduce their polluting activities; they are in a catch-22 situation. If they reduce the highly polluting economic activities, their economy will collapse and they will face calamities, including mass death. For instance, when polluting transport stops, they starve because of food scarcity, or when polluting energy sources stop, their internal climate conditioning and other vital equipment will fail and kill people. If they continue these highly polluting economic activities, pollution sickens them and intensifies global warming.

There is another catch: As we saw, the West must maintain its superiority. If developing countries excel, their markets will vanish and meet the above catastrophes. They are forced to act with greater speed, too. Desperate, speedy acts pollute far more than normal activities. Because of this entrapped situation, they could not fulfil the demands of Kyoto Protocol or promise pollution-reduction in Copenhagen.

It must be a lesson to the world, especially newly emerging polluters like India, China, and other developing countries, because they too are inching toward such a dangerous trap. If they fail to prevent such a course, their sufferings will be far worse than those of Western countries because of their additional curses, like HPD conditions.

Proxy Pollution

We saw that developed countries must maintain industrial superiority for various reasons, like keeping their global clients happy. Most of their client countries (poor and developing) do not have the economic and technological strength to create high tech and costly manufacturing facilities. Yet they need many scientifically and technologically superior products for communication, crime-fighting, fast transport, entertainment, medical services, and above all, military hardware (because of enemies within and around them). Thus, poor and developing countries are dependent upon polluting countries for many products.

Through this mutual dependence, third world countries transfer a lot of their highly polluting manufacturing activities to industrialized countries. Millions of third world migrants are manning those pollution industries, and thus transfer their share of pollution to the host countries.

Thus, considerable quantities of pollution which are supposed to originate in poor and developing countries are shifted to already highly polluting industrialized countries, and make them condemnable super polluters. We can call this transfer "proxy pollution."

Factors that Promote "Proxy Pollution"

Because of HIFs and HPD, poor and developing countries suffer every known evil. A huge percentage of their budget allocation goes for poverty alleviation and to fight crimes, violence, terrorism, civil wars or wars with neighbours, and other curses like contagious diseases and illiteracy. But a huge percentage of this is wasted because of many fooleries and large scale corruption.

The monumental fooleries of ignorant poor families (who create their own hells through HIFs) give immortality to all those evils. Under these chaotic and fund-starved circumstances, those poor and developing countries cannot think of huge and sensitive industries. Even if the government or the private sector starts such industry, their corrupt officials, greedy trade union leaders, irresponsible labourers, and selfish politicians will do all they can to devitalize or kill those industries. If they spend for research and discover and develop new gadgets, theft of technology, piracy, and faking will seal their fate. When someone is successful in an industry, many others will follow suit and then the glut brings down the prices and ruins the industry.

If one succeeds and comes out above all, one must be in a position to pay regular sums to a long line of criminals like "protectors," terrific trade union leaders, kidnappers, terror gangs, and of course, corrupt politicians and government officials. So, industrialization fails in such countries that are forced to source from polluting countries.

Speed Promotes Pollution

It is quite common to hear people, ranging from ordinary labourers to top professionals and from students to top business men, that they are very busy and do not have enough time to finish their routine jobs. Eating every meal together with all the members of a happy family is a celebration. But how many of us have time to enjoy this day-to-day celebration? Too many of us just gulp some fast food at some place near the work site to save time. Modern women do not want to waste time in cooking, and instead go for some profitable job. In my neighbourhood, even ordinary labourers buy polluting mechanized bikes to save time and to do more work. These are signs of unsustainability, deficits, and related hopelessness.

Nature has given us the anatomical structure and physiological functions to lead a calm life and has given a separate autonomous nervous system to deal with emergencies. The adrenalin-driven emergency function of speed is carefully choreographed to make us fly away quickly from danger zones or to resist them with all our strength. But if this emergency-function of speed becomes a permanent or continuous necessity, it is a highly abnormal and dangerous trend.

But for today's humanity, speed at every level has become a necessity to manage a life with unending scarcities, unhealthy competition, and dangerous challenges.

People of third world countries face unhealthy competition and challenges for resources, job opportunities, and to protect whatever they have. The unfortunate people with insufficient wealth migrate fast and run from place to place and to other countries, seeking work. Even their children are forced to learn a lot in a short time in order to compete with peers so that they can expect better jobs in future. Even for the employed or the business people, success and progress depend upon speedy travel, speedy work using advantageous gadgets, and speedy marketing. The challenges from corrupt people, criminals, terrorists, and traitors have to be tackled with speed.

Developed countries have to maintain their superiority through fast research, faster innovations, and frequent new products. They must travel fast around the world to introduce and sell their newer products. If they slow down, competitors will replace them and pirates will ruin their profits.

Speed, urgency, hurry, etc. require reckless spending of energy and are prone to costly complications which lead to far more polluting than activities done under hopeful, calm, and confident conditions.

Extra Pollution

Other than this widely discussed pollution, humans do a lot to harm everything which aids life. The many chemicals we use in our homes for cleaning and disinfection harm the environment and pressurized gases harm the ozone layer.

Even common salt and micronized particles make land less fertile (chapters 5 and 6.) Plastics remain in the soil for years and prevent rooting of plants and are hazardous to animals on land and in water. Heating and burning it liberates carcinogenic compounds. The toxic wastes of electronic goods, huge vehicles, effluents from factories, refineries, mining industries, etc. are of enormous quantities which spell disastrous consequences in many ways. The liberation of nitrogenous gases from petroleum, too, is a threat.

Humans are the only species who pollute more than the inevitable quantities of their metabolic/ physiological activities and are doing catastrophic damage to everything which is vital and precious. Incriminating other innocent animals for methane and for other damage is pure nonsense.

25

Reversing Pollution

Ravages of Pollution

Pollution is a real curse which directly sickens every living being and the host planet and indirectly threatens them through GW and CC. Yet we are the only species to create it in vast quantities and in unnatural ways. Pollution causes diseases ranging from simple irritation, inflammation, and allergic reactions to even cancer of almost every part of us, from the most exposed skin to the most protected brain.

The physical and chemical effects of it are many—like destroying the ozone layer, acidification of sea water, global warming, and many more. Further, the menace of non-biodegradable materials is also great.

Duty and Responsibility of Mankind

We, who are of the present generation, are the link between the past and future generations. We must recognize that all living beings, including us and our living green planet, are made for each other. We have no right to harm any of these and harming is pure madness and a crime. As intelligent species, we are supposed to hand over a better world to our future links, or at least in the same condition we received it from our parents. We boast about a million things, like computers, deciphering chromosomes, moon journeys, atomic energy, or medical triumphs, but it is an utter shame that we failed to control harmful pollution. If we continue to do this, we will be cursed as the most brutal animals the Earth ever had.

Rational Way to End Polluting

We have seen there is a pattern in the evolution of man-made ills, starting from deficits in families and ending with pollution, GW, and CC. But in the case of industrialized countries, evolution toward super pollution is slightly different and almost resembles a jump from early family or rural deficits to industrialization because of the advantages they enjoyed with inventions, innovations, better social order, and the global market they enjoyed.

To end pollution in poor and developing countries, the most rational path is to end the original sin (HIFs), and simultaneously mitigate those evolved evils like poverty, crime, and pollution itself.

But developed countries do not have such HIFs, and their rural population is a small fraction of the total. They must change this highly unsustainable population distribution pattern and support wholesome farming, including organic bio-energy creation, and improve renewable energy and "green" technologies. Above all, the most important factor to end their pollution spree is with poor and developing countries who aid super pollution through proxy-pollution and other market facilities; these will end when the former effort of ending HIFs yields results.

Original Sin and Rational Solution

The ultimate key that rationally and certainly ends pollution is with poor and developing countries. Since they initiated pollution by creating HIFs, they have the responsibility to end it. This primary family-deficit is created by illiterate, innocent masses. When HIFs are prevented and those innocent masses are saved from deficits, the evolution of the "chain of evils" and "proxy pollution" will stop.

Since it will take two or three decades to realize its full benefits, the present mitigation efforts must continue.

Planning for Carbon Neutral (Green) Living

We saw that urban centres are polluting furnaces which promote GW through greenhouse gases and direct heating. In contrast, well-planned rural living goes against that, or at least maintains neutrality. If mankind desires to protect its progeny, we must do all we can to promote the latter and prevent the factors which promote urbanization.

Building a Strong Carbon-Neutral Economy

Well-integrated natural (organic) farming creates real wealth. Its connected activities, like dairy, poultry, inland fisheries, etc., help each other and make it sustainable without creating any residual wastes or pollution. Even if external inputs become a necessity, they are meagre. Moreover, sustainable organic farming can sustainably employ more people than mechanized, unsustainable intensive farming. When the percentage of people enjoying sustainable living goes up, their economy stabilizes and brings down every factor that promotes pollution.

Evolving Opportunities and Benefits

As we discussed elsewhere, the global farming industry can be made to flourish if a small percentage of the huge funds spent on petroleum and coal is gradually diverted toward bio-fuels like vegetable-oils, alcohol, bio-gas, etc., and other efforts to harness sunlight and wind are encouraged in rural regions.

Encouraging horticulture, oil-yielding trees, forestry, and greening will clean our environment and prevent many diseases and, thereby, save funds and manpower. These activities will also help to sustain and protect endangered wild animals, birds, and plants, and help natural cattle farming and poultries (which also prevent many diseases and toxic contamination of food). Today, millions of retired people and ageing people are idling in cities, like "orphans" with nobody to take care of them, and nothing to do. The above greening efforts can certainly give them "new life" with great purpose and make life more meaningful, interesting, and healthy.

At last, these efforts reduce pollution, help carbon-fixing, reduce idle population in cities, and give sustainable energy. Then we can gradually stop digging for petroleum (which comes up to dig our graves) and can even fulfil needs like metals by recycling those we have brought out.

Reversing Urbanization and Encouraging Regional "Migrant Rotation"

We just saw how the rural economy can be improved to involve idle urbanites. Well-managed rural life is not at all dull or boring because they can gain a lot from loving and responsive beings like cattle, fowl, and pets. When we care for the plants, they never cheat us, but return love and gratitude through the timely yield of fruits, vegetables, flowers, etc.

When modern facilities and entertainments are added to such sustainable rural communes, life becomes pure joy which no one can resist. Other than the retired, the ageing, and the idle people of cities, the employed people and businessmen also can come back from the concrete jungles for longer vacations or for a permanent stay when they are fed-up or contented. By doing that, they can improve their physical and mental health and pay back their carbon debts.

When Nature attracts satisfied urban people, aspiring youths from villages can go to cities with full hope to fill those vacancies and to fulfil their ambition of using their talents and skills. These zealous workers do everything with joy and to perfection, and do more without boredom because they love it. They create and innovate and produce more. When they fulfil their ambitions, they, too, can go back to their roots to enjoy the wholesome life. All this—"migrants-rotation" and rural resurgence—favour sustainability and go against pollution, GW, and CC.

But Is that Possible?

These plans appear wonderful, but how can we make them happen? It is not at all hard, as one may doubt. All we have to do is to prevent the formation of deficit-causing HIFs. This would make people contented and happy. Smaller, sustainable families release huge quantities of resources for organic farming and reforesting, and these go against the "evil chain." With time, polluting industrial and other activities will come down to form an equilibrium with greening or even a healthier positive balance. (Ref. Chapters 30 and 31).

Because the causes of proxy-pollution decline, Western countries will be forced to correct their highly polluting economies and their irrational population distributions. Ending super-pollution of developed countries comes very late, after the progress of poor and developing countries toward sustainable living.

The people involved in climate change affairs like the Kyoto Protocol and the Copenhagen Accord and those with the desire to end pollution must go to remote regions to help people prevent the formation of the unsustainable debt trap of HIFs and to make the above described sane life a reality. It is easier to give a sustainable life to rural people than to "entrapped" Western urbanites.

Possible Economic Crisis in Industrialized Countries and Misguided Envy

The industrial economy is the last to gain a sustainable, respectable living in freedom. Today, we see many people envying the prosperity of developed countries, which comes at the heavy price of lethal pollution. It is not at all a commendable position. So there is nothing to envy. Instead of using the growing affluence for future industrialization, if present-day poor and developing countries sensibly utilize those manufacturing facilities in countries like Japan, South Korea, and Western countries, they can save their people from pollution. Then, both parties can mutually and economically support each other and save huge funds, which can be used for greening and other activities that end pollution absolutely.

26

Global Warming and
Climate Change are Real Threats,
Yet We Do More to Heighten Them

Global Warming (GW)

People from relatively poor rural regions (with too many HIFs) try to mitigate their deficits by destroying vast areas of nearby forests and other green covers and promote GW.

In contrast, the upwardly moved people living in urban regions pollute indiscriminately in many ways and thereby promote GW. They, too, do it to fulfil their very huge deficits.

The deficits of those rural people are mostly related to life-supporting resources like fertile lands and water.

The deficits of urban people are many; but the major deficit is energy. They need vast quantities of energy even for normal and idle living, and the quantities are enormous to fulfil their breadwinning, economic activities.

At last, both the rural and urban population contribute to GW.

Natural Doubts

Still, there are people who refuse to accept global warming (GW) and climate change (CC) as real phenomena and insist that these are natural cosmic cycles. Others doubt them because of contrasting events. It is natural that people expect hot summers and hotter heat waves, melting of ice caps and glaciers and rising sea levels with GW, but one often wonders why they face harsher winters, severe snow fall, or torrential rain. Doubters must understand that these contrasting events happen for scientific reasons according to the laws of physics.

Harsh Facts About GW

GW manifests in many ways that include CC. The direct effect of GW is experienced as harsher summers, which take more lives nowadays through heat stroke and other ailments related to higher atmospheric temperature and by starving people through droughts. We see more frequent and harsher forest fires and the gradually vanishing ice caps of mountains and glaciers near the poles. GW also causes more severe and more frequent hurricanes (cyclones), highly destructive torrential rains, and very heavy snow fall.

All this leads to unusual weather conditions, like extended summers and winters, faster droughts, disturbed rainy seasons, etc. We call the combination of these "climate change."

Some Aspects of GW and CC

Every element of Nature obeys the rules of physics and undergoes physical changes. We humans do not cause CC directly, but we just warm up the globe (GW). Atmospheric warming alters the physical equations that govern climate and creates many harmful effects which are the components of CC. Other harms, ranging from these physical changes to those related to health of crops, other plants (like forests), and living beings of land and sea, pests, disease carrying vectors, disease patterns, etc., are many and happen in direct proportion to GW.

Torrential rain: With GW, more water evaporates from the oceans, land-locked bodies of water, and from icy regions. Warmer air can hold many times more water as vapour/moisture. With rising temperatures, the quantity of water held by the atmosphere reaches the equivalent of many lakes and rivers. What went up must come down. When heavily-loaded moist air forms rain, it pours down as torrents and causes severe floods and extensive inundations. For example, the Australian

183

(Queensland) flood during the first half of January 2011 was so severe and devastating that they called it an inland tsunami.

Torrential rain and destructive floods cause landslides, crop loss, infrastructure damage, and loss of lives. Observations over the past decade reveal the gradual worsening of these events.

Heavy snow fall and harsher winters: The processes of evaporation, water formation, etc. involve a huge transfer of additional heat as latent heat. For instance, the latent heat of evaporation brings down temperatures even on summer days, and such changes in regions away from the tropics make winters harsher and longer.
When conditions favour snow formation, the heavily-laden atmosphere produces very heavy snowfall, as we have experienced in recent times.

Droughts: Despite torrents of rain and destructive floods, we face droughts because of faster evaporation due to a warmer atmosphere. Further, the faster air movements and lowering humidity after torrents results in faster depletion of water from the soil. So GW takes away many advantages of rain and favours severe droughts and desertification.

Vanishing rivers and lakes: When the temperature was lower, a vast portion of atmospheric moisture froze at the poles and over tall mountains. The latter melted at a steady pace and formed huge perennial rivers. These were further supported by seasonal rain. We affectionately named those rivers and lakes, which formed the basis of our civilization. For various reasons, like GW (failing ice-formation), changing climate, and over-use by humans, many rivers and lakes have disappeared or have become seasonal streams or ponds.

Worsening hurricanes: Temperature gradients are amplified by the events like faster evaporation, faster rain formation, snowfall, and faster drought, where a huge amount of heat is transferred in the form of the latent heat of evaporation and condensation. Urban centres act like harsh deserts in heating the atmosphere, which along with hotter deserts and new barren lands, heat the atmosphere faster. This hot, thinner air moves up, creating low pressure areas and prompts faster air movement toward it. When faster air is humidified and momentum rises, it becomes a hurricane, which further makes the seas rough and creates unusual winds, which are more frequent nowadays. Thus, they form unusual and unpredictable weather patterns.

Well Felt Deterioration

The harmful and destructive effects of GW and CC are obvious. Every observant person is anxious because of the worsening situation. If somebody over the age of about forty-five years denies these, such a moron can never be considered a normal human at all.

Green Cover and Global Warming

Forests and other green covers make use of tons and tons of atmospheric carbon dioxide (greenhouse gas) and release a proportional quantity of oxygen, and thus try to maintain a stable percentage of those gases in the atmosphere and keep under control the greenhouse effects of carbon dioxide.

Through photosynthesis, plants trap the sun's energy (heat and light), using the gases and water to create energy-packs, like food for the animal kingdom, and other useful products like timber, firewood, and oil (including potential bio-diesel) for us. In that process, they use trillions of calories of heat of sun light and reduce atmospheric temperature.

Thus, green covers bring down atmospheric temperature in two major ways—by bringing down greenhouse gases and by trapping huge quantities of the sun's heat into useful organic compounds. By Nature's arrangement, we are supposed to use these vast quantities of energy trapped by plants in various forms. If we do that, and use other renewable sources for our energy needs, the question of pollution and atmospheric warming does not occur.

Unfortunately, we destroy the green cover in many ways:

♦ Clearing forests for farming.
♦ Destroying forests for timber, paper, and firewood.
♦ Burning forests to make commercial plantations. It also heats atmosphere directly.

- Over-grazing creates dry lands and extends deserts.
- Growing urban centres remove green cover.
- Diversion of water that nourishes forests for human use dries up vast tracks of green cover.
- Pollution—gases, liquids, solids, and radioactive—directly and indirectly devitalize green cover.

Man-Made Evils and Global Warming

We have seen repeatedly how we create greenhouse gases like carbon dioxide, methane, nitrogenous gases, etc. through our activities related to travel, transport, manufacture of goods, energy creation, and in our day-to-day activities. In addition to the creation of greenhouse gases, those activities directly heat atmospheric air.

Every additional human beyond OPD hikes the deficits and so the above activities. Now, because of the continuing population explosion, huge deficits are added to the already heaped up debts, which worsen unsustainable living conditions to highly dangerous levels. Then desperate acts to fill up the shortages go up which promote GW.

Creators with No Control Over CC

We now know that GW happens because of human activities. CC does not happen directly because of our acts, but as per the laws of physics, and to some extent to those of chemistry, governing heat (GW). Any direct attempt to control CC is quixotic. If we wish to do anything to control CC, it must be directed at those activities which aid GW, like forest destruction, environmental mismanagement, the weakening ozone layer, urbanization, and pollution.

Unrecognized Burdens

We just saw that every added human beyond OPD is a deficiency creator. A report of the World Wildlife Fund says that, "overall, the Earth's population is consuming the resources of 1.5 planet—or it takes one and a half years to replenish the resources used in one year." (*The Hindu*, October 14, 2010:11). This report is too conservative because it does not mention the very huge unfulfilled day-to-day deficits suffered by billions of people despite over-use of resources and who live a subhuman life, facing premature death, or about the already accumulated deficits like carbon debt.

We take seriously factors like green cover destruction and pollution, which directly favour GW, but fail to understand how evils like corruption, criminal activities, terrorism, and wars contribute to it. For example, when a corrupt bureaucrat or politician exploits a sustainable, carbon-friendly family, he makes its life unsustainable. This forces the victim to do desperate activities to compensate for the loss or deficit, which favours GW. At the same time, the family of the corrupt goon leads a brutally lavish life without bothering the least about pollution, and pollute much more than their "quota." Thus, both these families are pushed into a situation that creates more GW than otherwise. Similar deterioration happens with every evil we discussed earlier.

Inability of the Debtors

When a country is unsustainable with too many HIFs (huge deficits), projects to protect and promote forests, renewable energy, and activities which check GW are pushed to the back burner because huge funds are required to fight other ills and evils, from poverty to terrorism. So it becomes a double loss with regard to GW because most of the precious funds needed for those projects are used for the very people who are engaged in damaging acts like greenery destruction and who cannot stop the acts unless they become deficit-free. Quite often they continue to have HIFs with the strength of the aid they receive and perpetrate even more evils. In that process, opportunities to promote renewable energy, etc. are lost. For instance, poor and developing countries of the tropical regions can beneficially use solar and wind energy to reduce their energy expenditure by 40 to 60 percent (chapter 21, *Book G*); but where are the funds?

Indirect Loss

Population pressure has led to the extinction of many plants, birds, and animals which once helped the maintenance of robust forests and green cover.

27

Ending GW and CC

Failed Efforts and Continuing Failures

It is a good sign that more and more people are coming forward to do something to end/bring down GW and CC. The efforts through the Kyoto protocol, the Copenhagen Accord, and subsequent meetings, the interests shown by independent organizations, several countries, and even ordinary people and school students are really appreciable. But so far, we could not count any appreciable success, and we can call those efforts to be costly failures because, despite huge spending and the use of vast manpower under the guidelines of the "best brains" for more than a decade, GW and CC have worsened when compared to what they were.

Now the world wants to evolve a definite formula that must work. The ongoing efforts, starting with the Copenhagen meeting, appear to be the repetition of the same failed efforts of the past. Every well-read person knows that such efforts will never work, and when we cannot explain a clear roadmap, we cannot expect any reasonable compliance of the "perpetrators" because of past failures with the same map. Continuing attempts to frame a formula evade success because no one has explained the foolproof roadmap with a wholesome understanding of GW and CC.

Other Outstanding Failures

This is not the first major failure by mankind. Our leaders and planners of the past devised the "best" policies and fought poverty. While fighting poverty, they faced crime and corruption and started fighting them, too. Before meeting with any success in these attempts, terrorism and war-like situations raised their heads around the globe. Huge funds and vast manpower were employed to contain all the above; yet millions die because of these curses—from poverty to terrorism.

While fumbling with those curses, we realized the dangers of pollution and started doing everything possible to control it. Yet, before we could make any progress, all those evils and curses, including pollution, combined to warm up the globe (GW), which triggered CC.

Promising Clue

Instead of an elaborate discussion of failures, I would like to go straight to the most rational idea. It is nothing but connecting deficits/ ULC and the evolving ills, including GW. If responsible thinkers, policy-makers, and leaders study any of the anthropogenic ills, evils, or curses, or the whole lot in relation to the level of deficits in various countries or regions, they will certainly find the right answer and can form a rational and worthy policy.

Anybody can do that by counting the numbers or the percentage of HIFs in a region or country and by understanding their proximity to Nature. The farther they go, the more are their requirements, which hike the deficits further. The deficits of developed rich countries can be understood from the quantities of polluting petroleum and coal they use in a year or fixed period.

Finding Key to End Curses

We do not have any time to waste, and we need very definite ideas which must yield measurable results with mathematical precision. I am sure that upcoming discussions will enlighten everyone on the imperatives and put them on the right path to end those curses we have discussed. (These ideas and schemes which help conquer all those evils and curses are derived from real life events.)

Understanding Green Cover Destruction and Pollution (and Other Evils like Crime and Terrorism) as Compensatory Mechanisms to Make Good the Deficits

We know that the human race has outgrown the natural resources meant for us. The excess growth remains as deficits. Deficits demand more natural resources and enormous quantities of energy which Nature doesn't possess. No one can live a full and worthy life with deficits so people struggle to make good the deficits. When something is too scarce and cannot be got even with hard work (billions of people face this difficult situation), the other options are "to beg, borrow, or steal," or "cheat, beat, and kill." In fact, we are doing exactly these very harmful and shameful acts and these prove the existence of the huge deficits and our over-growth.

Begging: Today, a vast section of global families suffers huge deficits and faces premature death. Billions of them try to live a full life out of charities (of various kinds, like food, education, healthcare, shelter, and many more) from other people or governments. Yet mankind as a whole does other shameful deeds besides begging.

Borrowing: The fossil energy we use is equivalent to borrowed resources. If we want to live with respect at all, we must give back the "borrowed" carbon to the bowels of the Earth. But we have not done anything tangible to reduce the need for this borrowed energy. On the other hand, we keep on using more of it and accumulate this carbon-debt in the form of accumulated pollution, especially in greenhouse gases, which destroy us and our innocent cohabitants. Now humanity has become a habitual borrowing community and has become dependent on it. Borrowing without plans for repayment amounts to stealing. When life is run on increasing quantities of borrowed resources, returning to sustainability (debtless life) takes a longer time.

Stealing: We need resources far beyond our share, and so we steal water, space, land, green cover, etc. rationally meant for other species of animals and plants, and in that process, we commit the following heinous crimes.

Cheating, beating, and killing: Since the number of needy humans multiplies like cancer cells, we grab more and more resources rightfully belonging to other life forms. Too many of those deprived species have disappeared from the face of our planet and too many are on the path to extinction. Is there a more serious crime than this heinous murder?

Other than these brutalities against the innocent, voiceless children of Nature, too many desperate, needy people indulge in corruption, crime, violence, and terrorism, and snatch the possessions and life of too many compatriots.

Springhead of All Evils and Curses

Now we must understand that all those man-made evils and curses are nothing but their efforts to sustain their life by minimizing deficits. Deficits evolve through HIFs and through irrational economic activities and lopsided population distribution (indiscriminate urbanization).

Urbanization and rampant industrialization can be checked if the formation of HIFs is prevented. In short, we can gradually correct all these deficits, ills, and evils, including curses like green cover destruction and pollution, by preventing the formation of HIFs.

Aggravating Factors

There are too many other factors, like faulty religious, socio-economic and political ideologies, superstitions, expensive religious rites, and events like natural calamities which further aggravate deficit-related evils, even to the point of "explosion" literally and metaphorically.

Blinding "Realities" and Causes for Their Failures

Today, almost all successful people, especially urbanites, do not recognize the precarious nature of modern living from the sustainability point of view. So they keep worsening the unsustainable conditions in the name of comfort and civilization. It is time to understand that the threshold of reaching unsustainability tends to come down and create more complications in direct proportion to their distance from Nature and the numbers of indispensable needs they add; undoing these must be part of any policy.

We have discussed the evolution of deficits through HIF, the augmentation of deficits through urbanization, and the evolution of evils and curses. Now we know that the unsustainable living condition caused by deficit is the real malignant disease—and not the evolved evils, including GW and CC. But deficits have failed to attract the right attention because of those harsher signs and symptoms. At last, those harsher signs and symptoms have been misunderstood as real, dangerous diseases, and have been "treated" accordingly. Because of this "wrong diagnosis," the real disease worsened even while mankind was fighting the symptoms.

The result: Present-day's multiplied and complicated curses, including GW and CC.

So management/treatment of these "wrong perceptions" must be replaced /supplemented by the efforts which end deficits.

Forgotten Deficiency Diseases

When I started medical practice in the early 1970s, I regularly treated children and adults afflicted with serious ailments due to deficiencies of the various components of food, ranging from carbohydrates and protein to vitamins and minerals. History says that, in the past, millions and millions of people died directly of these deficiency diseases or of causes associated with them or complications by them. Even today, millions suffer from such diseases in remote parts of developing and poor countries, but influential, civilized people suffer from the surpluses (like obesity) of those ingredients, and so have forgotten those serious deficiency disorders.

Diagnosing and treating those deficiency diseases was exciting to me because of the dramatic disappearance of the bizarre symptoms and signs and the impressive recovery of those patients. It was European scientists and medical men who first put forward the concept and established the link between deficiencies and those diseases. Humanity is highly indebted to them. We, the members of medical profession and our patients, enjoyed moments of pure joy because of their sacrifices.

Humanity will benefit a great deal and would experience such pure joy if they mind the deficiencies they cause by their wrong planning and wrong living.

Deficiency Diseases of the World

Today, humanity faces very huge deficiencies of basic resources like fertile lands and water, employment opportunities, shelter, energy, infrastructures, educational facilities, and also abstract deficits of virtues like love, dignity, justice, peace, equality, and many more. We must understand that each and every one of these deficiencies has its effect upon individuals, society, and the world.

Even now, to some readers, it may sound odd if I say that those huge and diverse deficiencies and sorrows started as small deficits in ignorant families in the form of HIFs (Huge Insatiable Families) but it is true.

Final Curative Treatment

The curative treatment (of all these evils, from poverty to GW and CC) is the act of ending unsustainable (deficient) living conditions at the family level—preventing HIFs. With time, it will reduce the need for urbanization and the industrial activities of polluting countries.

28

Cancer of Planet Earth

A Rational Comparison

Stupidities drag the stupid into troubles. Unending stupidities often drag even others and their benevolent, supportive guardians into painful and dangerous situations. Modern humanity, too, has been doing many rash and foolish acts, which have dragged them as well as the other millions of life forms and their motherly planet into a grim situation.

Mankind's imprudent proliferation and rash living have brought to it many ills and evils which we have already discussed. Their unending stupidities have driven many species to extinction and now threaten every living being and the whole planet—including the humans—with life-threatening pollution, GW, and CC. Yet humanity (the perpetrators), hasn't understood its calamitous stupidities which try to finish them off but leads an apparently "smooth" life as if everything is moving on smoothly, and this does further harm. I searched for some rational comparisons that could explain this terrible situation to indifferent people, and found cancer to be an appropriate one, where both the "guest" (cancer tissue = humanity) and the host (the person afflicted with cancer = Planet Earth) suffer.

What Cancer is to a Person, Mankind is to Planet Earth

Everyone knows the notoriety, pain, and fatality of fast-growing cancer. Because of its harsh consequences, cancer is also called malignancy, and it attracts the most urgent attention and "emergency" treatment. Like cancer tissues, which outgrow their limits at the expense of the other tissues and host, the human race has outgrown sensible levels and continues to grow to enormous size at the expense of other life forms and our host, Mother Nature, or Planet Earth. Like cancer, the human race inflicts painful and fatal harms to cohabitants and to the very planet on which humanity is dependent—Earth.

Cancer is the fast growth of a particular "species" of tissue without any purpose. Similarly, the human species grows too fast, like cancer cells, without any worthy purpose.

Cancer cells grow fast because they defy the controlling mechanisms. Similarly, humans, too, have overcome the controlling mechanisms of Nature and grow recklessly.

Cancer tissue "sucks" and over-uses nutrition meant for other tissues, and grows fast. Such stealing devitalizes other useful tissues, which weakens the patient. Similarly, mankind has usurped vast quantities of space and resources meant for others—the many plants, animals, birds, insects, and useful microbes—and is devitalizing them and even has exterminated many of them permanently. All this devitalizes Nature's mechanisms to ensure healthy sustainable living for all.

Cancer cells generate vast quantities of metabolic waste and create abnormal chemicals, like irrelevant hormones or proteins, which injure other normal tissues and affect their functioning and cause related symptoms like pain and fever, and those related to a particular organ's dysfunction or damage. Similarly, fast-breeding humans create huge amounts of "polluting wastes" like greenhouse gases, dangerous chemicals, non-biodegradable substances, etc., which upset the functions of many ecosystems and harm many life forms, and at last cause GW—similar to fever—and CC, which simulate serious symptoms like delirium and seizures.

By their physical growth, cancer masses press upon neighbouring tissues and organs and harm them. Similarly, the human pressure and presence push away other species into a threatened existence.

Because of unplanned and undisciplined fast proliferation, cancer masses outgrow their blood supply (with nutrition and oxygen) and create their own deficiencies and starvations. Cancer cells compete among themselves, which leads to the necrosis (death) of many of them. Similarly, people of crowded regions create their own deficiencies and poverty and then compete with and kill each other through crime, corruption, violence, terrorism, and wars.

Cancer cells detach from a primary site and metastasize (migrate and settle) in distant organs and ruin the health of the new region, too. Similarly, needy people from crowded, ungovernable regions migrate to distant places and countries, and do all sorts of unacceptable acts, like crime, treacherous acts, and even bomb the new hosts and also favour ruinous urbanization.

Above all, cancer tissue is a stupid, greedy tissue because by endangering the life of the host, it, too, meets premature death. Similarly, proliferating humans act foolishly with greed and in desperation, and thus harm their environment and devitalize many vital eco-systems, destroy green cover, and pollute extensively. These stupid acts write their own death warrants through GW and CC, and many other curses.

Thus there is no doubt that *Homo sapiens* do as much harm to the host, Earth, as cancer tissues do to their host.

Merciless, Tough Way of Saving the Person/ "Host"

In order to save a person from this scourge of cancer, we take very drastic steps. Surgical treatment includes merciless cutting away of the cancer tissue and related regions and even amputation of limbs, breast, or penis. The medicines (chemotherapy) used against cancers, too, have highly undesirable side-effects, yet are used without "mercy"—all with the sole aim of saving the person.

We, members of the "stupid" human race, endanger the well-being, sustainability, and even existence of our own race, other species, and even the host, Planet Earth, just like cancer tissue does to its "host." This situation demands urgent and determined remedial steps with no room for mercy or lenience. If we hesitate, we will have to face more sufferings and even extinction, along with many other innocent species—in the same way the "stupid" cancer tissue dies along with its host.

Here we are dealing with living humans and such drastic steps are not possible. So we must do the other best act, which prevents indiscriminate proliferation and thus prevents deficits at the family level, in the most determined way that gives predictable and measurable results.

29

The Panacea that Ends Man-Made Curses

Finding the Most Rational Solution for Global Curses

We, the human race, have degraded and endangered ourselves to the level to be compared to "stupid" cancer. The threats started as family deficiencies or unsustainability at family levels through HIFs (Huge Insatiable Families). Then we brought about generalized unsustainable living conditions (GULC/HPD) which cursed us with a variety of ills and evils, including GW and CC. Until we stop creating deficiencies and start a carbon-neutral or carbon-friendly sustainable living, we cannot hope for a worthy, peaceful living. Since the primary source of deficits is HIFs, preventing HIFs is the only remedy we have with us.

Evolving the Rational Formula

It is the balanced relation between life supportive resources (including the almost-fixed job opportunities) of a country and their beneficiary population which decides sustainability or OPD. The resources of any country are of fixed quantities and beneficiary humans are a variable factor. We cannot create even a molecule of life supportive resource, so the only option left is to regulate the variable factor (human population) to match the fixed factor. The only sensible and pleasing option is to help every newly-forming family and other eligible families to form a deficit-free, healthy, sustainable family.

The time-tested best option is the humane way of helping those families to exercise their fertility with caution and in the most rational way. By doing so, even the poorest of poor families will regain a respectable, sustainable living and enjoy life with hope, pride, and happiness.

Historical Plans

Vast numbers of families around the world have been sensible enough to form deficit-free, small families to suit worsening living conditions. Rationally, they must have enjoyed a wholesome, happy life, but the sustainability they are entitled to was hampered by the foolish acts of their compatriots. These latter people formed huge families with huge deficits and so their governments have been diverting a considerable part of the revenue to alleviate their poverty and the other evils evolved because of HPD. It was these evils and curses that have taken away the peace and happiness of those planned, contributing families and restricted the development of their countries.

The pragmatic governments of China and Singapore, and many regional governments around the world, understood the horrors of HIFs and HPD, and stressed the need to form sustainable, small families. Initially, they faced huge protests from ignorant people, from activists, and from certain "civilized" powerful governments around the world. Now, after three or four decades, the people who were "forced" to form happy, sustainable families enjoy a very high standard of living, the best nutrition, dignity, real freedom and comforts. On the contrary, the liberal countries suffered cancerous growth and suffer every known curse. Now, the "civilized" countries which criticized China and Singapore are in economic chaos and are doing smooth trade with them and again they prefer orderly, disciplined China and Singapore to disorderly democracies.

In some countries, including the "forced" states like Singapore, fertility levels have gone below replacement levels and so governments now request their people to have larger families and even offer incentives to support more children; but the people have realized the great life of smaller families and refuse to have more children. There is nothing wrong with a fall in fertility rate until they reach OPD.

Every sensible thought and study clearly indicates that implementing policies which guide people to have a Planned Small Contented Healthy Happy Family (PSCHHF) is the best and probably the only option we have to earn a sustainable, dignified living at all levels and freedom from the sorrows, shame, and pain associated with HPD.

Planned Small Contented Healthy Happy Family (PSCHHF)

This is a highly rational, no-nonsense plan, or one-line-policy, or a formula with a humane face and can be adapted easily or implemented without hurting anyone or endangering any genome. As the name suggests, this plan gives contentment, good health, and happiness, too. We will go through the components of this plan or formula, and understand how we gain the great life every normal human desires and how will it end all the evils and curses.

Planned Family

It is planning and disciplined living which lifted humanity to levels above other animals, so any negligence in this regard naturally curses people to suffer like endangered animals. Family formation is probably the most important part of one's life, and that of a nation, too, because families are the building blocks of nations. Making a family unsustainable, with more dependents than the ability of its breadwinners to support, ruins the life of the whole family as well as the well-being of their country. So it is the duty of both (the family and government) to evolve the most rational plan to ensure the freedom and honour of every family.

It is young, inexperienced couples who decide the size of their family. Even a small slip can push them and their innocent children into the hell of HIF. Those innocent, young couples must be enlightened to make an error-free, balanced decision by weighing their positive possessions, like life-supportive resources, and their abilities against their liabilities, like high unemployment rate, unhealthy competition, the presence of social, political, cultural, and religious evils like crime, corruption, violence, etc., which demand more of the couples' money, time, and energy and impose additional responsibilities and duties toward their children. Every planner must also take into consideration that most of the positive possessions, like physical abilities (health

200

and strength), naturally weaken with time and other possessions, like profitable businesses or professions, may lose the ability to support for various reasons.

A sensible plan gives them the best possible life, whereas fooleries ruin them entirely, as we have discussed in chapter 4, "Family," chapter 9, "HIF," and below.

Even with planning, things may go wrong because of unexpected events. Yet suffering families can normally expect only economic support from others and governments, because no one can play the role of a father or mother. During such difficult days, supporting a family with the least number of dependents is an easy task because their deficits remain low.

So, to ensure hopeful and confident living, it is always better to be on the positive side of the balance with a lesser number of children than the optimum, especially in HPD communities and countries.

Small Family

In addition to the above-mentioned external liabilities, modern, civilized humanity is over-burdened with too many needs. With time, the price of needs goes up, but the life-supporting resources and job opportunities go scarce. In addition to the growing cost of living, modern parents have far more responsibilities, like shielding their children (especially in crowded countries) from evil forces like criminals, terror groups, drug peddlers, sex perverts, selfish leaders in politics and religion, etc., who roam around to harm, indoctrinate, and exploit and to recruit the innocent children and youths into their outfits.

Because of all this, modern parents find it tough even to support two children. When they exceed their limits, caring and supporting children to satisfaction is not at all possible, so the children of huge families have more opportunities to go the wrong way and face too many "challenges" and temptations. One wrongly indoctrinated child is enough to take away the peace of the entire family and even that of the society. Even rich families are not exempt.

Under highly complex living conditions that demand more resources, efforts, energy, and time of modern parents, even a small slip of adding a child will deny the family a worthy life and adversely affect the pride, honour, dignity, and contentment of their innocent children. People in lower strata, living a hopelessly unsustainable life, must be very careful so that they must never repeat the mistake of their parents which ensured them their sufferings with insufficiencies and indignity. There cannot be a greater sin and mistake than "bestowing" deficits and related indignities upon innocent children.

When in doubt, the most sensible act of a couple is to stop with only one child, which is their right and duty, and that alone can give the best possible progress and prosperity. The children of such one-child-families naturally inherit more than double the wealth of their parents, which invariably frees them from the shame of deficits and unsustainability, so their children will sit equal with anyone, without any hesitation or low self-esteem.

Until a country recovers from HPD, it is always wise to have the smallest family. If not, their HIF and the country's HPD will make their life a real hell.

Contented Family

It is contentment which gives a person or a child the much-needed feeling of dignity and confidence, and so happiness and a positive, hopeful mind-set. Contented people never expect anything from anyone, so they feel equal with every respectable person of any status. Because of the freedom and mind-set, they can ignore the baits/ "traps" of the cheats, charlatans, or the crooked rascals, and protect their honour. Contentment comes naturally to any family when it plans rationally to have sufficient savings, ample family time, time for socializing and leisure activities. Contentment naturally strengthens their noble feelings like love, patriotism, gratitude, concern for others, and sacrificing for others. Such families are an asset to their nation and are its real pillars.

Healthy Family

Children of well-planned small families always enjoy the best care, timely immunization, medical care and nutrition, appropriate education, and above all, the loving "touch" of their parents. The parents in turn enjoy the love and gratitude of contented well-loved children, which are the best tonics to strengthen and motivate them to do more and to keep the family in the best health.

Children of very small families always have a very high proportion of highly responsible and dedicated adults like grandparents, uncles, and aunts to care for, watch over, and guide them. This circumstance further diminishes their chance to go wrong or to fall into dangerous traps. Other than the normal savings, they save more because of lower medical expenditures, freedom from litigations, etc. With such huge savings, they can keep their environment clean, have spacious shelter, and can procure provisions to ensure their safety. A healthy economy and family life naturally give them a healthy social life. Further, their savings can always help them face unforeseen difficulties and buy desired things without anyone's charity or help. All this naturally gives them the best physical and mental health.

Happy Family

Contentment, good health, a loving family, respectable social position, economic freedom, education, sufficient leisure, and satisfactory socializing and entertainment and, above all, much-needed hope, self-esteem, and peace give them a happy life as a family.

When all the families of a country adopt the PSCHHF norm, their children cannot have the inclination to harm others through exploitation, crime, or terrorism. Their time and energy will be directed toward healthy social functions and services, like protecting endangered species, reforestation, cleaning the degraded environment, and other nation-building activities. A life in peace, voluntary service, and amity will give them double happiness as a community and a nation.

Panacea that Solves All Ills

Helping families, especially ignorant and poor families, to form PSCHHF will slowly remove disparities, inequalities, and unsustainable living conditions, and will remove the connected ills and shame. With time, this great healer, the PSCHHF norm, endows a country with every desired virtue and blessing and moves populations toward LPD. LPD helps them to undo the calamitous mistakes (like carbon emission and accumulation) that threaten humanity with GW and CC.

Word of Caution

When the diagnosis itself is wrong because it is based on wrong premises, the prescriptions are bound to be wrong and capable of causing havoc. We now know that the evils we fought against—from poverty to pollution—are not at all real diseases. So with the wrong diagnosis, we fought them and failed; and at last brought about a more serious threatening situation with GW and CC.

Now we know the real silent disease and the only solution: the PSCHHF norm. If we continue to act foolishly, our children will never forgive us. Normal humans always prefer and love smaller numbers of trustworthy, loving, honest, and respecting people, and never a huge, unreliable crowd.

Good News for Those Who Do Not Believe in GW and CC

Even people who do not believe in GW and CC must help to propagate and practice the universal remedy PSCHHF, because this formula will end their worries, too—evils like poverty, unemployment, environment degradation, species extinction, crime, violence, and pollution—and lead everybody toward hopeful sustainable living.

Those are not at all boastful claims, but taken from real life situations. The PSCHHF norm, like any best policy, can give the expected results at the expected time, as described in chapter 31.

30

Toward a Stable and Sustainable Economy

Stable Economy Minimizes Factors Causing GW

A healthy, stable economy indicates fairly sustainable living conditions; yet, today we cannot call it a wholesomely sustainable (green) economy because the modern economy invariably depends upon petroleum. A chaotic and unstable economy means that the country concerned suffers from illogical and irrational policies, irrational population distribution (over-urbanization), and unsustainable living conditions caused by HIFs and HPD.

Modern economy leaves behind huge pollution, which favours GW and CC; but HIFs, HPD (as in poor and developing countries), and over-dependence on industry-based economies (as in developed countries) create more GW-promoting agents. The world cannot afford to continue this endlessly, so we must think in terms of Green Economy (GE) or Nature-based economy with zero pollution.

Mistakes Committed by Economists

Economies deal with almost fixed quantities of resources, job opportunities and business dealings and almost fixed or predictably varying numbers of people. With these data, economists and planners must be able to compute a clear picture of the economy of a given region in accordance with the changing time, and by giving ample space for unexpected natural calamities.

With the above computations economists dealing with a particular region or country can give only a one-directional prediction—either positive or negative—and an appropriate solution. But most of our economists have failed us regularly. It is an obvious shame that they do not agree with one another in most instances, and often predict in diagonally opposite ways. They have not been able to predict great falls which shook many apparently affluent countries, and often failed even to give the right "post-mortem" report or recovery course. The right solutions they rarely suggest appear to be predictions and are rarely based upon rational computations.

Despite them, recoveries happen as per the instinctual adaptation and adjustments of humans and, to some extent, due to the natural "pruning" of hapless people. The harms of wrong or irrelevant policies and faulty ideas are many and costly in terms of monetary losses and human life. There are uncountable examples. The most obvious is the failure to eradicate humble poverty. Another sorrowful instance is that wrong policies have created situations where those who have not even seen a paddy or wheat field or milk cow enjoy a lavish supply of food items and are not able to work because of obesity, while the farmers who produce these food items starve and even commit suicide to escape the miseries and humiliations of hunger.

Again, no one seems to understand that over-industrialization is a desperate act to fulfil some kind of deficiencies they have created inadvertently, as we have discussed repeatedly. They also fail to understand that over-industrialization and over-urbanization are highly unstable and unsustainable economic situations, which even take away their freedom—as we will see now.

Many industrialized countries experienced uncertainties, and the shocking fall of the Japanese economy is a stark example. At last, even those rich victims themselves have failed to learn the right lessons; but make many more mistakes and complicate circumstances even further. Because of such costly ignorance, many newly emerging economies, like China, India, and Brazil, are indiscriminately industrializing with high hopes.

Permanent Structures Need Strong Foundations

Every permanent structure, built to last long, must be raised upon a strong and wider base or foundation. The structure of an economy must also obey this common sense truth. Many seemingly unshakable economies fail around the globe because of this fault.

Disrespecting the Provider

Every living creature is made up of and sustained by the elements of Nature and so must live as per the wishes or schemes of this provider. We came from Nature and at last will surrender everything back to it; and in between, Mother Nature sustains our life by helping us in our agricultural activities, and not, certainly, by helping us develop our great industries. It is not uncommon to see leaders stressing the importance of the agricultural industry, but how many really try to build it as a strong one? Now, it is the "illiterate" and "ignorant" people of the bottom-most layers of society who are engaged in traditional agricultural activities; and the "progressive," "enlightened" people with power to govern and make policies go as far away as possible from Nature. But it is the latter "aliens" who make policies for the farmers, too, and weaken the farming vocation—the foundation of sustainable economy and the base of the economic pyramid.

Shaping the Economic Pyramid

With our share of natural resources, we are supposed to build a strong foundation for our economy by producing food, raw materials, and even energy without hurting the mechanisms which help Nature sustain its fertility, health, and sustainability. Other activities, like construction, industrialization, transport, bureaucracy, etc., must be built with its strength; activities like mining and scientific advancements must be complementary to that. And when people plan for a sustainable living, the need for the highly polluting, "borrowed," extra energy must not arise or must be used temporarily for emergencies.

Bio, nano, and molecular technologies have grown to very high levels and have huge potential. Now we can mass-produce the desired farm products and have the technologies to convert the energy-packed biomass into various useful products of daily use, construction materials, and fuel. Now, bio-fuel production shows great success. Bio-fuels and other renewable energy generation can economically help farmers and those at the bottom of society, and have the potential to gradually replace the huge petroleum-related industry, which must be the most desired ambition of Mother Nature. The potential earning and saving of funds in these ways is enormous, and if nature-based energy generation is developed with vision, farming and related industries can flourish as the top economies and employ many times more people, ranging from unskilled workers to highly specialized professionals. Such a strong economy can form the strong and wide foundation of the economic structure, similar to the wide base of a stable pyramid. ▲

Factors which Demolished the Stable Pyramid

Mankind has been misguided by two great successes:

♦ The advantageous use of dirty-energy (petroleum and coal) and the "success" and progress we enjoy because of them.
♦ Our ability to produce huge, surplus, quantities of food by employing a fraction of the people needed for Nature-intended, comprehensive organic farming.

These successes, along with the advancement of allopathic medicine, have given us comfort, longevity, great hope, and a feeling of triumph over Nature. Further the endless entertainments often divert our attention from reality. Comforts and over-confidence have led us to many foolish acts, which worsen sustainability.

There was a time when the world faced starvation and craved more food. Humanity thought that cheap and surplus food could end human miseries. In fact, it ended their fears and starvation and gave brutal confidence to vast sections of people to create huge families (HIFs). Improved survival rates (aided further by medical technologies, which can be considered another misleading triumph) and longevity rapidly pushed up deficits in families and created HPD. Deficits of HPD, growing unemployment due to better farm technologies (like mechanized farming, which needs far fewer workers), and shrinking land-holding per family forced more and more people to quit villages. Because of food security, all of them confidently engaged in and developed non-farming industries and service organizations, which gave them huge profits and enviable salaries. This fetched them food in far easier ways than the way the poor farmers manage their hunger.

With the power of cheap food and cheap energy, they developed more industries and enlarged urban life (cities) with lots of entertainments and other facilities. Such a comfortable life blinded them to facts like the unsustainability of their life, worsening energy debts, the harms of urbanization (discussed in chapter 18), and the primordial position of food and their parent industry.

Thus, those mirages helped and are helping industries and cities to grow far larger than the real supporting capacity of the foundation— natural resources and agricultural industry—which further worsens unsustainable conditions, causes more pollution and more of the other factors which favour GW.

Newer Jobs and the Haphazard Growth of Economy

Technological and scientific achievements continue to create newer jobs, more options, and better comforts. The ambitious among the growing population opt for these newer jobs and build the economy haphazardly upon the already weakened foundation.

Now, in most countries, the income from the foundation industry contributes just a fraction of GDP. From Nature's and a common sense point of view, such a growth is highly unsustainable and unstable. One can always compare such economic structures to a multi-storied building built upon a mud foundation, to the Leaning Tower of Pisa and even to an inverted pyramid.

How Do People Sustain Patently Weak Economies

It is common sense that something must be there to prop up or support any unstable or weak structure. What are the props these unsustainable and unstable economies use? And how do the farming people of crowded villages (the bottom of society) live with that weakened farm economy?

Sustaining through Destruction
(Economy Propped up by Destruction)

People of crowded villages, including starving farmers, around the world plunder forests and other green cover (as through grazing, as fodder, manure for other crops, etc.), exploit bodies of water, the environment, and the various eco-systems to "strengthen"/ support/compensate their weakened (unsustainable) economy. All those destroyed assets are of vital importance to the long-term sustainability of the very people who destroy them, for the survival of other life forms, and for the health of Nature. In many poor and developing countries, forest destruction and related activities are going on at industrial proportion and millions of HIFs live out of its proceeds.

They are weakening their already weakened foundation to "fulfil" the deficits of their own creation. Even this destruction could not support the growing population caused by HIFs and so they migrate to cities to enjoy that deceptively glittering urban economy.

Sustaining the "Glittering" Urban Economy with Crutches

From the time people start migrating toward cities, their "normal" life is supported to a huge extent by polluting, dirty energy. This petroleum energy is a double-edged weapon. It gives life to their economy and at the same time slowly devitalizes them and threatens the whole of mankind and Earth through pollution, GW, and CC. Yet, for the urbanites, it is better and "wiser" to prop up their unsustainable economy/life with this crutch and die a slow death with pollution rather than dying early by not using this polluting crutch.

Stability is never attained with that crutch alone, because industrialized urbanites cannot live with what they produce. The products of industries and other urban activities, like services, must be sold somewhere; and so they need another crutch—an external market, which means rural markets for developing countries and markets of other countries for highly industrialized, developed countries.

The economic instability is far worse in highly urbanized developed countries because the vast majority of their people depend upon this non-farming economy, where the agriculture industry just forms the small part of an inverted pyramid ▼. Because of such severe instability, they desperately need those two major crutches—dirty fuel and external markets—without which their economy will collapse. It is dependence, and these crutches have taken away even their freedom. Because of this dependence or slavery, we can never expect industrialized developed countries to comply with the efforts to mitigate CC, like the Kyoto Protocol or the Copenhagen Accord.

Persistent Emergency Situation is a Wrong Signal

We now know the harmful nature of polluting energy, yet we desperately suck more and more of it from the depths, because we cannot live without it. It helped humanity to make revolutions, but at the same time, harmed the benefited people by making them lazy, obese, and victims of its poisonous effects.

There is nothing wrong if we had used it initially when we faced an energy crisis or to tide over a crisis as an emergency act. But this "emergency" situation (along with others, like speed) has become a permanent feature of modern society. From this sorrowful condition of "persistent emergency," the intelligent human species must understand that something is terribly wrong with us which needs radical correction.

Distinct Deficiency-Generating Situations of Poor and Affluent Countries

The whole of humanity suffers deficiencies or unsustainable conditions, which have created this difficult and self-destructive situation. But the factors behind the unsustainability of poor and developing countries differ to a considerable extent from those behind developed countries, so the corrections, too, differ to some extent.

Two-Layered Deficiency of Poor and Developing Countries

They created unsustainability by creating more people than their country's ability to support. They suffer two-tier unsustainable conditions in the form of too many HIFs (family level), invariably at the bottom-most layers of society (lower tier), and generalized unsustainable conditions (HPD/GULC) affecting everyone (national level, the upper tier).

Two-Way Deficiency Creations by Affluent Developed Countries

As discussed earlier, they appear to enjoy LPD-like conditions, but face unsustainability because of their lopsided economic endeavours (industrialization beyond their requirements) and rampant urbanization.

While people of the third world are forced to migrate toward the developing urban centres because of highly deficient HIFs and HPD in rural regions, in industrialized countries the huge opportunities in urban centres attract people, including those who enjoy a sustainable living in rural regions.

So the major solution for poor and developing countries is the prevention of HIFs, and for the developed countries it is mainly a structural correction—favouring rural growth and rural economy, which reverses urbanization, slows down industrialization, and reduces their dependence upon dirty energy and external markets.

Anticipated Tricky Situations for Developed Countries

Industrialized, developed counties must anticipate certain tricky situations when the countries which provide them markets realize OPD and economic stability by preventing the formation of deficient families (HIFs).

At present, because of HPD, the third world has wars, ungovernable conditions, and the inability to manufacture high-tech products. So they import huge quantities of war-machines and high-tech products, which support the economy of industrialized countries and cause proxy pollution.

When the third world reaches OPD, their need for such imports comes down drastically. Growing affluence may induce some among them to industrialize to fulfil their needs. Industrialized countries will face the closure of those industries and growing unemployment. Still the silver lining is that the same progress in third world countries will encourage the markets for luxury products.

As a primary step, developed countries must prevent HIFs among their dependent populations suffering unsustainable conditions. However the primary aim must be to restructure their economic pyramid with the wider bottom constituting real green wealth from Nature—like sustainable organic farming, including bio-fuels and renewable energies. Organic farming needs larger land areas and more water, yet its yields are lower. But it helps farmers realize the true (high) price, and they can buy more industrial products and gradually free their countries from dependence upon external markets. Rising food prices naturally make urban life difficult for ordinary people, which motivate them to return to Mother Nature.

"Symbiotic" Global Solution

There is also a wholesome global solution to the above tricky situation which mutually benefits the developed as well as present-day developing and poor countries. Industrialized countries must continue to make their national economic pyramid stronger and must do all they can to build a healthy economic pyramid at a global level. This structure works in such a way that the already industrialized countries can continue their relevant industrial activities and present-day poor and developing countries must strengthen their farm based economy further to make it part of the integral, wide base or strong foundation of that global pyramid.

By these "symbiotic" arrangements, poor and developing countries, then sustainable countries, can enjoy the great benefit of affluence and stability without resorting to polluting industrialization (see chapter 25, "Reversing Pollution"). To make this a success, developed industrialized countries must use their markets on an equitable basis, so that global disparities vanish and a global village will unfold.

Mutual Help

Ending global deficits is a must to end the factors which promote GW and to realize a strong "global economic pyramid." The problem of poor and developing countries (the vast majority of people) is HIFs, so they must be enlightened to wholeheartedly accept the PSCHHF norm until they reach OPD. The rich countries can help the poor countries and communities to make that a success by helping them to build infrastructural facilities and by extending required assistance for about five years. From then on (as we will discuss in next chapter), those nations will save enough funds to sustain the schemes and to repay the debts. When they gain respectable sustainability with the worthy assistance of developed countries, these diverse countries naturally reciprocate with gratitude by helping developed countries to market their products and universalize contentment.

Successful Economy

Imagine a country with one million families. With the right plans (preventing HIFs), if every family is helped to save just one dollar per day, they save one million dollars per day for that small country. Along with the other regular revenues, such countries can really enjoy wholesome freedom and face any economic challenge with confidence. But if they have unsustainable huge families, part of the savings of contented families will go as aid and to fight evils like crime and violence, which will drag the country down in direct proportion to its HIFs.

The world wonders at China's great growth. China does not have any great policies other than common sense. They suffered the curses of deficits and helped their couples form deficit-free families so that every family could save part of its earnings, and they do all they can to control "parasitism" and reckless, destructive activities.

China deserves great praise for its common sense and the ability to learn from others' faults. China, as an emerging huge economy, industrialized fast and had to depend upon other countries for markets. Now, from the weakening Western markets, it learns its fault and has started the correction process by doing all it can to empower rural populations (*Newsweek*, "Farms matter more than skyscrapers," April 12, 2010:14).

Revolutionizing and Restructuring
Economy for Fail-Proof Stability

Growth of the GDP is considered a reliable sign of the economic health of a nation. Rationally, growth must mean a growth that happens after ending all the deficits. But, when we look into many growing economies, we can see the presence of millions of hard working people below the poverty line, suffering starvation and premature death. (Countries like India, Russia, and Brazil have the richest people of the world and also the poorest.) It shows the existence of huge deficits—either because of "exploitation" in some form (which appears as growth) or because too many families are so foolish as to form huge families with deficits. (Because of this chronic foolishness and the indifference of poor people, too many of their well-wishers of the past, who really sacrificed something to see the end of poverty, are fed up and now prefer to mind their own businesses.) So such countries have nothing to be proud of and must do all they can to end those deficits first and then to feel proud about their growth.

Misleading GDP Growth

In many other instances, such boastings can be termed absurd and misleading. Quite often, monetary dealings or transactions, like salaries, prices of commodities, and income from other sources, grow parallel to each other and augment everybody's income. But they cannot enjoy a more hopeful high quality life because the advantages of growing income are annulled by the parallel rise of prices. In other words, the work done to gain a particular object remains the same, despite economic growth.

So it is praiseworthy to give importance to the idea of a stable, sustainable, equitable economy where the economy is stabilized (need not grow) in such a way to give equal high quality life for every honestly working family. Attaining such a wonderful state is not at all difficult. It naturally happens when families do not over-do to expand themselves to cause deficits and their governments do all they can for the rational distribution of population to utilize their resources and opportunities in the most advantageous ways to ensure equitable income. Equitable income or pay can further be regularized by quantifying the work done with any job and, of course, giving reasonable incentives for quality, innovation, research, and specialization.

Ending Irrelevance

It is basic common sense that an economy cannot function with huge deficits. Both the popular forms of economic principles, communism and capitalism, failed when practicing countries accumulated deficits. Communism succeeded in the past when the communist countries had surplus resources (including those of brutally wealthy landlords) for disposal. Communists grabbed and distributed those surpluses to the landless and the other poor, and minimized deficits, which made the masses happy and improved their economy. But, when the population exploded to HPD levels, deficiencies soared and they could not do much. Then it was a policy similar to PSCHHF, which made China a respectable second biggest economy.

Capitalism needs surplus funds (profits and savings) and vibrant, free markets. Whatever success is achieved by them is a gift of dirty energy (which offsets the inherent huge deficits). So, if oil prices go up and their markets in other countries weaken, they cannot perform, and now they seek the help of "Communist" China, who now practice "commonsensism," not communism.

It is time common sense was applied and planning aimed at ending deficits and realizing contentment. Contentment supports a healthy way of living and goes against GW.

31

Timetable for a Great Green Living

Huge Profits and Benefits of a Simple Act

Ending unsustainable living conditions is of vital importance to ensure a hopeful, peaceful, and happy life and even for long-term survival. As we have already discussed, unsustainable conditions, as HIF and GULC/HPD, always complicate our life far worse than what is rationally expected from the quantum of deficits. For instance, poverty is the most common expression of unsustainable living conditions. We usually assess the enormity of poverty in terms of the shortage of wealth, but how many of us think of the enormous damage and loss suffered because of the determined efforts of billions of poor people to escape from poverty? In addition to the funds spent to alleviate poverty, a country loses huge wealth and revenue because of its effects in the form of forest destruction, corruption, crime, crime-fighting, terror acts, funds to contain terrorism, protection of VIPs, medical expenditures for preventable diseases, etc. Further, the income of the nation falls due to failing work efficiency and productivity.

Similarly, ending unsustainable conditions yields far more benefits and saves greater funds than what one normally expects. Deficits are created through HIFs, so ending HIFs means gaining sustainability. In practice, it is almost impossible to end existing HIFs and their deficits (unsustainable conditions) for about twenty years, because we cannot remove a (deficit-causing) dependent to correct the equation. But when the dependants grow to become earning adults, it corrects/ reverses the supporters-dependents ratio. Yet, by this time, the family would have lost most of the joy of living as a family and also would have caused considerable harm to the society by contributing to HPD and its evils. So the only option left is prevention of the formation of HIFs. The formula PSCHHF (Planned Small Contented Healthy Happy Family) is the only rational plan that can do that, and with time it ends unsustainability in the most predictable and respectable way.

Chain of Benefits Due to PSCHHF

We know that HIFs multiply to form GULC/HPD, which torture people with evils and favour GW and CC, so when there are no more HIFs, the evolution of evils stops and then reverses toward sustainability and serenity.

In today's world, a very vast majority of HIFs are in poor and developing countries, especially in rural regions and slums. Yet, as we saw, the effects of HIFs and HPD (accumulating deficits) reach even far-off, developed countries (through migrants and "proxy pollution"). So instituting the PSCHHF policy benefits poor and developing countries first, and when they defeat deficits/ poverty and save huge funds, this prosperity (as in China and parts of India) benefits the "unstable" economies of industrialized countries.

When global economy begins to stabilize, highly polluting industrialized countries can integrate their manufacturing activities with other countries and can thereby drastically bring down global pollution and help mitigate GW and CC.

The Most Advantageous Equation and Early Gains

The most advantageous PSCHHF is that with the most positive equation of two supportive parents (father and mother) and only one dependent child. The calculations given here are based upon such small families.

The needy poor people at the bottom of society are the happiest beneficiaries of this magic formula. When poor families, which were recipients of huge assistance from governments, get freedom from deficits, the aid they receive is gradually saved at a national level. It becomes a good savings/income to the nation. When those small families spontaneously save their surpluses, they naturally enhance money circulation and boost the economy, as in China and India.

The progressively prosperous course described below is commonly observed in communities and countries where a small family norm similar to PSCHHF has been in vogue for the last few decades. (The figures given here are too conservative and based upon published reports and observations. Even these modest quantities will certainly impress every reader.)

Socio-Economic Benefits

The new PSCHHFs which had been suffering poverty for generations now enjoy a debt-free, hopeful, happy, and dignified family life and respectable social standing. Thus PSCHHF initiates socio-economic revolutions at the bottom-most layers of society. The progress starts from day one, yet it will take a few years for the country to realize the visible changes.

Gains after Five Years of Strict PSCHHF Policy

Many countries spend huge sums for poverty eradication in many ways, like subsidized or free food, free medical care, free education, and other ways.

After five years of strict adherence to PSCHHF policy, the planned, small, debt-free families normally enjoy economic stability and reasonable sustainability. Yet, because of the HPD conditions which will exist for many more years, some of them may require continuation of some of the above-mentioned support. But, such requirements are negligible.

The parents of these planned families enjoy ample leisure and family time. For them, their only child is the most precious "bundle of joy" in the world and they care for their child in the best possible way, with timely immunizations, nutritious food, and timely medical care. At the end of five years, it is almost impossible to see an ill-nourished child below the age of five years and the mortality rate of under-five children falls to almost nil, and if death happens, it does not happen due to preventable diseases. Because of this success, the whole family enjoys the best mental, physical, economic, "social," and intellectual health. The medical expenditures of these new and young families fall and their productivity improves. All this helps them and their nation save very huge sums.

Since these new couples have only one child, and since other eligible couples also are helped to end fertility, the funds these countries and families traditionally spend for pregnancy-related care are saved.

At global levels, at the end of five years, even these early trickles of savings come to billions of dollars per year.

After Ten Years

The number of planned happy families (PSCHHF) doubles. They and their governments enjoy all the above. Further, they experience even greater benefits such as:

Best overall child-care, best education, and progressive prosperity and freedom from liabilities help **narrow socio-economic disparities** and discrimination. The needs of these new families are lower, so young fathers in their late twenties and thirties need not earn as much as their predecessors. This **brings down the competition** for jobs and resources. As these new families are contented and healthy, their mind-set promotes stronger bonds and cordial relationships with other families and people. Such a life in dignity and cordiality brings every adult and child into all the socio-economic and cultural circles (mainstream), a really **inclusive growth.**

Huge amounts of government spending on primary education in poor and developing countries are saved because of fewer children and because most of these fewer children prefer private schools. (In India, the state of Kerala and my district in Tamil Nadu were the first to enjoy a fairly successful PSCHHF norm, where hundreds of government schools were closed due to lack of pupils.) Students get the best care, vast playgrounds, and opportunities for wholesome physical activities, group games, etc., which promote sane interpersonal relationship and greater understanding. These conditions develop them physically, mentally, psychologically, and socially, so the expenditure for health care also comes down dramatically.

Monetary gains: The savings made at the end of five years almost doubles and the expenditures on health care and primary education and the spending on supportive care like the noon meal scheme come down dramatically.

Double savings: Because of self-reliance and savings, the number of families seeking government support comes down. Now, the new families as well as governments save huge sums. Because of these double savings, the total gain at global levels must cross trillions every year and can be used for environmental activities, reforestation, and renewable energy creation, to save threatened species and even to rebury carbon.

Vibrant markets: With comfortable savings, these new families strengthen market forces by opting for high quality branded items, which further generate revenue for the state and improve international trade and the general prosperity of the world.
Countries like Singapore, South Korea, and China crossed this stage a long time ago and counties like India and Brazil have started enjoying this prosperity because vast numbers of their families voluntarily adopt the PSCHHF norm.

The overall gains are uncountable: The real overall gains are almost immeasurable. The gains are multi-dimensional, namely huge economic gains, better infrastructures, psychological and social wellbeing, growing hope and security, realization of peace and happiness because of vanishing unemployment and falling crime, corruption, and violence, and much more.

On the GW front: The number of rural families that compensate for their deficits through forest destruction and such activities comes down and those who can spare funds, time, and manpower for environmental and other such activities goes up.

After Twenty Years

General gains: All the above-mentioned benefits and savings multiply far more than expected and the level of poverty comes down dramatically.

Literacy and safer childhood: School drop-outs are rare and this leads to a growing literacy rate. Children will not be available for child labour or other types of exploitation because in every family there are at least two adults to care for a child round the clock.

Respectable employment and decline in disparities, corruption, and crime: Youths who have passed eighteen years and have sufficient education must replace ageing employees and labourers. Since small families enjoy more savings and since their requirements are low, the craving for more earning comes down reducing further the competition for jobs. Scarcities of work-force prompt employers to hike salaries, to improve working conditions, to install safety equipment, and to offer other benefits with the aim of attracting workers. Such progress brings down industrial accidents, increases comforts and security of ordinary people, lessens socio-economic disparities, and eradicates crime and corruption.

This progress gradually ends the availability of cheap labour in poor and developing countries. For example, until now, China enjoyed the availability of workers for low wages who worked hard for a longer time and hiked production, so their economy flourished. Rich countries shifted their factories to China. But that advantage is vanishing now because of the end of HIFs and the end of poverty. It shows real progress of a people which may not be good news for those who exploit.

Today, many countries, including small African and Central American countries, suffer hatred, suspicion, divisive thoughts, and chaos (like Rwanda or Afghanistan) because of HPD. If every HPD country of the world implemented the PSCHHF norm, all those repulsive traits would end and give way to love and trust and bring people and countries closer, like the EU. (Such a commendable progress and inclusive growth is not at all possible with any other policy.)

Monetary gains: Governments around the world are spending trillions to eradicate poverty and to fight crime, violence, and terrorism. Twenty years into the PSCHHF norm eradicates a very high percentage of the above evils and so the budget allocations for them also fall dramatically. The very huge parallel economies with black money and ruinous black deeds also start vanishing.

Simultaneously, most of the former aid-receiving poor families come to a stage to pay taxes. All the above huge revenues put those countries in good stead to create the best infrastructures and comforts to the people. The economy flourishes with a vibrant market force. With stability, peace, and hopefulness, countries come closer to sustainability. Now, governments can reduce the work-force dealing with poverty, policing, judiciary, etc. Or they can be diverted to valuable activities like reforestation and revival of a clean environment.

The yearly monetary gains at global levels come to many trillions.

On the GW front: As we see around the world, an unexpected harm is done at this stage; it is the trend toward more pollution. People with ample funds and leisure go for luxurious goods, especially personal automobiles, and boost the travel and tourism industry. All this tends to create more pollution.

Yet, vast migrations for economic reasons fall dramatically. When huge funds and a redundant work force engage in re-forestation, oil seed cultivation (for bio-fuels), and other such activities discussed earlier, like renewable energy creation, these can certainly bring down the pollution level. With time, these will turn the carbon-equation to the favourable side.

After Thirty Years

Socioeconomic life: Now every child and youth of the new generation (from the new-born to thirty years old) comes from a contented, happy family, and those between thirty-one and sixty years old are successful, happy parents. A small section of people above sixty may require some kind of support from governments. The number of ageing population will remain higher until the population stabilizes at OPD or LPD. That may take one or two more generations, depending upon their HPD. Yet the sustainable, small, happy families can look after their dear parents and grandparents with gratitude and love. The grandparents are the best baby-sitters and nothing can be more pleasant for them than spending years with their grandchild. Their experience is useful to manage household, farms, and other affairs. The number of ageing dependents can be brought down by improving rural life, as discussed earlier. Even if the family rejects and governments are indifferent, those well-lived old people can always buy care and comfort with their savings if they lived a planned life (see chapter 27 of *Book G*).

Toward a wholesome hopeful society: Unhealthy competition, unemployment, crime, and terrorism face a natural death if every family of the world has enjoyed PSCHHF all these years. Some issues, like unemployment, can remain at insignificant levels despite vast progress and prosperity in countries with too high HPD. China has successfully enjoyed the PSCHHF norm for more than thirty years, yet suffers some of these evils because of HPD, which will have a natural end with OPD or LPD, and taking care of their rural economy and restrictions on urbanization can do more for faster wholesome sustainability. Newly emerging economies like India, Brazil, South Africa, etc. will suffer unemployment and related evils for a longer time, even if their population declines, because still they have too many HIFs and suffer very high HPD because of the absence of proper guidance to form sustainable families (PSCHHF). Therefore, HPD will remain for a longer time than China. (This is the cause for more corruption, crime, and poor infrastructures in India when compared with China.)

Desired jobs increase productivity: Because of favourable employment conditions, almost every eligible person gets his/her desired job, earns comfortably, and becomes a dignified taxpayer. Such satisfactory jobs, close to one's heart, facilitate inventions and innovations.

Even for positions in politics, bureaucracy, judiciary, and other such jobs, only those with a real liking will take them up. Efficient and honest functioning, then, becomes natural and corruption and indifferent attitudes vanish naturally.

A tough time for vices: When people are educated, satisfactorily employed, and live as closely-knit, affectionate, small families, it is almost impossible to get youth to replace ageing criminal or terror groups, so such groups face natural death.

Opportunities for timely married life: All these growing "only-children" (now youth) of small families start earning with dignity and contentment, so they can marry at the right age (unlike those from HIFs). This can prevent sexually transmitted diseases and AIDS, and many other psychological and social ills related to sex.

Great inheritance: When these youths marry, the new families inherit the wealth of two families, and since they are comfortably employed, they enjoy a standard of living far higher than their poor grandparents and parents. When these new couples give birth to children, these fortunate children will have at least six adults waiting round the clock to care for and support that "bundle of joy." From then on, the naturally inherited resources become surplus for every new family. Such surpluses further boost forestry and other activities as discussed above.

A comparison with post-World War II Europe: We know how Europe earned LPD status in a ghastly way. Now, poor and developing countries have the formula to earn OPD or LPD status in the most humane and smooth way with no need to suffer like pre-1945 Europe. Hatred and discrimination of every kind will fade away. Then every people of every corner of the world will respect and love each other spontaneously and come closer, like the EU.

Savings on every other front and the clean-up: By now, normal state expenditures plummet to insignificant, low levels, and every country possesses huge funds, manpower, and other resources to do every act that takes their country back to the pristine status (with all its diverse inhabitants, including other life-forms) it enjoyed a long time ago.

Sudden fall in population and the need for more children: When PSCHHF is a universal policy for thirty years, population starts stabilizing in most regions, especially the regions which had a low HPD.

From now on, another dramatic change happens spontaneously for about five to six decades. Because of PSCHHF, the age group below thirty years (children and youth) remains half of that between thirty-one to sixty (parents), and those above sixty (grandparents) are of considerable numbers. Those above sixty years will exit within the next thirty years, which will stabilize the population. During the next (succeeding) thirty years, those parents will exit, which will bring down the population faster. Yet an HPD country need not worry at all, because even then it cannot reach LPD.

The fast decline gets arrested with the exit of the parents' generation. Most European countries and Japan have already experienced the first phase of stabilization and are continuing with the latter phase. The decline is felt in countries with low fertility rate. China will experience it in the coming decades.

As we see, governments of such countries encourage people to have larger families, but people are reluctant because of the wonderful life they enjoyed as small families. Yet, by now (from thirty years into PSCHHF), people must come forward to have families with two or even three children, in accordance with the prevailing population density.

Reverse migrations: Every country and racial group has migrants living among different cultural groups or countries, like "foreign bodies," socio-cultural orphans, and objects of curiosity. When crowded countries reach the second phase discussed above, migration becomes a curse of the past. Those who migrated away in desperation in the past can now go back to their roots with confidence.

Monetary gains at global levels: The global gains come to many trillions per year, with which a lot can be done as discussed above, including reburial of carbon, and can help victims of unexpected natural calamities (man-made calamities disappear to a great extent) anywhere in the world. No one can be greedy to grab wealth, and even if we heap money and gold on the roadside, no one comes to touch those "silly" things, because everyone has everything beyond his needs and enjoys a wholesome, high quality life. That extra wealth becomes a burden. (Ancient Tamil literature says that people in parts of India enjoyed such a life during the Tamil Sangam era about 2000 years ago.)

Wholesome Global Integration—Global Village

The economy of industrialized countries will suffer because of their faulty "foundation," unstable structure of society and economy, falling global markets, and industrialization of other countries. Yet, the huge savings and accumulated earnings of the former poor and developing countries can do a lot to stabilize the economy of unstable industrialized countries, provided the global leaders come together to form an integrated global economy as discussed earlier.

Wholesome life in freedom attracts people toward each other as respectable and trusted friends, so national boundaries become irrelevant and start fading. We can call such a reality a global village. A global village means real peace and happiness, and the most economical way of living, which goes against pollution, GW, and CC.

The Ultimate Formula

This timetable for great progress is not my imagination, nor is it some boastful utterance, but is taken from real life situations and historical happenings. Thus, PSCHHF is not just a formula or policy but a respectable liberator and a phenomenon, and it alone can save modern humanity from the dangers—from poverty to huge accumulated pollution and then GW and CC—they have created. The results of the PSCHHF norm are predictable and measurable.

The above progress is assured if every family of the crowded communities and countries of the world comes forward to stop with only one child for just one generation—for about thirty years. With larger families, it takes a longer time to realize that wonderful life.

32

Implementing PSCHHF

Deadly Consequences of Neglecting Simple Math

People of most countries have dangerously outgrown their resources, and the total global population has exceeded the supporting capacity of the planet. We committed this highly consequential mistake because we failed to mind the most simple arithmetic, that four cannot be subtracted from three, or $3 - 4 = -1$, and even the conspicuous $3 - 6 = -3$, while forming our own families. Under present-day conditions, an ordinary couple can earn enough just to maintain a family of three (two parents and a child) in a moderately sustainable manner. Every excess causes deficits in their families, which then affects the sustainability of their countries, creates the evils we have discussed, and drains nations' wealth.

One Cannot Cut the Feet to Fit the Shoes

We know that the life-supportive resources of our planet are of fixed quantities, and for a right balance, we can do only one act—regulating the variable human population against the life-supportive resources.

There are two options to bring about this correction:

♦ Leave the correction to Nature. Nature normally culls excess population in brutal ways—as it has been doing.
♦ Plan sensibly to voluntarily regulate the human population.

Nature always tries to restore the right balance in a hard way, by pruning the excess beneficiaries through starvation, crime, violence, terrorism, wars, infectious diseases, accidents, forcing to use poisoned food and water, suicides, poisoning through pollution, and at last, through the effects of GW and CC. Thus, millions of people die prematurely (culled or pruned) every year through these horrible processes.

The other method is voluntarily correcting the indiscriminate growth with suitable policies. We now know PSCHHF is a respectable liberator from man-made evils and the most wholesome policy for the HPD countries. Millions of families around the world enjoy the benefits of the small family norm. But unfortunately, many millions of families are too ignorant or oblivious of this plan and waste their lives in a horrible hell called HIF.

We have seen that life as HIF is horrible to the extent to institute continuous emergency services. Hence, there is no room for sentiments or ego related to religions, cultures, race, traditions, or anything which adversely interferes in implementing the formula which definitely prevents the above sorrows and pain and ensures dignity.

Most Appropriate Mode

For many reasons, it is ideal to have two children, per PSCHHF. Yet, in crowded regions, families find it hard to support even one child satisfactorily. One child is every couple's right and governments have the duty to support them, if necessity arises; but creating damaging deficiencies by having more children shows their intellectual poverty, as commonly observed in families which create economic poverty. It is wise to live with contentment and dignity as a three-member family rather than suffering pain and indignity as a huge family. So it is most rational to have only one child per family (the best ratio) in crowded regions for at least one generation, or until HPD falls to OPD.

Shed Fooleries and Learn From Achievers

We now know that PSCHHF is necessary for the well-being and the very survival of humanity. Every human must strive for its success. Unfortunately, there are Quixotes who trivialize the tormenting

HIFs and HPD for various reasons, like ignorance, contrasting perceptions (as discussed in Chapter: 33), wrong information, and faulty indoctrination.

The leaders of huge China and tiny Singapore implemented the small family norm (PSCHHF) with patriotic fervour when they understood its benefits. I say that it was with patriotic fervour that they did it, because that scheme was highly unpopular in those days with vast sections of their own ignorant people and attracted condemnation from almost all the Western countries and many human rights groups; yet those leaders were firm in their determination to implement that policy because they had the vision and were so sure that it was the only way to end the starvation (about forty million people died in China during the early 1960s due to famine/starvation), sorrows, and pain of their compatriots. Now their people enjoy real economic freedom and freedom from most of the social, cultural, and religion-related strife because of those visionary patriots.

Forty or fifty years ago, China and Singapore were teaming with hungry, angry people, but their government-sponsored PSCHHF did the magic that ended those miseries in the most painless way and made them stand equal with the most developed people within a space of about thirty to forty years. Their "humane" neighbours and other liberal countries around the world were in far better condition then, but are experiencing hell-like conditions at present because of the steadily growing population. Now, those very countries which condemned China and Singapore are soliciting their cooperation to end Western and global financial difficulties.

Unfortunately, even today, some Western countries, religious bodies, and organizations are committing many wrong acts in the name of humanism and rights without properly understanding the impact of deficits. This heaps sorrows and pain upon the people they sympathize with and also upon the world. If the world wants to recover from the huge deficits and sorrows and if the poor and developing countries want to see real happiness on the faces of their citizens, they must adopt the PSCHHF norm wholeheartedly as their national policy.

Hardships of Implementing PSCHHF Norm

For a distant well-wisher, implementing the PSCHHF norm may look simple because, for an ordinary poor family, it is nothing but the easy task of not going beyond the first childbirth. But poor and developing countries around the world and even poor communities in developed countries face many practical difficulties. So every country, poor or rich, must take this into account while implementing poverty alleviation schemes and as part of the fight against other evils.

Hurdles Between Poverty and PSCHHF

Ignorance: Family formation and childbirth are normal and natural events which must happen spontaneously at the right time in everybody's life. But modern realities expect people to be cautious. Millions of very poor young couples of our globe form huge, unsustainable families because of their ignorance about those realities. They often think that poverty and related sufferings are inseparable parts of worldly life and fail to plan rationally, so enlarge families as per instinct.

Absence of facilities: There are other millions who have passed the above stage and want to limit the number of their children with the aim of saving their families from poverty, but they do not have facilities for contraception.

Economic constraints: There are needy families living near well-equipped medical centres but avoid availing themselves of their services for social and economic reasons.

The misguided millions: There is another huge section of people who are fooled with wrong socio-cultural-religious ideologies propagated by irresponsible, ill-informed people. They even include educated people and trust that children are gifts of God or a strength to their families and communities and so feel that they must not interfere in any way with anything which brings in a new life. They fail to understand that the same God won't like to see His followers in poverty and indignity and so has given them brains to analyse existing difficulties to plan a worthy life. At last, when families suffer sorrows, starvation, and exploitation, those instigating preachers never come to their rescue.

Removing Hurdles

So enlightening the ignorant masses about the prevailing difficulties and need to plan a deficit-free family must be a priority. Then governments must create the best facilities for contraception and related care, support, and follow up, and warn the misguiding elements appropriately.

Enlightening and Educating

When ignorant people in misery are made to understand what is deficit, how they inadvertently create it, and how the deficits curse them with unending hunger, sufferings, sorrows, and premature death, and are made to realize the benefits of a deficit-free family life in dignity and helped to appreciate the easy ways to adopt PSCHHF, they will certainly cooperate.

It is high time every responsible leader and well-informed citizen took it as a patriotic service to teach the ignorant masses the prevailing truths like the following, in addition to the above.

- The needs of modern families are far more than they were in the past. Hence the modern families cannot support as many children as their grandparents could.
- Despite great progress in many fields, they have outgrown their fixed resources and job opportunities.
- Every family can certainly enjoy contentment and dignity by preventing its deficits.
- Alleviation efforts may end hunger, but they will never give the respectable life earned by preventing deficits. Every alleviation method falls into the undignified acts of "beg, borrow, or steal," which hurts the sensitivities of their growing children.

We now have wonderful tools like radio, TV, internet, print media, and film to carry messages even to remote regions. School education is another reliable influencing tool. When children are educated to understand the facts and real life situations in a graded way through school curricula, they will avoid those mistakes in the future. They will certainly propagate such knowledge among their relatives and ignorant neighbours.

Caring for the Remote Poor

Our world has pathetic people like gypsies, hill tribes, and marginalized, discriminated, and exploited poor who cannot be reached by any of those methods. But they are the people who need PSCHHF most. So it becomes the patriotic duty of every worthy government and service organization to do everything possible to reach them.

Zero Failure Means Great Future

Every worthy government has village-level health visitors, administrative officers, teachers, and workers of public (food) distribution sectors. Their services can be used to gather information, to teach the above, to motivate people to adopt deficit-free family planning, to take the innocent people to the right place to get the right care (like contraception) and other benefits, and for follow up care and to guide further.

Medical and Contraceptive Facilities and "Inclusive" Progress

Good health and timely contraception (that free families from deficits and debts) are the key elements which bring about a healthy deficits-free society in crowded (HPD) countries. As far as the poor are concerned, health and contraception go hand in hand, because almost all their health hazards, like malnutrition, prevalence of preventable diseases, high infant and child mortality, high maternal mortality, etc., are related to their huge deficits caused by their HIFs. Timely contraception certainly prevents those sorrows, ensures health and longevity, and above all, a respectable contented living which brings (includes) them into the mainstream of social and economic activities. As per my first-hand observations, studies, and experiences with thousands of families, this is the only way for the "excluded" poor to get included respectably in the national or global streams. Expecting others (as often promised by ill-informed leaders and economists) to take them into "inclusive growth" or as part of the respectable mainstream of people will remain a mirage until they remain deficient; because no one likes to be associated with needy people who "beg, borrow, or steal."

Importance of Rural Medical Facilities

Most urban areas of developing and even poor countries enjoy most of the modern medical facilities; invariably on a commercial basis. But rural regions lack even basic facilities for medical care and contraception. Because of this negligence, mortality, especially child mortality, remains high among the rural population. Hence, most of them think that if they deliver more children, at least a few will survive to see adulthood. They do not understand that the natural deficits associated with the huge families are the cause for their sufferings and premature death. Consequently, they often resent the idea of contraception and dig their own graves.

It becomes our duty to help them prevent such calamities. Establishing appropriate health care facilities under the supervision of a qualified medical team and employing health visitors will do wonders on the health front, which will build confidence in the minds of the ignorant poor to limit their families to one or at the most two children.

Facilities for Contraception

Prevention of birth (contraception) before ordinary families cross their limit of sustainable conditions is the ultimate act to ensure their health and happiness. The major target of campaign for contraception must be the young couples who are likely to have a baby soon, and the other target is every family with the potential to have more children. This simple-looking ultimate act is the magic which will end tough-looking poverty, crime, violence, forest destruction, species extinction, and pollution; and at last apply a brake to GW and CC.

We have two types of contraception, permanent and temporary. Each of these has its own place and importance.

As we have seen, it is the duty of every family to deliver one baby, even in the poorest regions, and to raise that child as a respectable, healthy citizen. But that noble aim will be marred when the number is exceeded. So, advising and performing contraception, preferably after the first birth, is the best option for underprivileged, innocent people. There can never be a greater help for such poor families than helping them to earn a sustainable, respectable living.

Permanent sterilization can be done to women a few days after childbirth, and after confirming the health condition of the baby. When in doubt, it is always wise to postpone permanent sterilization for a few years until that precious baby is in the best of health and progressing. In the meanwhile, temporary contraceptive methods like IUCD (intra-uterine contraceptive device) or other methods can be recommended. When the child becomes a healthy, active member of the family, parents can opt for permanent sterilization, which can be done to the mother or to the father.

Temporary methods are used even to postpone the first pregnancy with the aim of improving living conditions of the couple in order to receive the precious child with respect.

Health Care Facilities

Leaders and the medical fraternity often trivialize the act of sterilization because it is a very simple surgical procedure, but do not look into the psychological and other aspects of the ignorant poor villagers. Sterilization does not involve any vital organ at all. Yet complications due to unrelated causes can mar the sanctity of this noble act. One such complication is enough for those with vested interests to make wrong propaganda. If complications occur despite the best care in the best set-up with the best medical team, people accept that as an inevitable or "natural" happening. But when it happens in a not well-equipped set-up, it is always taken as negligence and irresponsibility. Too many families avoid sterilization because of the unavailability of reasonably equipped, accessible health care centres. Governments must do all they can to create such facilities in remote regions and improve transport facilities, too.

The ignorant poor who come for sterilization must be made to enjoy the best medical facilities in the best hospitable environment because it is the first major step in their journey toward a hopeful, happy life with dignity. Every person must be treated with utmost care and respect to prevent any ill-feeling or complications.

Pre-Natal Care

It is very common to see young brides coming from huge poor families suffering with anaemia, malnutrition, vitamin deficiencies, worm infestation, and diseases related to poor hygiene. Such are the young and ignorant girls/women who will soon become pregnant and come for the first delivery. Failure to correct those deficiencies can lead to complications during pregnancy and childbirth which affect the health and economy of the whole family.

These illnesses can adversely affect the development and health of the foetus, too. Under such circumstances, sterilization is risky for the mother, but unfortunately, these are the women who need sterilization most because their next pregnancy will be more risky and can even cost her the precious life or can cause severe health hazards. And again, with the next baby, that family will become an unsustainable HIF.

Improving the health of soon-to-become pregnant (newlywed) women with nutritious food, appropriate vitamins and minerals, de-worming, hygienic care, etc. is very important because they are the affectionate, responsible mothers who are going to take care of the development of a new pillar to their nation.

Post-Natal Care

Childbirth is a highly stressful period for every woman and even for their families. But quite often, the poor women with ignorant people around suffer difficulties. Newborn babies need the best care and disturb the sleep and rest of the poor mothers; that is the time they themselves need sufficient rest, care, and timely nutritious food, which are scarce in poor families. The comprehensive services of health workers and related village institutions can fill that vacuum to a great extent. Such timely services make a pleasant impression in the minds of those new mothers that will go a long way in their determination to form a respectable, happy family and be part of inclusive growth.

Monetary Support

The well-to-do families of the upper strata of society voluntarily adopt PSCHHF and they do not require any kind of support in this respect. But, for many reasons, those from lower strata certainly need monetary support, along with other help.

When a poor couple chooses to have the smallest family with only one child, they can easily procure their requirements. Yet in crowded countries, unemployment, unhealthy competitions, and other socio-economic evils will remain as nagging problems until they reach OPD, which will take about three decades, even if they adopt one-child families. Until then, some new families may need help in order to gain a healthy, respectable life in a smooth way.

It is Not at all Charity

We must understand that monetary support of couples who adopt PSCHHF is not at all charity. If the same couples prefer to have huge families, as they traditionally do, say, with three children, all of them—five people—require assistance from the government for at least two decades, and such assistance comes to enormous amounts. But when they form small families, they may require just a small fraction of that for a short period during the family's early, stressful days. Again, if huge families remain imprudent and indifferent, their next generation also seeks freebies and initiates social, political, and other evils; thus they waste huge national wealth. So we can say that the small funds required to support poor families to form PSCHHF are their own savings. In the normal course, they soon become contented, contributing tax-payers and support other such families.

It is an encouraging fact that benevolent governments have to spare funds just for about five years in these accounts, because by then those progressive countries save huge sums, as we discussed in the previous chapter, which will take care of those schemes. And with time, they will have surplus funds for nation building and carbon-reduction activities. But if left to form huge families, poverty, crime, and such evils, and the huge funds required for fighting such evils, will ruin the whole nation.

Socio-Economic Support through Reservations in Jobs and Concessions

HPD regions suffer evils like unhealthy competition, corruption, favouritism, and crime, which directly affect the members of small poor families, especially those with only one child, because of their small size and relative prosperity. It becomes a very definite duty of governments to protect those PSCHHFs from aggressive, malicious, and corrupt people. Prompt action against intimidators certainly gives them great hope and ensures their dignity.

Further, when small families, especially the urban poor like slum dwellers, are given preferential allotments in housing schemes, they live as mutually supportive groups and their children find like-minded companions and playmates. With such cooperation, they can resist the intimidation of huge families.

It is natural that the second and successive children of any family has an edge over single children in skills and knowledge; the only child often faces difficulties and so must be given sufficient concessions during admission to higher education and in employment and other opportunities. Extending reasonable lenience for appointments in departments like policing, judiciary, etc. gives them the much-needed feeling of safety and security; and when youths of contented families are in vital positions, corruption comes down.

Economic support for self-employment schemes easily strengthens the economic stability of PSCHHFs and they become taxpayers faster than the huge families.

There cannot be a greater service from the side of leaders and administrators than that which empowers the marginalized, includes the "excluded," and ensures the dignity of ordinary people. Implementation of PSCHHF norm does it in the most pleasing way.

33

Crossing the Hurdles

Sentiments which Help Poverty/Deficits Flourish

There is nothing that justifies any system, policy, ideology, sympathy, or service that imposes or helps impose deficits in families that curse the "recipient" with life-long sufferings and premature death (unless compensated for in shameful ways). Humanity could not end poverty because almost all policies and efforts aimed at its mitigation/eradication exhibit the sentiments and "virtues" of those handling it and not their understanding of it. These influential people as heads and planners of countries, service organizations, religious institutions, and even international bodies often repeated those "failed" acts in the name of fundamental rights, human rights, humanism, compassion, and such noble ideals, because they thought what they did was noble and right. The misery of the majority of present-day poor people, numbering billions, is the "gift" of those "noble" people with power.

Ignorance and arrogance form a bad combination, and when power joins them, the blend can cause havoc. Humble visionaries have often suggested near-perfect policies to end poverty, but they often faced the above combination. Vast sections of ignorant poor masses have wrong understanding, and so they appreciate the above "compassion," and often think that they suffer deficits/poverty because of rich people and "impotent" governments, and so feel that the rich people and governments have the duty to sustain them. In such contexts, democratic governments fear flak and fail to adopt the most rational policy.

Grant the Poor the Opportunity to End Deficiencies

Instead of trying to end their poverty or unsustainable living conditions in a humiliating way through freebies and other helps (which failed them time and again), they must be helped to end or prevent their unsustainable wrong family-equations. Experience says that ending the wrong equation is more important than giving material support, and now we know that the PSCHHF norm does that job with dignity and without any room for the humiliating "beg, borrow, or steal."

Historical Interference and Indifference

There are many past instances where vast groups rose against "cruel" visionaries and governments when they introduced "small family norm" in the name of family planning, and even condemned them as anti-poor and inhumane monsters. Those with vested interests and loud foul mouths created the feeling that such policies were created by enlightened people to cheat the ignorant, hapless poor, so many poor families ignored wise voices and suffered. Often, those "sympathetic" morons were really ignorant about the facts behind poverty.

The horrible experiences say that being a party to the creation of poverty (HIF) or being a silent spectator of poor couples begetting children beyond their ability to support, amounts to a crime and is an anti-national act (treachery). With PSCHHF, or rational family planning, families create three or four contented, respectable citizens (parents and one or two children), but by misguiding them or by failing to act, those directionless leaders help ignorant couples create five or more discontent, undignified, starving people per family. It pains those families and drains national wealth and peace. Is that not treachery? Would those traitors ever allow their children to share the starvation and miseries of the poor they created?

Anticipating the Quixotes

There were huge protests and riots when the life-saving smallpox vaccination was made compulsory, but visionary patriotic leaders courageously stood against those morons. Because of Edward Jenner and the wise and courageous visionaries, smallpox is now history. Similar morons are present even in these enlightened days, and we can always expect some protesters even when benevolent policies like the PSCHHF norm are implemented. To avoid strained situations, distractions, and failures, attempts must be made to enlighten ill-informed activists, too, about the worth of PSCHHF, and provisions must be made to reprimand and punish those irresponsible, misguiding people for the sufferings of those huge miserable families.

The Result of Quixotic Interferences

Because of declining populations, certain developed countries recommend more children per family, but conditions are just the opposite in poor and developing countries. So their understanding/perception of poverty and population differs, too. That is why organizations, governments, and even people of rich and contented countries condemn any policy that recommends the curbing of childbirth. Quite often, the comfortably-living arm-chair activists, irresponsible political and religious leaders of poor and developing countries join the above.

In the past, such people obstructed population-related policies and even threatened to stop aid to poor countries that wanted to implement the small family norm. So poverty was created again and again, even in the families which had already suffered enough and survived on humiliating aid. With time, they create HPD and suffer more. If those Quixotes did not exist, our world would have been a far better place to live in.

Safeguarding Freedom Gives Us Rights and Privileges

It is the fundamental right of every human to enjoy every freedom like economic, social, religious, political, "personal," etc. But no one ever pours or donates those gifts like rights and freedom upon the needy. Hence, it is the duty and responsibility of people as individuals and as families to earn all those freedom and rights by fulfilling their duties and responsibilities and with rational plans and discipline. Moreover, freedom is not at all a permanent gift; absolute freedom must be earned and possessed with continuous efforts and, if needed, with struggles and sacrifices. When all those different freedoms are earned and protected, the question of rights never arises. But, when irresponsible couples make their families unsustainable, they lose economic freedom first, and then the other freedoms. After indulging in such foolish acts of forming HIFs, fighting for their "rights" and privileges becomes an awkward act.

Help People Earn Respectable Freedom

Quite often, a contented life with rights and freedom is inherited from parents or grandparents who, in their turn, have earned them through their hard work and sacrifices. But the beneficiaries often fail to understand the value of their freedom and the sacrifices behind it because of unchallenged living. As we saw earlier, it is not uncommon to see such rich youths or people, and even countries, squandering away or misusing their inherited wealth and freedom.

Most of the "enlightened," developed countries enjoy prosperity and freedom from many evils because their forefathers suffered and sacrificed their comforts. But the present generation of "ignorant" leaders, activists, and educated people are squandering away those freedoms and rights. It is the height of foolery on the part of any people to demand something as their rights after foolishly losing the possession of them through irresponsible acts.

No government can ever enrich irresponsible people and it is not the duty of governments to shower freebies and comforts indiscriminately and indefinitely upon indifferent people, especially upon those with healthy limbs. These thoughtless handouts amount to plundering the contributions of patriotic, hard-working people and tax-payers to the development of their country and safeguard its freedom and dignity. In practical life, such spontaneous freebies often misguide irresponsible recipients and blunt their sense of responsibility and the need to plan.

In such circumstances, it is always better to make the targeted people understand their responsibilities and ability to prevent their family-deficits. Setting reasonable conditions, including quid-pro-quo, really helps the dependent poor earn respectable freedom and dignity.

It is the duty of every government to do all it can to maintain peace, to prevent exploitation, and to guide people to form the right size families, so that citizens will (must) earn their freedom and dignity with pride and respect.

Kindly Act on Behalf of Unfortunate Children

We know that the acts of fulfilling deficiencies of huge families fall within "beg, borrow, or steal." No parent has the right or "freedom" to subject his children to those humiliations. But HIFs certainly do that. We punish people when they harm others; but we do nothing when irresponsible parents make their children subhuman, disrespectful creatures. There are innumerable instances where ignorant parents, rather foolish traitors, make their children earn for the family as child-workers, neglect and throw them into streets, sell some of the children to support the others, make them sex workers, and even force them to beg for the family. Yet no one comes forward to prevent such shame from happening again and again in families, and no one indicts the barbarous parents.

Now it becomes the duty and right of children to force their parents to adopt the PSCHHF norm. Since those children are minors, powerless, and do not have much knowledge of how to make such demands, governments must act on behalf of children and force parents to "plan" a deficiency-free family.

Dangerous Right to Fertility

It is a right argument that no one has the right to curb the fertility of others. But one's fertility must not create situations which curb their and others' freedom, honour, hope, and well-being.

Child Mortality and PSCHHF

A high rate of child mortality is natural to any region with a very high presence of unsustainable, poor families. Too many activists and ignorant masses think that when poor couples deliver many children, at least a few will survive to create the next generation. But this statement or thought is the mother of all stupidities, because child mortality is the result of the prevalence of unsustainable living conditions as huge families with the deficiency of every good thing.

When children of HIFs suffer from insufficient care, malnutrition, unhygienic environment, unsafe shelter, and exposure to repeated infections, they easily succumb to even trivial infections. I have treated children of both extremes. The survival chances of the well-cared for, well-loved, regularly-immunized, and well-nourished children from infectious diseases is as high as about five hundred to a thousand times, and even more when compared with those of severely malnourished children.

Maternal Mortality as a Cause for Activism

There are activists who take maternal mortality as the reason to fight any effort which tries to limit pregnancies. They do not want anyone to interfere in the fertility/pregnancy-related affairs of poor people. From my own experiences and other studies, I can say with 100 percent certainty that high mortality among poor mothers occurs because of indiscriminate childbirths and related complications and curses; and such sorrows can be prevented only with PSCHHF.

As we saw, it is very common to see among poor, crowded communities a very high percentage of young wives and mothers suffering from malnutrition, anaemia, and other deficiencies. When their families and countries care for the young pregnant wives satisfactorily, their first childbirths go smoothly.

If those new mothers stop with only one child, they can get nourished to good health and look after the child and family. But if they become pregnant again and again, their sufferings multiply and lead to risky pregnancy and labour; because:

- They have to look after their existing children and family, despite pregnancy.
- Successive pregnancies make them weaker, anaemic, and exhausted.

♦ Their health often worsens because of lack of rest and sleep.

♦ When a family grows, poverty and starvation also grow and affect physical and mental health.

♦ They cannot have the best personal hygiene and clean environment, which exposes them to many infections and worm infestations.

♦ A huge family prevents the mother from getting timely medical care.

♦ Even among well-nourished women, mortality tends to rise with successive pregnancies because of a scarred, malfunctioning uterus which often fails to contract soon after childbirth. This causes severe bleeding.

♦ With ageing and because of above stresses and strains, they develop diseases affecting other organs which also contribute to mortality.

It is clear that allowing a poor woman to have more deliveries is an unpardonable sin and inhumane act, so encouraging such dangerous acts is barbaric and must be stopped at any cost.

Derangement of Sex Ratio

There are people who argue that the sex ratio is deranged in favour of male children in regions where pregnancies are restricted.

In fact, this happens because of selective abortions for various social and economic reasons. But the ratio never deranges due to honest adherence to the one-child-family formation.

Unusually High Ageing Population

As we have discussed, the percentage of the ageing population remains high for about two generations when families of crowded countries strictly adopt the one-child formula. They face certain economic difficulties; but wise management of this state, as described already, eases it. All those difficulties will get corrected when the children of a universal PSCHHF policy become grandparents, because of the faster decline of population caused by the exit of the previous two generations which constituted the majority. This brings the population density near OPD. When they regain OPD, it is advisable for families to have two children, which would ensure the most advantageous population with almost an equal representation of all different age groups.

Children of one-child families naturally inherit more than double the wealth of their parents. Such prospering children and families cannot shy away from the responsibility of caring for their ageing people. Moreover, because of the intimate, well-bonded family life of one-child families, ageing grandparents and parents get seamless and smooth care in most families; they are neglected in huge families for reasons we discussed earlier.

Even if those ageing couples do not get the care they deserve, the well-planned old people naturally have enough savings to buy the services they require. But problems are natural in countries (like the developed) where more and more families split without understanding the importance of family life and where governments indiscriminately shower on aged people what they call old age benefits. If those governments help their people understand the value of a planned family life and encourage them to develop and sustain the habit of saving from younger days, such pains never occur. Further, governments and service organizations must help people have healthy and frequent social interactions and teach every age group the psychological, social, economic, cultural, and political advantages of wise use of a worthy and liberated religion.

Religious Hurdles

Various religions were formed at different points of time many centuries ago when the global population was just a fraction of what it is now. Despite surplus resources, many died early in the past because of infectious diseases, rampant exploitation, and wars, so having more children heightened the chances of their survival. But today, it is just the opposite, and yearning to have more children means leading those children to poverty and sorrowful death. There cannot be a greater cruelty, sin, and treachery than this foolish act, yet people keep committing this unpardonable cruelty, sin, and crime in the name of

God and religion. No worthy religious leader ever allows its followers to "beg, borrow, or steal," or "cheat, beat, or kill." Yet our world has too many fraudulent preachers, priests, and other religious leaders who exploit the poor in too many ways, to enjoy a lavish life. Since ignorance, illiteracy, poverty, and desperation of people are the capital of their "business," they never help remove such shame and even promote huge families, which naturally acquire those sorrows. If they face rivalry or challenges, many of them do not even hesitate to promote hatred, violence, and terrorism. Such malevolent people (intellectual terrorists) in religion (and in other spheres, too) must always be identified and indicted sternly in the most appropriate manner.

Humble Request

Never be a hurdle on the way of any people trying to form a sustainable, respectable life through PSCHHF, because that alone will narrow disparities and an unequal distribution of wealth (see chapter 63 of *Book G*) and slowly curtail the acts which lead to GW and CC. Ordinary people must be enlightened to understand all the above hurdles, and governments must be serious about those who misguide and exploit innocent poor people.

34

The Cost of Imprudent Benevolence

Wholesome Understanding of Problem Gives Effective Solution

The aim of this book is to enlighten the world on the real starting point of the evils we live with (creating unsustainable families) and the only solution (creating sustainable families) that ends them. These facts appear to be too simple and often make me wonder why humanity has failed to end the evils.

Most humans are prudent enough to find a solution when they have a wholesome understanding of a problem. So when mankind, especially the suffering poor people, understands HIFs, HPD, and the way they created the ills and evils, they certainly appreciate the importance and efficacy of PSCHHF and accept it. But imprudent handling of these affairs denies the affected people the opportunity to learn the facts and so worsens the situation further as is happening now. Until the poorest of the poor understand the various aspects of deficits, the situation will continue to worsen.

Hopeless Scenario

Aiding the poor and the needy is a necessity, but it cannot go on endlessly. Prudent schemes aimed at ending poverty must end it in about twenty years (ending poverty doesn't always mean sustainable living), and must give the beneficiaries dignified freedom from wants. Unfortunately, in many regions, it has gone on for generations, yet the number of people seeking aid is going up. The gigantic stupidities of the aid-giver and the beneficiaries further are exhibited by the stark fact that there are chronic aid-receivers who demand such assistance and other benefits as their rights and privilege, and even stage huge protests in this regard. Such scenes including the demand for reservation for jobs and education facilities (even by well-educated rich people) are very common in India because these schemes have not ended their feeling of hopelessness and deficits despite enjoying benefits for more than six decades.

Unfortunately, no one, including the government, taught them their role in creating deficits/ poverty and their ability to end it. Humanity must end such a sad state of affairs because such long-term assistance affects the honour and dignity of the sensitive aid-receiver, affects a nation's progress, and makes tax-payers furious and cheated (a major cause of tax-evasion), and thus creates social disharmony.

Benevolence That Obstructs Introspection

Studies show that most organizations and governments which help the "well-settled" poor (as against the victims of calamities) do so as a routine and the poor, too, utilize that help as part of their normal life. Such spontaneous and "routine mitigation" takes away the need of the aid-receiver to introspect and understand why they require freebies and others enjoy economic independence. Then how can those ignorant masses act rationally to end their deficits?

At last, those people with unending deficits never understand that they alone can and they alone must end their deficits and the related pains they suffer.

Studies very emphatically assert that educating the beneficiary poor people and training them how to use incentives and quid-pro-quo judiciously help them recover fast from economic dependence and so education and training must be part of the schemes aimed at ending poverty.

How People Lose Touch with the Original Deficit

We know that the deficits primarily evolve in HIFs. Poverty is the foremost visible expression of deficits, and the other evils evolve after poverty. Most often, victims or perpetrators of the "earlier evils" like crime, corruption, or violence do not bother or know anything about deficits because they are in a confused state with too many problems on hand to be solved. Those who are well adapted to these parasitic jobs are often "content" with what they do and if we try to enlighten them on this problem by saying that they do such acts because of the deficits created by their families, they are certain to abuse us because they are far away from the original deficit and oblivious of those situations.

As far as other people are concerned, as we have repeatedly discussed, every evolved evil acts in a vicious fashion and worsens the other evils, augments their deficits and changes the scenes. That is why a vast section of our leaders, planners, and aid-receiving poor say that poverty is there because of corruption, crime, violence, terrorism, illiteracy, exploitation, etc.

Thus the passage of time and changing scenes hide the real cause, so governments simply alleviate poverty and at last fail to eradicate it, but even worsen it.

Additional Blinding Factors

In addition to the above, there are many selfish, lazy, cunning "leaders" in religion, society, cultural circles, and politics who misguide and exploit the ignorant poor in many ways and invariably put the blame upon others for their poverty and sufferings. It is very easy to cheat the desperate, ignorant poor by many a devious way, and as long as the poor remain desperate and confused about their unending sorrows, they will succumb to those fraudulent "saviours" in any field.

Intensive Education of People

For the above reasons, expecting the ignorant poor to earn a dignified life by ending deficits is wrong and most of their leaders of the above category cannot be trusted. So, intensive and proactive education using every opportunity and the various media (discussed earlier) must be considered a national duty. It is not just the poor who must be educated, but all sections of people—those in responsible positions and those dealing with the evolved evils including GW and CC—so that prudence will prevail at every level to end deficits.

Double Whammy

Millions of migrants are enjoying a more peaceful and orderly life with many benefits and rights that they do not enjoy in their own countries. Developed countries enjoy a kind of OPD-like condition because of the employment opportunities created by heavily polluting economic activities and keep on attracting more migrants. Thus, they, in fact, are worsening their already worsened huge energy deficits and also demography and population density.

The emigration of job-seeking youth from poor and developing countries eases their unemployment levels and unhealthy competition, and their huge remittance to their home countries improves the living conditions of millions of families in poor and developing countries. All this gives deficit-prone societies and countries a feel-good situation which makes it unnecessary for them to think of their deficits and, thus, they continue to do the wrong acts of deficit creation.

Thus, deficiencies of both countries—the industrialized and the poor—worsen.

Using the Stability of Opportunist Regimes

As we saw earlier, many countries have been groaning under autocratic and authoritarian rule or "pseudo-democracies" for a long time. All of them suffer huge deficits, and in one sense it is these deficits, their ignorance, and the ensuing crimes, corruption, and ungovernable conditions that help the brutal and cunning rulers impose their authority. External interference in any name—like promoting democracy or ending suppression—worsens the already pathetic situation, because it gives many reasons for rulers and other vested interests to vitiate the scene. Many such regions suffer chaos and violence for decades. (Historic happenings in Vietnam and present-day Pakistan, Cuba, and North Korea are a few among too many examples.) Instead of disturbing whatever stability those people enjoy, it is prudent to use that stability to teach them the lessons of deficits through common friends and other friendly channels. Such non-interference gives those people and leaders enough opportunity for introspection and to prove for themselves the existence of their huge deficits. With time, such a prudent approach gives them economic freedom and hope, which naturally pave way for saner natural democracy.

Conclusion

This prudent way of handling and educating the poor and ignorant people and countries can change the course of our world and confer a sustainable, happy life upon every section of people faster than any other means.

35

The Precious By-Products of the PSCHHF Norm

Contrasting Worries and Concerns

Today, the anxieties and worries of educated, well-informed people are about pollution, GW, and CC because they can visualize their catastrophic consequences. But a majority of mankind bothers the least about these or does not know much about them. For them, poverty, unemployment, crime, corruption, intolerance, fanaticism, violence, etc. are the curses to be eradicated. In contrast, the worry of the lovers of Nature is about the threatened and vanishing precious species of life forms and their habitats, like virgin forests.

Yet there are power-hungry, money-loving, immoral exploiters who have no worry about anything except their position, "pound of flesh," and pleasure. Unfortunately, these are the people who work tactically to occupy powerful and influential positions in many third world countries and plan for their "hopeful" future.

By-Products of One Group's Triumph are the Desired Gifts of Others

Because of day-to-day experiences and the awareness created, the attention of responsible people of the world is focused on pollution, GW, and CC to an appreciable extent, but as we have seen, the worries of most others are different. Fortunately, all those diverse people can realize their noble ambitions and even those power-hungry people will lose their greed and madness when the win-all formula of PSCHHF is implemented.

Thus, when one group sincerely tries to eradicate an evil—for instance, crime—by using the formula PSCHHF, the other evils like poverty, violence, forest destruction, polluting activities, etc., too, gradually end. Similarly, when efforts are taken to end GW and CC through PSCHHF, all the sequential evils and ills which appeared before these will vanish naturally.

Thus, one person's success gifts other people with their desired freedom (end of evil) as its by-products. So the cooperative efforts of every different people fighting the diverse evils become mutually complimentary and make everyone happy in the shortest possible time. Utilizing this formula in any name, under any banner, or for any of the above evils will give relief to all. That is the worth of PSCHHF.

Emotional Sacrifices versus Rational "Enforcement"

I know politicians, bureaucrats, religious leaders, philanthropists, service organizations, social workers, professionals, and many others working honestly and with passion to end socioeconomic evils. I personally know people who sacrificed their precious time, wealth, and professional skills for the benefit of the needy with the hope that all of them (the benefactors as well as the beneficiaries) may see happy days within their lifetime. Because of such sincere sacrifices, some of those noble souls became paupers in their latter days and even passed away as unsung "orphans" because they "wasted" their prime days and precious wealth for others. Because of them, millions of families are living a respectable life; yet the noble souls invariably count themselves as failures because, despite those successes, the ills like poverty and social vices they targeted remain strong and kicking, and they could not see for themselves the hopeful, harmonious society they wanted to create.

But in regions or countries where policies similar to PSCHHF were "forced" upon needy people or when the poor were coaxed to adopt PSCHHF, evils vanished spontaneously, to give a hopeful happy life for all.

Do Not Blame Politicians, Bureaucrats, or Service Organizations

It has become a habit of long-term sufferers of curses to curse and blame their leaders, officials, other enthusiasts, and even happy neighbours for keeping them in poverty and allowing other evils to flourish.

We cannot blame anyone for somebody's sufferings, because every one of them had opportunities to form deficit-free families. Almost everybody living today is a victim of some evil, in some way or the other. Even powerful politicians, bureaucrats, religious leaders, and those in service organizations suffer evils like unhealthy competition and crime, and feel the impact of violence, terrorism, pollution, GW, and CC.

Because of such unfavourable conditions, everybody is forced to be busy and to ensure his safety, rights, and position. For instance, leaders in any democratic country spend a considerable part their lives convincing people and moving to the top; the officials do everything to satisfy their superiors so that they can get promotions in time, and they even use corruption and crime as ladders. Thus a huge part of their precious time is wasted. For various reasons we have discussed, unlike in the past, most of them choose those "professions" as a socio-economic necessity and not out of dedication. Most of them become selfish and try to safeguard their interests and those of their own people. In that process, the people who render a more sincere service with dedication and vision become a minority and they invariably remain voiceless amid ambitious sharks.

Under these circumstances, expecting others, especially in poor and developing countries, to lift the poor and other sufferers up is foolishness, so everybody must try to understand the obvious realities and act with reasonable sense to prevent/minimize deficits in their families.

Necessity for Fail-Proof Policies

We don't have time to waste, so patriotic people in responsible positions must come out with failure-proof policies to end the targeted curses and dangers in a predictable way.

When a policy is made with basic common sense and with the right understanding of the problem, that problem ends in a predictable way within a timeframe. Policy-makers must be able to explain step by step how their policy works to end the problem. Even a common man can verify the worth of a policy by asking why, what, how, and go step by step to reach the target. If not, that policy will become another curse. Our universal formula PSCHHF passes all those tests and can be applied to solve every problem related to HIFs and HPD.

Everybody's Responsibility

For various reasons, like urban living, other harsh impacts of unsustainability, and lack of time, policy makers fail to go to the bottom layers and remote regions to understand the problems firsthand. Most policy makers do so with the knowledge of their college education and with unreliable statistics and second-hand information. That is why the world suffers poverty and other evils and that is why the Kyoto Protocol met a premature death and its "responsible" authors are not even able to give an "autopsy" report of it nor could find a solution in Copenhagen and its follow-up meetings. It is time everyone asked the authors of any policy to explain its practicability and time-linked progress.

For the reasons discussed above, entirely depending upon such people in high positions often will give heartaches, as we suffer now. So it becomes the patriotic duty of every citizen and globalist to understand the degree of unsustainability or quantum of deficits and help innocent people around them form sustainable families through PSCHHF. Then it will prevent any more deficits in ignorant families and end their curses as the main product or by-product. With time, general deficits (GULC/HPD), too, shrink and abolish the ingredients of the various "recipes" behind the evils and curses, including terrorism, pollution, GW, and CC.

36

Rational Action-Plans to Regain Sustainability

Critical Agenda

We know that deficits, deficiencies, or shortages created by people, ranging from the poorest of the poor to the most developed and rich, act like invisible infection by disease-causing bacteria (the real disease), as we discussed in chapter 3 ("The Simile"), and create threatening signs and symptoms which we mistook for the real disease. People in general create deficits through HIFs, and highly industrialized and over-urbanized countries cause deficits through their lopsided economic activities. PSCHHF is the only "formula" that can gradually end HIFs and indirectly correct the unsustainable deficit-causing economic activities of industry-dependent and over-urbanized countries. So, if we have the will to implement the PSCHHF norm, we can end or drastically reduce the factors which promote GW and apply brakes to CC. And, as a bonus, PSCHHF ends almost all the social, economic, political, religion-related, and other evils and curses, as we have discussed repeatedly.

Under present-day conditions, bringing down pollution levels and green-cover destruction to an equilibrium with Nature's ability to manage (zero pollution and zero destruction through OPD) alone cannot ensure the wholesome, sustainable life we desire because we have accumulated those damaging pollutants, like greenhouse gases, to highly dangerous levels and have destroyed far larger areas of green-cover than the levels which can be renewed by Nature at the present pace.

We must reach a position to release more of the natural resources we control and to spare our energy, funds, and time to assist Nature to do its noble job, and also to find alternate sources of energy to reduce the use of polluting fuels and then to dispose of the accumulated pollution. Such a rational and "penitent" act can be done only when we reach LPD, so the aim of the whole plan must be LPD.

Until then (and even afterward), we must do all we can to contain GW and continue present-day mitigation activities like:

♦ Improving technologies for efficient use of fuels.
♦ Substituting petroleum with bio-fuels.
♦ Harnessing the energy of wind, sunlight, bio-mass, tidal waves, small streams, etc.
♦ Containing forest destruction and promoting green cover.
♦ Forging international understanding/accord to strengthen the above efforts.
♦ Discouraging carbon-guzzling industrial and other activities; a carbon-tax can be imposed, but those funds must be wisely used for the above and to bring about LPD.

Indifference Withholds Progress

Humanity suffered costly defeats in its fights to eradicate the evils it has created because we never told people the "secret" behind these evils (deficits) and their solution (PSCHHF). Further, spontaneous poverty alleviation services (from the time of one's birth) take away one's opportunity and need to think (introspect) and plan. Vast numbers of families around the world are forming small sustainable families and alleviation efforts have brought millions of poor families above the poverty line, but the benefits are not at all realized to the extent they should have been because still thousands of families cross their limits every day to create HIFs. A small percentage of such indifferent families (about 10 percent) is enough to nullify the positive achievements of other families.

The Foolery of Creating More Deficits at High Cost

Often, the freebies give the beneficiaries sufficient hope and "contentment," which takes away the compulsion to have small families, and they perpetuate the necessity for more assistance. Thus the precious mitigation funds help many families create more deficits and more evils. Is it not foolery? To avoid this foolery, implementing 100 percent PSCHHF must be part of the policies and programs aimed at ending poverty, crime, violence, terrorism, and even pollution, GW, and CC. Global organizations and rich countries must help the needy countries and people until they reach LPD.

End Cannibalism to Save National Pillars

It is the moral duty of every able human to support the victims of unexpected catastrophes, but no healthy, normal individual or family has the right to live for a long time (for decades or generations) at the expense of other people. It is the duty of such dependent people to plan meticulously to end their shameful dependence at the earliest possible time. If not, such dependence silently devitalizes or even kills patriotic, hardworking, ordinary people, like farmers and honest tax-payers, as is happening now. Is it not cannibalism?

Many planners and people fail to look into the details of the sources of huge aid. Other than taxes collected from well-to-do people, vast quantities come directly or indirectly from the hard-working, self-respecting, poor farmers and such people whose labour and products, like food materials, are heavily undervalued to satisfy irresponsible and indifferent poor people, the common man, urbanites, and even rich people. Their sweat, blood, and even life go as unsung sacrifices to keep alive the aid-receiving irresponsible people. In India alone, thousands of hard working farmers and their family members die every year for causes related to these.

Ending such chronic dependence is a vital necessity to save the honour and life of honest, hard-working people who are the vital pillars of any country

Do Not Repeat Mistakes

In addition to huge funds spent by poor and developing countries to end their poverty, developed and rich countries had been supporting many of them. Now, despite the chaotic economic conditions, attempts are made to extract huge funds from industrialized countries in the name of carbon compensation. Before these carbon-trading days, the same rich countries donated huge funds to the third world to strengthen democracies, for education, healthcare, to fight terrorism, to rehabilitate displaced people, and many such noble purposes, and now to improve energy efficiency, reforestation, and such acts; but none of those recipients claims appreciable success. If all those transfers of funds and other material aids happened with the clause to make every recipient family a deficit-free sustainable family within a reasonable time through PSCHHF norm, many of these evils would not have evolved or would not have attained dangerous proportions. Then, the necessity for the carbon-tax would not have come.

Repeating such careless use of funds, including those like carbon-offset money, would perpetuate poverty and other evils and cause more pollution through the resultant evils and "proxy pollution." So a part of those precious funds, including the carbon-tax, must be diverted to avert the formation of HIFs. Then, with time, all those families would smile with joy and all the targeted evils would meet with a natural death.

How Does It Act?

When compared with the decades-long, huge assistance in HPD regions, the funds needed to educate poor families (about deficits and PSCHHF) and to build facilities for contraception are very meagre. Efficient running of these schemes reduce and, with time, would end all the evils like poverty, crime, corruption, etc. and give people real peace. It would further save funds in two ways: the funds spent on alleviation and the funds spent to fight crime, violence, and other evils (see chapter 31).

Wasting any more time and funds in foolish ways is a crime against humanity and if the same funds create more evils, it is a tragedy and a catastrophe. Wasting a day will add more filth to the atmosphere, damage huge areas of forests, and add thousands of new HIFs to perpetuate that dangerous course. So the world must act fast.

Ugly Encouragement

Even today we have powerful people to "assure" mankind that our world has enough resources to support still more people and thus they misguide ordinary people. A saner world must make everyone, including those "optimists," understand that the human population has outgrown its limits and we now live a complicated and compromised hopeless life with the help of "prohibited filthy" energy and by sacrificing many precious species of flora and fauna and other gifts of Nature, and by continuing to usurp the share of basic resources and space meant for endangered species. Further, a large number of people live as parasites; they use crime, violence, terrorism, and such immoral acts to fulfil their deficits, and in that process force innocent fellow humans to starve and die early. Does anyone need any other proof to understand the very serious deficits we are living with?

We have too many facts to prove that human population has exceeded its limits. Every common sense estimate says that our world cannot even support half of the present-day population in a wholesome way. Misguiding innocent people with such pulpy assurances would create situations which wipe out more and more of the hard working, innocent, "voiceless" humans and other species.

Gauge the Degree of Deficits

We cannot satisfactorily manage something which we cannot measure. So it is appropriate to create some kind of measure or scale and index to estimate the level or degree of unsustainability (quantum of deficits) and related evils. Such scales can help people understand those in a practicable and useful way.

Deficits are quantities. We can certainly measure them by direct and indirect means. Then we can assess their magnitude, relative levels in different regions, their progress or worsening with time, etc. Thus, by using these, we can also judge the worth of related policies and mitigation efforts.

By direct methods, we can measure the quantities of various resources and other things people lack. For instance, the additional fertile lands the farmers of a country need for sustainable organic farming and thereby sustain their country, the area of land a city needs to supply it with enough sustainable fuel and to detoxify its wastes, the quantities of additional water required for agriculture and other use, the amounts of necessities like infrastructures, living space, educational facilities, etc. we require, give a clear idea about their deficits in a direct way.

By indirect methods, we can assess the levels of deficits by assessing their impact upon society, economic activities, and other aspects of living. We know that poverty, crime, violence, forest destruction, terrorism, ungovernable conditions, migration, polluting activities, GW, and CC are curses caused by deficits. The prevalence of these curses— like the number of families below the poverty line, the area of forests destroyed per year, the crime rate of a region, the quantity of polluting energy consumed in a year, the area under ungovernable conditions or terrorists, the number of migrants per million people, the number of people wishing to migrate away from their motherland, the number of premature deaths, deficit-related suicide, the prevalence of malnutrition, and many more issues—and their intensity roughly reflect the level of deficits or unsustainable living.

One of the direct acts of GW is evaporation of water from the surface of Earth. We cannot measure the evaporated water to assess the intensity of GW, but we can assess its seriousness by measuring the total rainfall and snowfall for a year.

All these measures can be used to assess our progress toward sustainability and the efficacies of our policies.

A Saner Action-Plan for Today's Ungovernable States

Too many countries and regions are badly governed by ill-informed tyrannical leaders. As we have discussed in chapter 34, they thrive because of the prevailing poverty, ignorance, illiteracy and desperate disorderly conditions caused by HIFs and HPD. It is a mutually complementary or viciously complicating situation, where the above worsened living conditions bring wily, tyrannical leaders to a top position and give them "stability." Such wrong leadership worsens people's living conditions further. The PSCHHF norm is the best solution for them, and not the removal of the tyrant or installation of democracy; even if we remove the rulers, chaos will prevail because of HPD (Iraq, Libya and Egypt).

As we have discussed, saner humans cannot reach them to implement the PSCHHF norm, so attempts must be made through common friends to earn the trust of rulers and then to use the "orderliness" and stability created by those tough rulers to end their HIFs and HPD.

Recent Upheavals in the Arab World

Recently, country after country, from Tunisia to Syria, experienced revolt against their long-term rulers. They had enjoyed some kind of order and stability for many decades, and if these had been used to give the people a hopeful, sustainable, contented life by ending deficit-creating HIFs, these same protesters would have praised their leaders and advisers and even could have come forward to give their lives for such foresighted benevolent leaders, and could have had a lot of reasons for celebration. But now, no one knows where they are heading, with the huge deficits they carry.

Millions of migrants from such countries had been working in developed and rich countries. If the host countries had emancipated them through the "migrant-rotation" technique (discussed in chapters 20 to 23) and enlightened them about HIFs, it would have done wonders. But that did not happen. Even now, the hosts could initiate such services. Would they take up this noble job as a humane service?

Worst Contribution of Religions

In the past, every religion favoured huge, healthy families. With time, certain sects realized the hardships of huge families and so encouraged manageable, small families. Yet too many Catholic and Islamic countries/societies did not practice the small family norm till recently because their preachers did not guide them to do so. And so they suffered in the past, and still suffer all the evils and shame of HIFs and HPD. Countries like Bangladesh, Indonesia, and many Catholic countries realized these faults and are now correcting their mistakes. Yet the religious preachers of too many societies misguide their people in this respect or never bother to guide them to have deficit-free families, and so, too, many poor Islamic, Catholic, Hindu, and Buddhist societies and certain sections of Protestant Christians still do not care to form sustainable small families and so are making their life an ordeal or hell.

Religion is a sensitive issue, and if others interfere in its matters, it backfires; respectable and responsible people of respective religions must try to give their people a respectable life by removing ignorance. There cannot be a greater service to their God than making their poor people contented, happy, and grateful followers.

Wrong Notions Misguide Developing and Poor Countries

We have already seen the sorrowful dependent economy of industrialized developed countries and their unquenchable thirst for energy. Yet others envy their life without understanding their precarious situation. Most other countries live a well-adapted deficient living (WADL), but have not gone to the sorrowful extreme of industrialized countries. Now, if every country of our planet sincerely does all it can to correct things to end deficits, industrialized countries will be the last to see a wholesome sustainable life, because they are farther away from wholesome sustainable conditions than the others.

In all the meetings related to climate change, poor and developing countries accuse developed countries for their high pollution per head and even do all they can to penalize them through carbon charges, without understanding the "proxy pollution" (by the same accusers) and the entrapped (enslaved) sorrowful position of those polluters. Such demands and accusations can never serve any worthy purpose, but distract the attention of the world away from rational policies and practicable solutions. So it is a rational and worthy act for all poor and developing countries to do all they can to end their own deficits so that they can earn wholesome sustainability sooner (like China).

When poor and developing countries earn a wholesome sustainable life, the factors which cause "proxy-pollution" vanish and force developed countries to downgrade their polluting economic activities without anybody's compulsion.

No More Procrastination

We have discussed the contrasting perception of developed and other countries on matters concerning population. And so, when influential people from any side interfere in such matters of others, they often do wrong and complicate matters, as we see around the globe, and thus they obliterate the chances of optimal recovery. So, unwarranted interferences of any country or organization must be ended, especially in matters concerning population policies, migration, and demography; but they can certainly promote PSCHHF.

Now, every policy and effort must be aimed at restoring LPD and sensible population distribution. Compelling poor families to end deficits (accepting PSCHHF) may appear harsh and against fundamental rights, but the respectable, great life it gives justifies such "harsh" acts. Hesitation or procrastination would deny those poor families their only chance to enjoy their only life.

Delay Continues to Create Bizarre Creatures

HIFs and HPD are horrible conditions with the power to "morph"—literally and metaphorically—every victim into many forms, ranging from totally surrendering "slaves" to those who commit the most heinous crime.

HPD forces many people to commit unhealthy acts, like forest and environment destruction, corruption, violent activities, theft, "rowdyism", irresponsible polluting activities, and many more. As we saw, it makes even parents commit crime against their own children, voluntarily and involuntarily.

Society often gives names or prefixes to such people, in accordance with their "profession," trait, and way of life. They call or refer to them as thief, rowdy, beggar, forest plunderer, cheat, scammer, gangster, trickster, rapist, rascal, etc., or metaphorically as mosquito, leech, beast, worm, etc., and add similar prefixes to their real names given by their dear parents. Society calls irresponsible parents, too, reprehensible names and the uncared for and "thrown away" children are referred to as vagabonds, orphans, "intellectual or ideological bastards," dirt, etc. Very few sympathize with such unfortunate people because, in an HPD society, everybody carries some sorrow, grudge, burden, or grievance.

Even those "rejected" people call "normal" people miser, parasite, money-bag, stony heart, unkind, etc.

It is not at all a healthy situation. No sane person or society can tolerate it. Can you imagine, then, the condition of a society, even if it has a small percentage of such despised or untrustworthy, bizarre creatures?

Humane and Benevolent Act

Thus HIFs, the sources of deficits, are real hells and they deny a worthy life to their members, hurt others in many ways, and devitalize the world through pollution, GW, and CC. Preventing the formation of HIFs through the PSCHHF formula is the most urgent and rational and sensible service today. Interpreting this noble act as an injustice or denial of fundamental rights is wrong; PSCHHF alone confers upon them all the basic possessions and necessities by default, including fundamental rights, dignity, hope, real freedom, and above all, peace and happiness.

It is not at all an act against humanism; it is the most humane and benevolent act, because it gives a respectable life to miserable families and saves humanity and our planet Earth from the ravages of pollution, GW, and CC.

Priceless Rewards

Recovery from deficits, ills, and evils grants humanity the most desirable mind-set with love, gratitude, friendliness, hope, security, and trust, which ends national borders and brings people together as global villagers. Such a happy, peaceful life eradicates every remaining residual factor which favours global warming and climate change.

What else can be the ambition of mankind today?

That is the power of PSCHHF—the ultimate solution.

The End

Notes